Microsoft System Center Data Protection Manager 2012 R2 Cookbook

Over 100 recipes to build your own designs exploring the advanced functionality and features of System Center DPM 2012 R2

Robert Hedblom

BIRMINGHAM - MUMBAI

Microsoft System Center Data Protection Manager 2012 R2 Cookbook

First published: April 2015

Production reference: 1270415

Published by Packt Publishing Ltd.
Livery Place
35 Livery Street
Birmingham B3 2PB, UK.

ISBN 978-1-78217-271-0

www.packtpub.com

Credits

Author
Robert Hedblom

Reviewers
Steve Buchanan
Adrian Costea
John Joyner
Michael Seidl
Yegor Startsev

Commissioning Editor
Kevin Colaco

Acquisition Editor
Kevin Colaco

Content Development Editor
Neeshma Ramakrishnan

Technical Editors
Ruchi Desai
Shali Dheeraj
Nilesh Mangnakar
Edwin Moses

Copy Editors
Sonia Michelle Cheema
Sonia Mathur
Stuti Srivastava

Project Coordinator
Danuta Jones

Proofreaders
Safis Editing
Lesley Harrison
Paul Hindle
Chris Smith

Indexer
Mariammal Chettiyar

Production Coordinator
Komal Ramchandani

Cover Work
Komal Ramchandani

About the Author

Robert Hedblom has a well-known System Center and cloud MVP profile. He is often seen as a presenter or speaker at large global events, such as TechEd, Ignite, System Center, and Azure gatherings. Within his line of work at Lumagate, he delivers scenario-based solutions in complex environments, empowering the Cloud OS strategy from Microsoft.

Backup, restore, and disaster recovery have always been a part of Robert's work, and now, he is trying to make a point that it is not about the implementation of different products that matters anymore, it's all about building cost-effective, optimal, and well-designed services.

"All good designs come from knowing your data services' dependencies" is what Robert believes in.

Robert was a coauthor on *Microsoft System Center Data Protection Manager 2012 SP1, Packt Publishing*, and has also written other books and given training. His expertise is often utilized by Microsoft's MCS and PFE organizations in Europe, and he is an elected member of the development process of the System Center stack and Azure at Microsoft Redmond.

The most important part of my life is my family and I'm grateful for having their support all the way through the process of writing this book. Words cannot express my love and gratitude. I also want to send a big thank you to Mr. Shivam Garg, who is the lead program manager at Microsoft in India; thank you for your support and fun talks over messed-up time zones. Last but not least, I would like to say a sincere thank you to all the reviewers who helped out with the review of this book.

Most importantly, thank you Packt Publishing, especially Neeshma Ramakrishnan, for making this journey a constructive and rich experience.

About the Reviewers

Steve Buchanan is a regional solution lead with Concurrency, a three-time Microsoft System Center MVP, and the author of several technical books focused on the System Center platform.

He has been an IT professional for over 15 years and has held various positions, ranging from infrastructure architect to IT manager. Steve is focused on transforming IT departments through DevOps, service management, systems management, and cloud technologies.

He has authored the following books:

- *System Center 2012 Service Manager Unleashed*, published in 2014 by Sams Publishing
- *Microsoft System Center Data Protection Manager 2012 SP1*, published in 2013 by Packt Publishing
- *Microsoft Data Protection Manager 2010*, published in 2011 by Packt Publishing

Steve holds certifications in A +, Linux +, MCSA, MCITP: Server Administrator, and MCSE: Private Cloud.

Steve is active in the System Center community and enjoys blogging about his adventures in the world of IT at www.buchatech.com. You can also follow him on twitter at @buchatech for his latest blog posts.

Thank you, Robert, for including me on this project. Nice work on the project; DPM's future looks bright!

Adrian Costea is an information technology enthusiast, and his primary focus is datacenter infrastructure and virtualization projects across a number of industries, including government, healthcare, finance, gas, and oil. He likes to discover new things and also likes to write on his blog at http://www.vkernel.ro.

Working in the field of IT infrastructure for over 8 years now, he has developed expertise in VMware, Windows, Linux, Citrix, and other technologies. Currently, he holds a number of technical certifications, including MCTS, MCITP, MCSA, MCSE, VCP5-DCV, and CCA for XenApp 6.

Outside of work, Adrian enjoys sports, traveling, and meeting new people. You can contact him on twitter at @vkernelRO for questions or to just say hello.

John Joyner has been a Microsoft MVP for System Center Cloud and Datacenter Management for 8 years. He is the director of product development at ClearPointe, a provider of Management as a Service from their System Center-based Network Operations Center (NOC). He is a coauthor of a four-book reference series in *System Center 2012 Operations Manager: Unleashed, Sams Publishing*, and holds MCSE: Private Cloud, Azure Architecture, and Azure Infrastructure certifications.

Michael Seidl is a senior consultant who works for Base-IT, a Gold Partner in Systems Management, located in Austria. His experience as an IT consultant has been growing since 2001, and he is mainly focused on SCDPM, SCO, SCSM, and PowerShell. Working with some of the biggest companies in Austria gives him the opportunity to work on great projects with complex requirements. He regularly shares his experience on the TechNet Forum and on his blog at www.techguy.at.

Yegor Startsev is a former System Center Cloud and Datacenter Management MVP from Samara, Russia. He has worked in the IT industry for over 12 years, starting as a systems administrator and working up to his current role as a chief information officer. He is focused on managing IT departments and budgets and architecting and developing IT projects in a large group of construction companies. He is a regular speaker at regional Microsoft and IT Pro community events. He was a technical reviewer for *Microsoft System Center Data Protection Manager 2012 SP1, Packt Publishing*. He also runs the DPM blog titled *Recovery Point* (http://ystartsev.wordpress.com). He is married and is a proud father of triplets: two boys and a girl.

www.PacktPub.com

Support files, eBooks, discount offers, and more

For support files and downloads related to your book, please visit www.PacktPub.com.

Did you know that Packt offers eBook versions of every book published, with PDF and ePub files available? You can upgrade to the eBook version at www.PacktPub.com and as a print book customer, you are entitled to a discount on the eBook copy. Get in touch with us at service@packtpub.com for more details.

At www.PacktPub.com, you can also read a collection of free technical articles, sign up for a range of free newsletters and receive exclusive discounts and offers on Packt books and eBooks.

https://www2.packtpub.com/books/subscription/packtlib

Do you need instant solutions to your IT questions? PacktLib is Packt's online digital book library. Here, you can search, access, and read Packt's entire library of books.

Why subscribe?

- ▶ Fully searchable across every book published by Packt
- ▶ Copy and paste, print, and bookmark content
- ▶ On demand and accessible via a web browser

Free access for Packt account holders

If you have an account with Packt at www.PacktPub.com, you can use this to access PacktLib today and view 9 entirely free books. Simply use your login credentials for immediate access.

Instant updates on new Packt books

Get notified! Find out when new books are published by following @PacktEnterprise on Twitter or the *Packt Enterprise* Facebook page.

Table of Contents

Preface

This book will give you the information needed to get started with System Data Protection Manager 2012 R2. Also, it will cover the important facts regarding how to design, implement, and manage the solution that you set up from an optimal and supportive perspective.

What this book covers

Chapter 1, Pre-installation Tasks, gives you a good start in understanding what is needed for a successful DPM deployment.

Chapter 2, Installation and Upgrade, walks you through installing and updating DPM.

Chapter 3, Post-installation Tasks, gives you the facts regarding what it takes to get the solution up and running in a production environment.

Chapter 4, File Server Protection, explains how you should back up and restore your file workloads.

Chapter 5, SQL Protection, builds up on the concept of protecting and restoring the SQL server workload.

Chapter 6, Hyper-V Protection, provides the information needed to understand the protection and restoring of Hyper-V.

Chapter 7, SharePoint Protection, gives you a deeper understanding regarding SharePoint backups, most importantly, restore.

Chapter 8, Exchange Server Protection, covers the backup and restore scenarios for the Exchange server workload.

Chapter 9, Client Protection, teaches you how to build solid backup and restore scenarios for Windows clients.

Chapter 10, Workgroup Protection and CBA, covers how to protect servers that are not joined in the same domain. You will also understand workgroup protection and the Certificate-Based Authentication (CBA) mechanism.

Chapter 11, Azure Integration, deals with integration with Azure, which is a hot topic. In this chapter, you have recipes that explain how to integrate your DPM server solution with the Microsoft Azure Backup Vault services.

Chapter 12, Disaster Recovery, covers recipes on disaster recovery scenarios that you can use DPM for.

Chapter 13, Tape Management, has recipes that give you a deeper understanding when it comes to tape management from a DPM perspective.

Chapter 14, Monitoring and Automation, covers proactive monitoring and automation, which is crucial for any Backup-as-a-Service (BaaS) solution.

What you need for this book

You will need a running DPM server solution in a lab or production environment, which you want to manage in an optimal way.

Who this book is for

If you are a DPM administrator, this book will help you verify your knowledge and provide you with everything you need to know about the 2012 R2 release. No prior knowledge of System Center DPM is required; however, some experience of running backups will come in handy.

If you have some experience of running backups and are looking to expand your horizons with System Center DPM, then look no further, as this is the book for you. No prior knowledge about System Center DPM is required. If you have never worked with System Center Data Protection Manager, this book will be your travel companion in your learning journey, starting with the fundamentals and finishing off with advanced concepts.

Sections

In this book, you will find several headings that appear frequently (Getting ready, How to do it, How it works, There's more, and See also).

To give clear instructions on how to complete a recipe, we use these sections as follows:

Getting ready

This section tells you what to expect in the recipe, and describes how to set up any software or any preliminary settings required for the recipe.

How to do it...

This section contains the steps required to follow the recipe.

How it works...

This section usually consists of a detailed explanation of what happened in the previous section.

There's more...

This section consists of additional information about the recipe in order to make the reader more knowledgeable about the recipe.

See also

This section provides helpful links to other useful information for the recipe.

Conventions

In this book, you will find a number of text styles that distinguish between different kinds of information. Here are some examples of these styles and an explanation of their meaning.

Code words in text, database table names, folder names, filenames, file extensions, pathnames, dummy URLs, user input, and Twitter handles are shown as follows: "The DPM 2012 R2 software depends on both local security groups that are referred to when the DCOM object that controls the DPMRA service is used to initiate a VSS Request for the protected data source."

Any command-line input or output is written as follows:

```
Set-ReplicaCreationMethod -ProtectionGroup $newpg -Now
```

New terms and **important words** are shown in bold. Words that you see on the screen, for example, in menus or dialog boxes, appear in the text like this: "In the **Select protection group type** step, choose **Clients** and click on **Next >** to continue."

 Warnings or important notes appear in a box like this.

 Tips and tricks appear like this.

Reader feedback

Feedback from our readers is always welcome. Let us know what you think about this book—what you liked or disliked. Reader feedback is important for us as it helps us develop titles that you will really get the most out of.

To send us general feedback, simply e-mail `feedback@packtpub.com`, and mention the book's title in the subject of your message.

If there is a topic that you have expertise in and you are interested in either writing or contributing to a book, see our author guide at `www.packtpub.com/authors`.

Customer support

Now that you are the proud owner of a Packt book, we have a number of things to help you to get the most from your purchase.

Downloading the color images of this book

We also provide you with a PDF file that has color images of the screenshots/diagrams used in this book. The color images will help you better understand the changes in the output. You can download this file from `https://www.packtpub.com/sites/default/files/downloads/Microsoft_SystemCenter_DataProtectionManager_2012R2_Graphics.pdf`.

Errata

Although we have taken every care to ensure the accuracy of our content, mistakes do happen. If you find a mistake in one of our books—maybe a mistake in the text or the code—we would be grateful if you could report this to us. By doing so, you can save other readers from frustration and help us improve subsequent versions of this book. If you find any errata, please report them by visiting `http://www.packtpub.com/submit-errata`, selecting your book, clicking on the **Errata Submission Form** link, and entering the details of your errata. Once your errata are verified, your submission will be accepted and the errata will be uploaded to our website or added to any list of existing errata under the Errata section of that title.

To view the previously submitted errata, go to `https://www.packtpub.com/books/content/support` and enter the name of the book in the search field. The required information will appear under the **Errata** section.

Piracy

Piracy of copyrighted material on the Internet is an ongoing problem across all media. At Packt, we take the protection of our copyright and licenses very seriously. If you come across any illegal copies of our works in any form on the Internet, please provide us with the location address or website name immediately so that we can pursue a remedy.

Please contact us at `copyright@packtpub.com` with a link to the suspected pirated material.

We appreciate your help in protecting our authors and our ability to bring you valuable content.

Questions

If you have a problem with any aspect of this book, you can contact us at `questions@packtpub.com`, and we will do our best to address the problem.

1

Pre-installation Tasks

In this chapter, we will cover the following topics:

- ▸ Changing tracking process
- ▸ Planning DPM pre-installation tasks
- ▸ Planning the DPM disk pool
- ▸ Firewall configuration

Introduction

Within a modern data center there are new and interesting challenges that the IT department needs to address to adapt to the new way of thinking regarding building services instead of focusing on an explicit product. The most important fact is that there will never be a product in the market that will cover or solve all the needs of a company or organization. Today's IT department must change the way it looks at solutions; a single product will never be the answer but combining different technologies and building up services will provide a much higher value for the organization or company regarding both time consumption and cost.

The modern data center is all about building services that empower the possibilities the different products bring to the table. By combining your backup software with the monitoring software and using the concepts of automation, you can create something that will develop with time. There is no whitepaper that you can simply download that will let you in on all the secrets to build a flawless **Backup as a Service** (**BaaS**), **Restore as a Service** (**RaaS**) or **Disaster Recovery as a Service** (**DRaaS**) solution.

System Center Data Protection Manager 2012 R2 (**DPM**) is the latest release and with it comes a new product group team in India. The team has in the few past months provided high scale development and improvements to the product and they will strive even harder to optimize DPM and also bring new features and supported scenarios to the table.

In this chapter, we will cover the pre-installation tasks for DPM 2012 R2. We also will provide you with the information you need to understand how DPM 2012 R2 works and get started with a well-planned implementation of your backup, restore, and disaster recovery scenarios.

What is System Center Data Protection Manager 2012 R2

The recipe will cover an introduction to what DPM 2012 R2 is and explain the product.

For many years, the focus for protecting a data center has always been backup. There are many vendors and third-party solutions still claiming in the market that they are the best and most suitable backup solutions for your data center. If your purpose in performing the backup operation is being able to perform a restore, then the majority of the third-party software and vendors out in the market will not be able to help you. The most challenging part of providing a restore plan or a restore scenario for a service is that the third-party software and vendors are focusing on providing you just a backup, not the ability to restore. This is where DPM 2012 R2 comes in. It all started with the release of the Windows Server 2003, and with that release came the possibility of providing online snapshots using a new feature called **Volume Shadow Copy Services** (**VSS**). The APIs for the solutions were quickly adopted by third-party software and vendors but no one could, in the beginning, get it up and running in a fully optimal way. The idea regarding the VSS architecture was a great one and a big step forward regarding how to manage snapshots of different workloads like file, SQL, or Exchange in order to provide a consistent data snapshot.

Microsoft understood that if this architecture was to blossom in the way that they wanted it to, they needed to create backup and restore software themselves. In 2006, the first version of DPM was released with the focus only on protecting the file workload. A lot of companies tried it but few were adopting the new software since they still hosted and ran their data center with the traditional IT mindset.

During the past years Microsoft did not invest heavily in DPM, but under the new team that is driving the DPM solution from India, there have been a lot of investments, making DPM the primary choice for private cloud protection. Microsoft has invested in both developers and experts, pushing the product forward and making it a natural choice of the modern data center.

You may ask what is the thing that differentiates DPM from other backup software on the market. The answer is quite simple; restore based on supported and optimal scenarios with the power of easy integration building the BaaS, RaaS, and DRaaS for a modern data center. DPM knows the Microsoft stack architecture the best as it was written by Microsoft for the Microsoft technologies present in the data center. Combining DPM with the majority of the System Center family members and Azure technologies, you are able to provide an extremely high-end solution for your data center; it is all about design.

DPM only adapts to the current technology and solutions that Microsoft has developed for their workloads. DPM will never, for example, make any decisions on its own regarding SQL restore. The SQL team has clearly defined how a supported and optimal restore should occur and this is what DPM understands and adapts to; the same goes for all the Microsoft-branded workloads.

DPM always focuses on the restore scenario, since providing supported and optimal backup scenarios is not a challenge.

DPM 2012 R2 has the capability to back up production data sources to disk, tape, and Azure. For more detailed information regarding the DPM disk pool please read the _Planning the DPM disk pool_ recipe. For more information regarding how DPM uses tapes, tape management, and Azure integration, please read _Chapter 11, Azure Integration_.

With DPM you are able to back up the most common workloads in a modern data center. The workloads that DPM will natively back up using the underlying VSS are:

- Exchange Server
- SQL Server
- SharePoint Server
- Microsoft Dynamics
- Windows Server
- Hyper-V
- System States and Active Directory
- Windows clients

The following figure shows the DPM back up process:

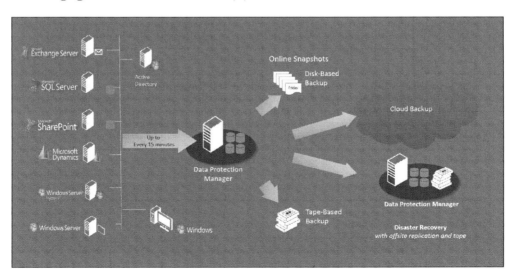

For detailed information regarding the different versions DPM 2012 R2 can protect, please read the support matrix `http://technet.microsoft.com/en-us/library/jj860400.aspx`.

The primary DPM server is the first line of protection that you deploy for your production workloads. For systems that use transactional log systems (Exchange and SQL), you are able to replicate the production data from the protected data source to the primary DPM server every 15 minutes. This is also applicable to the file workloads.

Regarding the DPM disk pool, DPM has only one demand: the disk that should be used for the DPM disk pool must be presented in the operating system that has the DPM software installed as a local disk. DPM is able to operate with pass-through disks, **Direct Attached Storage** (**DAS**), **Network Attached Storage** (**NAS**), or **Storage Area Network** (**SAN**) storage. It is also possible to communicate directly with a storage using the iSCSI initiator within the operating system of the DPM server. Please note that this is not a good, optimal, or in any way decent approach to a DPM disk pool; never use iSCSI.

When DPM 2012 R2 starts protecting a workload, it creates an initial copy of the production data source that it has to protect. This is stored in the DPM disk pool in a dedicated volume that uses the same GUID ID as the protected data source. This volume is called the **replica volume**. The replica volume will hold the only full back up that the DPM ever will do of the protected data source. All changes in data, also known as data churn, that occur after the replica has been created, will be synchronized to DPM disk pool. When creating a recovery point, the data is stored in the recovery point volume that also uses the GUID ID of the protected data source for identification.

The most important component of the DPM server architecture is the DPM database also known as the DPMDB. The DPMDB holds all the configurations made on the DPM server, protection groups, agents, backup schedules, and so on. It is of great importance that the DPMDB is protected via a secondary DPM server when you build the DPM-DPM-DR scenario, copied to file, or archived to tape.

DPM depends on its DPM agents that will perform a VSS request for the protected data sources and have that data replicated from the production environment to the DPM server.

For further information regarding DPM, there are numerous places you can visit online. There are both Microsoft websites and MVP blogs that provide you with good content and decent information:

- The DPM TechNet forum `http://social.technet.microsoft.com/Forums/en-us/home?forum=dataprotectionmanager`.
- DPM TechNet web pages `http://technet.microsoft.com/en-us/library/hh758173.aspx`.

- ► DPM survival guide `http://social.technet.microsoft.com/wiki/ contents/articles/11867.system-center-2012-data-protection- manager-survival-guide.aspx`

- ► RobertandDPM `http://robertanddpm.blogspot.com`

What's new in the R2 release

This recipe will cover the news in the DPM 2012 R2 release.

As the market develops, Microsoft understands the new challenges that companies and organizations face and therefore constantly develops its product stack to be able to meet the new requirements.

Microsoft has made some improvements and added some more architectural functions to DPM 2012 R2 release. The following list presents and explains the enhancements made to the product:

- ► DPMDB cluster support: The database that stores all the configuration for DPM (DPMDB) can now be placed in a SQL cluster environment. This removes the standalone challenges that existed in the previous versions. With this enhancement comes reliability, consistency and most important, scalability.

- ► Backing up of virtual Linux servers: DPM 2012 R2 can now protect virtual Linux servers running on Hyper-V using the technique "Backup using child partition" or "online snapshot" in Hyper-V. Note that only file-level protection is supported, not application-based protection.

- ► Virtual deployment: It is now possible to deploy and manage DPM via **System Center Virtual Machine Manager** (**SCVMM**). You can install DPM on a virtual machine, and configure storage using `.vhdx` storage pool disks that are shared through the VMM library.

- ► Optimization for online protection using Azure: Microsoft has optimized the **express-full** technology used when synchronizing the protected data from the DPM server on-premises to Azure via the Windows Azure Backup Agent.

- ► SQL server media: For any new DPM 2012 R2 installation, the SQL server now needs to be pre-installed locally or remotely.

The new releases in the R2 version of the DPM software will make it possible for companies to meet some of the new challenges they are facing.

With the constant releases of **Update Roll-ups** (**UR**), Microsoft is meeting the new challenges that companies are struggling with.

The architecture of System Center Data Protection Manager 2012 R2

This recipe will cover the architecture of the DPM software and explain the local security groups like DCOM objects and others, to make your understanding of the product more clear.

There are some parts of DPM that are very important to have knowledge about. They are:

- ▶ Specific catalogs
- ▶ DCOM
- ▶ VSS interaction with mini drivers and the DPM filter
- ▶ Local security groups

The following are some catalogs under `%systemdrive%\Microsoft System Center 2012 R2\DPM\DPM` that are important to the DPM server functionality:

- ▶ End User Recovery
- ▶ Protection Agents
- ▶ Temp
- ▶ VMMHelperService
- ▶ Volumes
- ▶ XSD

The **End-User Recovery** catalog contains the MS file for the active directory schema extension and configures the DPM server to enable the feature **End-User Recovery**.

Protection Agents contains two catalogs, which are **AC** and **RA**. The **AC** catalog is used by the DPM agent coordinator when pushing new DPM agents to the server hosting the data sources that it needs protection for. The **RA** catalog holds the binaries for the DPM agent and can also be used as a remote repository when manually installing the DPM agent.

DPM provides a lot of logs that you can read to gain an understanding of what has happened and why. All logs that the DPM server software produces are stored in the **Temp** catalog.

For DPM to be able to continually provide data source protection, even if protected virtual machines are making an outer-cluster migration that also includes the migration of storage, DPM needs to integrate with SCVMM. The catalog **VMMHelperService** contains the binaries and DLL files for creating the integration between the DPM server and VMM server.

The catalog **Volumes** actually contains four catalogs, and three of them are important to know about. The **DiffArea** catalog contains shortcuts to the recovery point volumes in the DPM disk pool. The **Replica** catalog contains shortcuts to the replica volumes in the DPM disk pool. The **ShadowCopy** catalog contains the catalog **Database Backups**, which will hold the backed up DPMDB when you trigger a DB backup using the DPMBackup executable.

Last but not least is the **XDS** catalog, which contains all the XML schema files for the DPM software.

The DPM 2012 R2 software depends on both local security groups that are referred to when the DCOM object that controls the DPMRA service is used to initiate a VSS Request for the protected data source. If there is a problem with rights in the DCOM object, the DPMRA will not be able to provide a snapshot since the chain of configuration is broken.

Since the local security groups are critical, it is important that their purpose is explained. The local security groups are:

- Distributed COM Users
- DPMDRTrustedMachines
- DPMRADCOMTrustedMachines
- DPMRADmTrustedMachines
- DPMRATrustedDPMRAs
- DPMSCOM
- MSDPMTrustedMachines
- MSDPMTrustedUsers

The members of the **Distributed COM Users** group are the computer accounts that the current DPM server has access to. You will also find specific service accounts here regarding your SQL server hosting the DPMDB as well as user accounts.

DPMDRTrusedMachines members are the other DPM servers that provide a DPM-DPM-DR configuration and via the membership of this group, have access to listing the protected data sources on the primary DPM server and take usage of the DPM writer.

The group **DPMRADCOMTrustedMachines** contains the primary and the secondary DPM server computer accounts.

DPMRADmTrustedMachines contains the computer accounts that have an associated DPM agent with the DPM server.

The group **DPMSCOM** contains the computer account for the SCOM management server that is used for monitoring and management of the DPM server via SCOM and the Central Console feature.

MSDPMTrustedMachines contains the computer accounts that have an associated DPM agent for the DPM server.

The last group is **MSDPMTrusedUsers** and this group is used by the centralized management features.

Change tracking process

This recipe will explain how DPM will identify block-level changes.

Getting ready

With the introduction of VSS, the purpose of making a full copy of the production data is obsolete. Using the VSS as a starting point, DPM provides an extremely fast and reliable change identification process.

How to do it...

DPM 2012 R2 relies on the VSS architecture and provides advanced change tracking functionality based on the mini-filter driver stack along with a DPM file filter.

How it works...

The change identification process relies on VSS as the core component. Within the VSS architecture, there are three different snapshot technologies that you can use:

- ▸ Complete copy
- ▸ Copy-on-write
- ▸ Redirect-on-write

The Copy-on-write technique is the one that provides the possibility of making online snapshots during production hours. This technique identifies the block-level changes and "freezes" the blocks making them ready to be copied. If there are other blocks that were changed during that process, the VSS identifies those. Once the initial identification has finished, the VSS starts managing the changed blocks.

Describing the whole picture, there is more to it than just using the standard VSS architecture. Not only is Microsoft DPM dependent on the VSS functionality but it also uses parts from the mini-filter driver stack and a dedicated file filter named DPM file filter to make the change tracking process of block-level changes fully supported, as well as optimal and fast for a DPM protection scenario.

There's more...

For further and deeper information regarding how Volume Shadow Copy Service works, refer the MSDN website `http://msdn.microsoft.com/en-us/library/windows/desktop/bb968832(v=vs.85).aspx`.

When DPM creates a recovery point, there are a number of underlying technologies that make it possible. As mentioned earlier in this chapter, the DPM server can take advantage of a system that uses transactional logs and adapt to the change journal. Creating a recovery point in DPM is a part of what Microsoft calls Express-Full. The Express-Full operation is the function that is triggered when the backup job is initiated from the DPM sever.

 When DPM backs up server workloads, the DPM server triggers the backup job. When the DPM server backs up Windows clients, the client triggers the backup job.

The Express-Full consists of the following:

▸ Block-level change tracking process

▸ Synchronization of changed data

▸ Creation of a recovery point

Planning your DPM pre-installation tasks

This recipe will enable you to plan your DPM server deployment and most importantly, make it possible for you to provide a starting point for your BaaS, RaaS, and DRaaS. The recipe will also cover network consumption and archiving possibilities.

Getting ready

There are a lot of questions that must be sorted out before you start planning your DPM server deployment. First is the classification process of the data sources that you would like to protect. A very common strategy that many companies that are still providing traditional IT to the company or organization are using is to back up everything they can backup once a day. However, this is not a good approach. There are, of course, several servers within your data center that need a high frequency of backups but not all the servers are equally important. It is essential that you adapt your business continuity plan before you have any implementation done. Start by identifying your services and then break down the services into components to clearly see how or why they are of importance to your business.

Use the different classes and sort the components that build up the service into these three categories:

- ► Gold
- ► Silver
- ► Bronze

As you may realize, the Gold class is more important than the Silver and the Bronze ones. Use these classes to differentiate your data and services so you get a clearer view.

How to do it...

From a more technical perspective, there are some considerations that need to be addressed:

- ► The total amount of data that should be protected
- ► Untrusted domains
- ► Internet access to remote sites and cloud services
- ► SQL Server installation
- ► Virtual or physical deployment of the DPM server
- ► Archive management

To be able to understand the number of DPM servers that you need to deploy, you must first know:

- ► How much data to protect
- ► Untrusted domains
- ► Network limitations between different remote sites
- ► The need for building up disaster recovery scenarios

Every DPM server can manage 120 TB of storage for its disk pool. For example, 40 TB of those could be addressed to the file workload or 25 TB could be addressed to the SharePoint workload. In the scenario where you are managing multiple domains that you need to provide protection for, you can create a two-way transitive trust between the domains. In that case, the DPM server will operate in both domains without any limitations. This, however, comes with a security risk and if you have not created a two-way transitive trust between the untrusted domains you should think twice before you go for it. If you are able to set up a two-way transitive trust without causing any security risk, follow this blogpost to learn how to do it: `http://robertanddpm.blogspot.se/2011/09/backing-up-cross-domains.html`.

For the other scenario, to provide restore capabilities for untrusted domains, refer to *Chapter 10, Workgroup Protection and CBA*.

DPM can be deployed and provide a global restore capability strategy for your company or organization. If your bandwidth is greater than 512 kb then DPM will be able to provide its services. However, you should always include the restore scenarios when you are building up your backup strategies that reflect your business continuity plan. In many cases, you should deploy a DPM server on-site or build up your BaaS service using Windows Server Backup feature and have that integrated with Azure for archiving purposes, if you don't have the funding. Nevertheless, you are able to both throttle the DPM agents that are installed in the remote office protecting data sources and enable the **on-the-wire compression** for optimizing network consumption.

The SQL Server is no longer a part of the installation media for DPM 2012 R2, which is a good thing. Now you need to think before you act. A majority of the consultant companies needs to understand SQL more and also realize that if you have a poorly set up SQL, you will have a bad experience with the product hosting its database on that SQL server. Remember to set up your SQL server using service accounts, dedicate a RADI 1+0 for the DPM and monitor the SQL performance using System Center Operations Manager with a proactive monitoring approach.

With the release of the UR3, DPM 2012 R2 can be completely virtualized in all thinkable scenarios. You have the ability to use Synthetic Fiber Channel for accessing and using a physical tape library and also the ability to provide deduplication of the DPM disk pool using the SOFS architecture. When building a BaaS, RaaS, or DRaaS for a modern data center or a data center that still adopts the traditional IT approach, it is crucial that the DPM server is running on Hyper-V and is of instances that build up the service. Since a service in a modern data center is highly resilient and highly automated, you will benefit in many ways by building your BaaS, RaaS, and DRaaS using virtual DPM servers.

When it comes to archiving possibilities, there are currently three different solutions:

  ▶ Physical tape library
  ▶ **Virtual Tape Library (VTL)**
  ▶ Azure

You should not just consider one of these three as an option. Focus instead on the requirements of the BaaS, RaaS, and DRaaS. Some protected data sources should be provided as archiving possibilities but maybe only once per month, go with Azure. Where protected data sources need an archiving solution but should also be able to restore quickly, go with VTL. In case the data sources need an off-site secure solution, go with physical tapes.

How it works...

Having all the information presented in an organized manner, you can now start designing the structure of the BaaS service. A piece of advice here—take small steps towards your goal and never rush an implementation. You will probably bump into a challenge or two, so it is of key importance to work using a well-defined structure.

There's more...

For more information regarding the setting up of SQL as a part of the prerequisites, please read *Chapter 2, Installation and Upgrade,* which also provides you a walk-through guide of the steps for DPM 2012 R2 installation.

Planning the DPM disk pool

This recipe will cover the information needed for planning the DPM disk pool.

Getting ready

The best way to start the planning phase for the DPM disk pool is to have the initial amount of data that you would like to protect and also a theoretical data churn. With these two components, you can easily determine the exact storage needed for your DPM disk pool.

How to do it...

System Center Data Protection Manger is able to use any type of disk that is presented as local attached storage in Disk Management.

[It does not support the use of USB/1394 disk for the DPM disk pool.]

From the UR3 release, you can now build a total virtual solution for the DPM server technology using Hyper-V. This also comes with the great possibility of building a virtual disk pool with VHDX files that could be stored on a **Scale Out File Server** (**SOSF**) and enabled for deduplication. With the approach of making a virtual solution you can save and optimize disk consumption very easily.

DPM 2012 R2 is able to use:

> ▸ Direct Attached Storage
> ▸ Fiber Channel Storage Area Network (FC SAN)
> ▸ iSCSI

A very important fact is that iSCSI should not be considered your primary choice due to some challenges that often occur when leveraging that technology. The most common challenge is that the initiation of the iSCSI target fails and therefore the entire DPM disk pool fails. iSCSI will work in smaller deployments with DPM but if your ambition is to provide a more stable solution, you should consider SOFS. If your company does not provide an SOFS, you should use a DAS and provision VHDX files to the virtual DPM servers. As you can clearly see, the recommendation is to build as much virtually as possible.

 It is not advised to use any virtual RAID controllers that are hosting the DPM disk pool.

Keeping track of the storage performance is also of key importance. Providing a decent proactive monitoring and performance approach is something that you will benefit from in the long run. Build up a proactive monitoring concept using System Center Operations Manager and see how the impact of the performance will change according to the number of backup jobs, workloads and synchronization frequency of the DPM servers.

How it works...

Microsoft recommendations regarding how to determine the actual size of the DPM disk pool are from a minimal perspective. Multiply the total amount of protected data size by 1.5. For instance, if you want to protect 10 TB of data you need 15 TB of storage from a minimal perspective. The recommended approach is to multiply the total amount of the protected data size by three. So if you want to protect 10 TB of data, you need 30 TB of storage. These calculations will, of course, generate a lot of overhead in the DPM disk pool since there are several factors that are not presented in the equation.

If you want to determine a more exact number for the size of the disk pool, you can use the following formulas.

Replica volumes:

- ▶ Exchange data = Data source size x (1 + log change) / (alert threshold - .05)
- ▶ SQL Server data = Data source size x (1 + log change) / (alert threshold - .05)
- ▶ Windows SharePoint Services data = Total size of all databases/ (alert threshold - .05)
- ▶ Virtual Server data = Data source size x 1.5
- ▶ For Windows Server system state = (Data source size x 3) / 2
- ▶ For file data = (Data source size x 3) / 2

Recovery Point volumes:

- Exchange data = 4.0 x retention range in days x log change x data source size + 1600 MB

- SQL Server data = (2.5 x retention range in days x log change x data source size) + 1600 MB

- Windows SharePoint Services data = (1.5 x retention range in days x log change x total size of all databases) + 1600 MB

- Virtual Server data = (Data source size x retention range in days x 0.02) + 1600 MB

- For system state = (Data source size x retention range in days x 2) / 100 + 1600 MB

- For files = (Data source size x retention range in days x 2) / 100 + 1600 MB

The log change is:

- 6% for Exchange

- 6% for SQL

- 10% for SharePoint

As you can understand, you will get a nearly exact estimation but the downside is that it will take a long time to calculate.

If you are protecting just Exchange, Hyper-V, and SharePoint you should use the storage calculators that are available for download at this site: `http://www.microsoft.com/en-us/download/details.aspx?id=24375`.

There's more...

Providing decent hardware that hosts the DPM disk pool is very important. You don't need premium disk solutions for the DPM disk pool but can use decent hardware that can easily scale out.

Adding the DPM disk pool could be done via the DPM console or via PowerShell. For more information regarding the subject, please read the *Adding disks to the DPM disk pool* recipe in *Chapter 3, Post-installation Tasks*.

It's important to know the limitations of the Windows Server operating system. DPM 2012 R2 has the following limitations that you should keep in mind while designing BaaS, RaaS, and DRaaS:

- 600 volumes in the DPM disk pool

- 32 spanned disks in Disk Management

▸ The disk that should be used for the DPM disk pool must be a Dynamic disk in Disk Management

▸ The DPM disk pool can store 9000 snapshots

 If you collocate the Hyper-V, SQL, and client workload, you can protect a larger number of data sources. Please refer to *Chapter 5, SQL* and *Chapter 6, Hyper-V* for more details.

Firewall configuration

This recipe will cover the firewall configuration that is needed to establish a successful communication between DPM 2012 R2 and the data source that should be included in the DPM protection.

Getting ready

Opening just the right amount of firewall ports with the right direction of communication will provide you a more high-end security approach. DPM uses Microsoft standard communication ports, but for some features, there are a few other TCP ports that need to be opened.

Protocol	Port
DCOM	135 / TCP
DPM specific ports	5718 / TCP
	5719 / TCP
DNS	53 / UDP
Kerberos	88 / UDP
	88 / TCP
LDAP	389 / UDP
	389 / TCP
NetBIOS	137 / UDP
	138 / UDP
	139 / UDP
	445 / TCP

Protocol	Port
Centralized Console	6075 / TCP
	1433 / TCP
	1434 / UDP
	80 / TCP
	443 / TCP
	50000 – 65000 / TCP
	4022 / TCP
	5723 / TCP

How to do it...

Having the Windows firewall enabled would be considered the most natural thing. However, many companies rely on a physical firewall as their first line of defense meaning that their Windows firewalls are disabled.

An easy approach is to create a **Group Policy Object** (**GPO**) that holds the configuration for the Windows firewalls. Use the **Advanced** mode for firewall configurations so you can easily provide the necessary configurations.

How it works...

One important thing regarding the direction of communication is to understand who is initiating the communication. When DPM is protecting server workloads, the DPM server will call for the DPM agent to start its VSS request, but when DPM is protecting clients, the DPM server will wait for the DPM agent present on the client to call in.

There's more...

You could also limit the actual port range for the high-end ports to a specific port range. For instructions on how to do this, you can refer to this article: `http://blogs.technet.com/b/dpm/archive/2011/06/28/how-to-limit-dynamic-rpc-ports-used-by-dpm-and-protected-servers.aspx`.

2
Installation and Upgrade

In this chapter, we will cover the installation and upgrade for System Center Data Protection Manager 2012 R2. We will also understand the prerequisites to start your upgrade process.

You will learn how to:

- Install a SQL Server locally on the DPM server
- Prepare a remote SQL Server for DPMDB
- Install SCDPM 2012 R2
- Install SCDPM 2012 R2 using a remote SQL Server or cluster
- Install SCDPM 2012 R2 in optional scenarios
- Understand the supported upgrade scenarios

Introduction

The final result of an installation will never be better than the dependent application design and implementation. A common mistake discovered frequently is the misconfiguration of the SQL configurations that the System Center applications depend on. If you provide System Center a poorly configured SQL Server or insufficient resources, you will end up with quite a bad installation of the application that could be part of the services you would like to provision within your modern data center. In the end, a System Center application can never work faster than what the underlying dependent architecture or technology allows.

By proper planning and decent design, you can also provide a scalable scenario for your installation that will make your System Center application applicable for future scenarios.

One important note regarding the upgrade scenario for the System Center Data Protection Manager software is the fact that there is no rollback feature built in. If your upgrade fails, you will not be able to provide an easy approach for restoring your DPM server to its former running state. Always remember to provide supported scenarios for your solution. Never take any shortcuts because there aren't any.

Installing a SQL Server locally on the DPM server

This recipe will cover the installation process of a local SQL Server that is collocated with the DPM server on the same operating system.

Getting ready

SQL Server is a core component for System Center Data Protection Manager. It is of major importance that the installation and design of SQL Server is well planned and implemented. If you have an undersized installation of SQL Server, it will provide you with a negative experience while operating the System Center Data Protection Manager.

 Before continuing the installation of SQL, please read the *Planning DPM pre-installation tasks* recipe in *Chapter 1, Pre-installation Tasks*.

How to do it...

Make sure that your operating system is fully patched and rebooted before you start the installation of SQL Server 2012 and that the DPM Admins group is a member of the local administrators group. Now take the following steps:

Insert the SQL server media and start the SQL server setup. In the **SQL Server Installation Center**, click on **New SQL Server stand-alone installation...**

The **Setup Support Rules** will start and will identify any problems that might occur during the SQL server installation. When the Operation is complete, click on **OK** to continue.

In the **Product Key** step, Enter the product key and click on **Next >** to continue.

The next is the License Terms step where you check the **I accept the license terms** checkbox if you agree with the license terms. Click on **Next >** to continue.

The SQL server installation will verify if there are any product updates available from the Microsoft update service. Check the **Include SQL Server product updates** checkbox and click on **Next >** to continue.

Next is the **Install Setup Files** step that initializes the actual installation. When the tasks have finished, click on **Install** to continue.

Verify that all the rules have passed in the **Setup Support Rule** step of the SQL server installation process. Resolve any warnings or errors and click the **Re-run** button to run the verification again. If all the rules have passed, click on **Next >** to continue.

In the **Setup Role** step, select **SQL Server Feature Installation** and click on **Next >**.

In the **Feature Selection**, choose the SQL server features that you would like to install. System Center Data Protection Manager requires:

- ▶ **Database Engine Service**
- ▶ **Full-Text and Semantic Extractions for Search**
- ▶ **Reporting Services – Native**

As an option, you can also install the SQL Server Management Studio on the same operating system as the DPM sever. Those components are found under **Management Tools**, check both **Basic** and **Complete**. Click on **Next >** to continue.

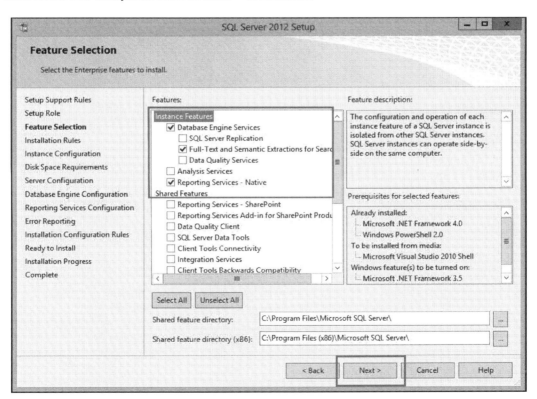

Verify the **Installation Rules** step, resolve any errors, and click on **Next >** to continue.

In the **Instance Configuration** step, select **Named instance** and type in a suitable name for your SQL server instance. Click on the button next to the **Instance root directory** and select the volume that should host the DPMDB.

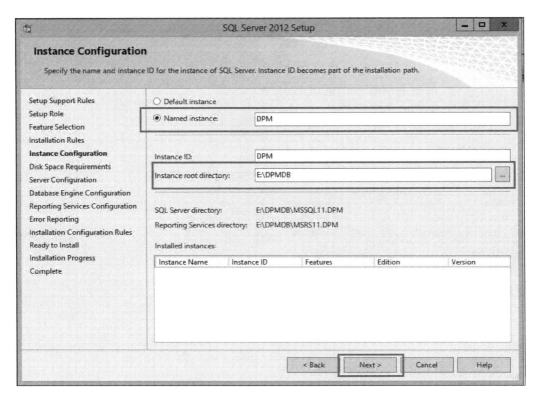

Click on **Next >** to continue

Verify that there are no problems in the **Disk Space Requirement** step, resolve any issues, and click on **Next >** to continue.

In the **Server Configuration** step, type in the credentials for the dedicated service account you would like to use for this SQL server. Switch the **Startup Type** to **Automatic** for the **SQL Server Agent**. When all the credentials are filled in, click on the **Collation** tab.

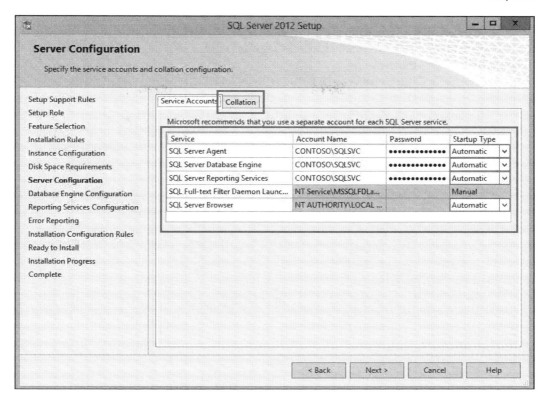

In the **Collation** tab, must enter the collation for the database engine. System Center Data Protection Manager must have the **SQL_Latin1_General_CP1_CI_AS** collation. Click on the **Customize...** button to choose the correct collation and then **Next >** to continue.

The next step is the **Database Engine Configuration** step and here you enter the authentication security mode, administrators, and directories. In the **Authentication Mode** section, choose **Windows Authentication mode**. In the **Specify SQL Server administrators** section, add the DPM Admins group and click on the **Data Directories** tab to verify that all your SQL server configurations point to the dedicated disk. Click on **Next >** to continue.

In the **Reporting Services Configuration** step, configure **SSRS or SQL Server Reporting Services**. For the **Reporting Services Native Mode** choose **Install and configure** and click on **Next >** to continue.

The next step is **Error Reporting**. Choose the **defaults** and click on **Next >** to continue.

In the **Installation and Configuration Rules** step, verify that all operations pass the rules. Resolve any warnings or errors and click the **Re-run** button for another verification. When all operations have passed, click on **Next >** to continue.

Verify the configuration in the **Ready to Install** step and click on **Install** to start the installation.

The **Installation Progress** step will show the current status of the installation process. When the installation is done, the **SQL Server 2012 Setup** will show you a summary of the **Complete** step. That is the final step page of the SQL Server Server 2012 installation wizard.

Click on the **Close** button to end the **SQL Server 2012 Setup**.

How it works...

SQL server is a very important component for the System Center family. If the SQL server is undersized or misconfigured in any way, it will reflect negatively in many ways on the performance of the System Center.

It is crucial to plan, design, and measure the performance of the SQL server so that you know it will fit the scale you are planning for, and the workloads that it should host.

There's more...

For more information regarding supported versions of SQL and how you should plan your installation for an optimal scenario for hosting the DPMDB, please refer to the *Planning DPM pre-installation tasks* recipe in *Chapter 1, Pre-installation Tasks*.

Preparing a remote SQL Server for DPMDB

This recipe will cover the procedure to prepare a remote SQL server for hosting the DPMDB.

Getting ready

In the scenario where you build a large hosted DPM service solution delivering BaaS (Backup as a Service), RaaS (Restore as a Service), or DRaaS (Disaster Recovery as a Service) within your modern data center, you may want to use a dedicated backend SQL server that is either a standalone SQL server or a clustered one, for high availability.

 It is not advisable to use SQL Server Always-On to host the DPMDB.

Regardless of whether you put the DPMDB on a cluster or a backend standalone SQL server, you still need to perform some initial configurations prior to the actual DPM server installation.

How to do it...

After installing your backend SQL server solution you must prepare it for hosting the DPMDB.

Insert the DPM2012R2 media and run the setup. In the setup screen, click on the **DPM Remote SQL Prep** link.

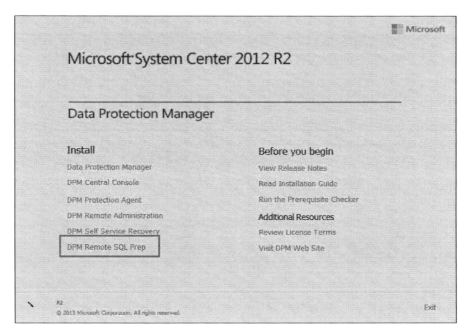

The installation wizard will start and install the DPM 2012 R2 Support Files; this is a very quick installation.

When the installation has finished, a message box prompts that the installation has finished and that the **System Center 2012 R2 DPM Support Files** have been successfully installed.

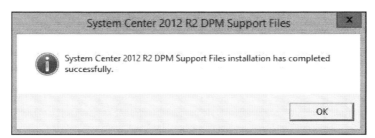

How it works...

The support files for SQL server will be installed on the backend SQL server box and will be used when the DPM server connects and creates its database.

There's more...

For the DPM server installation to be successful, when you place the DPMDB on a backend SQL server solution, you need to install the SQL 2012 SERVICE PACK 1 Tools that are located in the `catalogue\SCDPM\SQLSRV2012SP1` directory on the DPM media.

See also

For further information regarding design considerations, preparing service accounts, and other important pre-installation tasks for SQL server please read the *Planning DPM pre-installation tasks* recipe in *Chapter 1, Pre-installation Tasks*.

Installing SCDPM 2012 R2

This recipe will cover the installation process for System Center Data Protection Manager 2012 R2.

Getting ready

Before you start installing System Center Data Protection Manager 2012 R2, it is recommended that you read the *Planning your DPM pre-installation tasks* and *Planning the DPM disk pool* recipes in *Chapter 1, Pre-installation Tasks* regarding DPM prerequisites and SQL server planning and design.

How to do it...

Insert the DPM 2012 R2 media and start the setup for System Center Data Protection Manager 2012 R2. When the installation list is presented click on **Data Protection Manager** to start the installation.

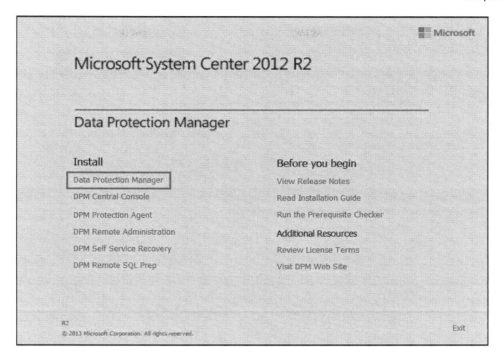

The installation wizard starts and prompts you with the **Microsoft Software License Terms**. Accept the license terms by checking the checkbox **I accept the license terms and conditions** to continue the installation.

The installation wizard will now prompt you with eight different installation steps. Currently you are on the **Welcome** step. To continue the installation, click on **Next >**.

The next step is the **Prerequisites check** where you can choose to install DPM using a standalone or a clustered SQL server.

 This recipe will cover the standalone scenario, for remote or cluster installation please read the *Installing SCDPM2012 R2 using a remote SQL server or cluster* recipe in this chapter.

In the **Instance of SQL Server** type in your server name and the instance name that should host your DPMDB.

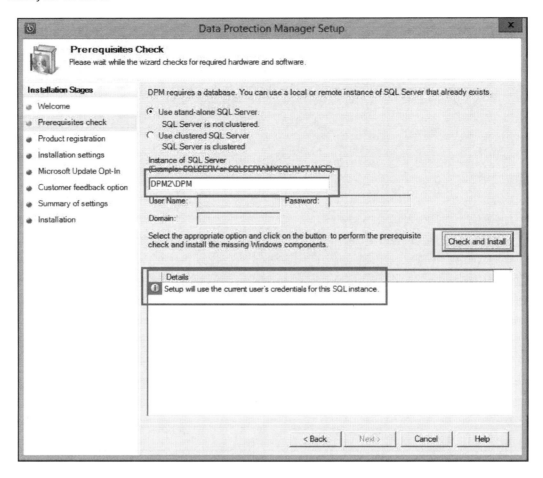

Please note that when you install DPM and use a local SQL server installation, the setup will use the current user's credentials for the SQL server instance. If the domain account that is logged on and performing the installation is not a member of the DPM Admin group in the Active Directory, the installation will fail. Click on the **Check and Install** button to run a verification that all the prerequisites have been met before the installation can continue.

If you haven't installed the SIS filter before you started the DPM server installation, the installation setup will install the SIS filter but will require a restart of the DPM server before the installation can continue (`https://technet.microsoft.com/en-us/library/hh758058.aspx`). Simply restart the DPM server and start the installation wizard one more time. When you run the prerequisites checker in the **Prerequisites check** step, it will be successful. Click on **Next >** to continue.

In the **Product registration** step, enter the **User name**, **Company**, and **Product key** and click on **Next >** to continue.

The next step of the installation wizard is the **Installation settings** where you specify the location of the DPM files and read the summary of the **Space requirements**. If you want to place the DPM files in a specific location, click on the **Change...** button and specify the new destination. To continue to the next step, click on **Next >**.

You can specify in the **Microsoft Update Opt-In** if the local Windows Update should be redirected to use Microsoft Update instead.

 Be very cautious regarding automatic update of the DPM server. Before you apply an update rollup for DPM, there are some considerations that you should verify. This is discussed in detail in the *Upgrading the DPM agents* recipe in *Chapter 3, Post-installation Tasks*.

Choose the most appropriate option for your implementation and click on **Next >** to continue.

If you would like to submit feedback to Microsoft regarding your usage of DPM, this is highly appreciated and is done in the **Customer feedback option**. There are dedicated technicians who will read your submitted logs and your contribution means a lot to Microsoft. Click on **Next >** to continue.

In the **Summary of settings**, you can verify your installation configuration. If everything looks good, click the **Install** button to start the installation.

The last step is the **Installation** step and here you can keep a watch on the installation progress in real time. When the installation has finished, click on the **Close** button.

How it works...

The installation media for System Center Data Protection Manager 2012 R2 will provide you with the installation bits for the DPM software. Since the 2012 R2 release of DPM, the SQL media is no longer included on the DPM media, so you need to consider how you design and install your SQL server that will host the DPM server software.

There's more ...

When System Center Data Protection Manager 2012 R2 is installed, you need to perform a number of post-installation tasks before your DPM servers are able to start protecting your production environment. Please read *Chapter 3, Post-installation Tasks* for further information regarding post-installation tasks.

Installing SCDPM 2012 R2 using a remote SQL server or cluster

This recipe will cover the installation of DPM 2012 R2 using a remote SQL server or cluster.

Getting ready

▶ This recipe will cover and explain the configuration needed to complete a DPM 2012 R2 installation when you are using a backend, standalone server or a SQL cluster for achieving a high-availability scenario.

[It is not advisable to use SQL Server Always-On to host the DPMDB.]

Before you can start your DPM sever installation you need to configure the SQL server to be able to host the DPMDB.

The only difference in the installation wizard when you install the DPM server software is the **Prerequisites check** step.

How to do it...

This recipe assumes that you have your SQL server installed and that correct configurations have been made according to the recipes in this book.

Regardless of whether the DPMDB is placed on a SQL cluster or a standalone SQL server, you must install the DPM 2012 R2 Support Files on the SQL server node(s) that will host your DPMDB. Please read the *Preparing a remote SQL Server for DPMDB* recipe in this chapter, since it is a prerequisite.

In the **Prerequisites check** step of the Installation Wizard, you have an option to choose whether you would like to place the DPMDB on a remote standalone SQL server or a SQL cluster.

For a standalone backend SQL server hosting your DPMDB, enter the SQLSERVER\INSTANCE in the **Instance of SQL Server** field.

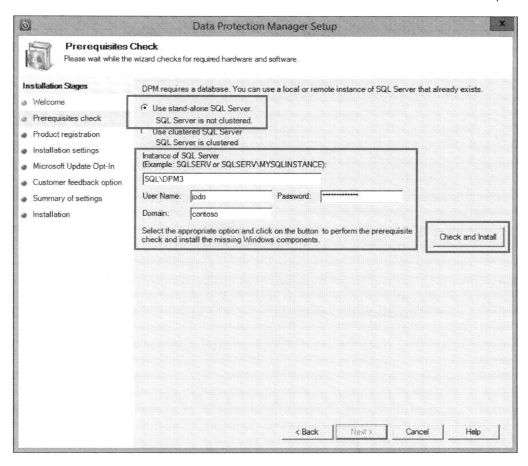

Enter the **User Name**, **Password,** and **Domain** for the account that has the appropriate rights for the SQL configuration. Click on the **Check and Install** button to verify the prerequisites.

 The account used for the configuration must be a member of the DPM Admin group.

In the case of a SQL clustered environment you must specify both SQL server and instance for the DPMDB and also where the **Instance of SQL Server Reporting Service** is located since this is not supported to be clustered.

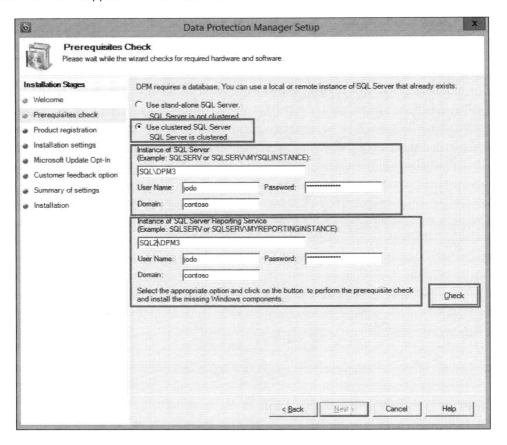

Enter the **Instance of SQL Server** for the DPMDB and also provide information for the **Instance of SQL Server Reporting Service** that will host the reporting for the DPM server. Provide credentials that have the rights in the SQL server configuration; the accounts should be members of the DPM Admin group. Click on the **Check** button to check the prerequisites.

Click on **Next >** to continue the installation.

How it works...

The DPM server Installation Wizard will provide you with the right configuration needed regarding the SSRS configuration for the DPM reports. SSRS or SQL Server Reporting Service is not supported to be clustered.

There's more...

For a detailed guide on the installation steps, please read the *Installing SCDPM 2012 R2* recipe in this Chapter.

Understanding the supported upgrade scenarios

This section will cover the supported upgrade scenarios that also apply to installing DPM rollup updates on the DPM server.

As a DPM administrator, one of the most important maintenance tasks is to apply update rollups, service packs, and also upgrade to the latest version.

There are some considerations that you should think of before you apply any update rollups, service packs, or upgrade to the latest version of the DPM software:

- ▶ Back up your DPMDB
- ▶ Solve any inconsistencies and alerts in the console
- ▶ Have a recovery plan

When you apply update rollups, service packs, or upgrade to the latest version of the DPM software, the installation will update both files and in some cases the DPMDB. Since there is currently no roll back function for the DPM software updates, it is very important that you understand the importance of having your configurations backed up in case of data corruption or hardware failure and so on.

You can backup your DPMDB using a DPM-DPM-DR scenario where a secondary DPM server backs up the primary DPMDB and vice versa. This is also called chaining.

In the upgrade scenario where you have a primary and a secondary DPM server, the above recommended strategies apply. However, it is recommended that you always start the upgrade process with your secondary DPM Server and then upgrade your primary DPM server; this is to avoid any unnecessary disturbance.

Always have a decent restore plan but most importantly have set routines regarding the backup of the DPMDB and have a proper design for your DPM servers and their disk pools. For more information regarding design considerations and valuable advice, please read *Chapter 1, Pre-installation Tasks* and *Chapter 3, Post-installation Tasks* of this book.

3
Post-installation Tasks

In this chapter, we will cover the post-installation tasks for System Center Data Protection Manager 2012 R2.

We will cover the following topics:

- Understanding the DPM terminology
- Configuring the DPM disk pool
- Adding disk to the DPM disk pool
- Growing volumes automatically in the DPM disk pool
- Creating a replica manually
- Installing the DPM agent via the DPM console
- Installing the DPM agent manually
- Upgrading the DPM agents
- Configuring DPM agent throttling
- Understanding DPM Protection Groups
- Optimizing the Protection Group
- DPMDB optimization
- Report management
- Configuring a dedicated backup network
- Configuring e-mail notifications
- Applying update rollups (UR) to the DPM server
- Working with filters

Introduction

After the planning and installation of System Center Data Protection Manager 2012 R2, the next challenge of your setup is to make the DPM design adapt to your business needs. This chapter explains the important terminology used, how to actually get started with your Protection Groups, and the points to consider while setting them up.

What is of major importance here is to understand that System Center Data Protection Manager 2012 R2 is not just a focused backup software that provides you with snapshot data. DPM creates the possibility for you to build backup, restore, and disaster recovery services for your company or organization. There is more to DPM than meets the eye; under the hood, there are great possibilities and, of course, challenges that you must face. In the end, it all comes down to, is for you to have a decent and proper restore plan that you can adopt to your business continuity plan and to always have your critical services up and running. Meanwhile, you continuously offer optimal, supported, and sufficient data restore capabilities within your modern data center.

Understanding the DPM terminology

During the setup of System Center Data Protection Manager 2012 R2, you probably saw one or two words that were, perhaps, new to you. When you work with DPM, you will encounter new terminology that are important for you to fully understand. This is what will be covered in this recipe.

There are many thoughts and interpretations about the different terminology that System Center Data Protection Manager is build up on, but the best source for this particular subject is TechNet.

At the site `http://technet.microsoft.com/en-us/library/gg597301.aspx`, you will find the DPM Glossary that will provide you the basic understanding of the DPM terminology.

The community has always provided decent and good information to Microsoft regarding what could be improved. Since the DPM team is highly committed to push the product forward, they are working on rebuilding the content of TechNet.

Configuring the DPM disk pool

This recipe covers points to be considered when configuring the hardware that will store the DPM disk pool.

Getting ready

System Center Data Protection Manager consumes a large amount of disk space to be able to provide suitable data protection. The product group for DPM understood the pain of this and has provided deduplication of the DPM disk pool if you place the VHD or VHDX files on a **Scaled-Out File Server** (**SOFS**) that has deduplication enabled.

It is important to purchase the right kind of hardware for your solution that will also map directly to an optimal ROI. The recommendation is, of course, to empower your solution using SOFS but if you do not have the required budget, there are some important facts that you need to consider.

How to do it...

There are some do's and don'ts for choosing the correct disk storage for the DPM disk pool. Keep in mind that being supported does not always go hand in hand with being the most optimal solution. Of course, you should not spend a huge amount of dollars on your storage solution for storing backed up data, but keep it simple in order to achieve your ROI easily.

First thing to keep in mind is to never use a software raid controller that could, for example, be found in an NAS solution using iSCSI protocol. Using a software raid controller is not supported and in some environments, it will create a bottleneck for performance. This should, however, not be associated with DPM using a SOFS that hosts its VHD or VHDX files for its disk pool as the setup is different in many ways.

If SOFS is not possible, you should purchase a DAS storage solution and a physical RAID controller that has a high value of throughput. The best recommendation is to use a RAID5 configuration for all your arrays. Never use ADG (RAID6) due to performance latency.

How it works...

There are many good hardware vendors out there who claim to be the market but the best advice is to keep it simple. Don't purchase expensive SAN solutions for your DPM disk pool as that will only result in a poor ROI. The hardware that you should consider buying is a storage solution that supports the SOFS configuration, so you can enable the DPM disk pool for deduplication.

There's more...

Summarizing this recipe, you should remember the following:

- ▶ Do not use a NAS solution based on iSCSI access to your DPM server
- ▶ Do not use a software RAID controller
- ▶ As a primary choice, you should place your VHD or VHDX files on a SOFS that enables the DPM disk pool for deduplication

- ▶ If you don't have the funding to set up an SOFS, you should purchase disk storage that uses a physical RAID controller and also a SATA disk interface for achieving a good ROI.

- ▶ Use RAID5 for your arrays.

 You can enable deduplication for the DPM disk pool by placing your VHDX files, that are members of the DPM disk pool, on SOFS.

Adding disk to the DPM disk pool

This recipe explains how to add a disk to your DPM disk pool either via the console or by using PowerShell.

Getting ready

Before you start protecting your production environment, hosting your company's critical services in your modern data center, you must add disk storage to the DPM server disk pool. This can be done either via the DPM console or via DPM PowerShell.

How to do it...

When adding disk storage to the DPM disk pool via the console, start by clicking on **Management** to get to the management pane on the console.

 Before you are able to add disks to the DPM server disk pool, they must be present in **Disk Management** under **Computer Management**. It's recommended that you convert your disks to dynamic disks before you add them to the DPM server disk pool.

On the left hand side of the console is the **Disks** link. Click on it to list the **DPM Storage Pool Disks**.

 You do not need to create any volume yourself; System Center Data Protection Manager will allocate and handle the disk allocation itself.

Click on the **Add** button on the top left side of the console to start the **Add Disk to Storage Pool** wizard. Choose from the **Available disks** on the left side and mark the one that you want to add to the DPM disk pool. Click on the **Add >** button.

If you have not converted the disk to a dynamic disk, you will see an information box saying that before DPM can use this disk, it must be converted to a dynamic disk.

Your new disk will appear on the right hand side under **Selected disks.** Click on **OK** to make the disk available for the DPM disk pool.

If you want to add a disk via DPM PowerShell, you must open the **DPM Management Shell,** which is located on your desktop, by default.

Adding the disk to the DPM, via the **DPM Management Shell,** is covered in two steps. First, you must list all the disks available in the operating system via the following syntax: `$DPMDisk = Get-DPMDisk -DPMServerName "Contoso-DPMServer".`

Remember that the disks presented in Disk Management are indexed in the `$DPMDisk` variable; if you would like to see the third disk in the, simply type `$DPMDisk[2].` When you have identified the disk you want to add to the DPM disk pool, type the following syntax: `Add-DPMDisk -DPMDisk $DPMDisk[n].`

Here, `n` is the number of the disks in the array for `$DPMDisk.`

How it works...

System Center Data Protection Manager manages and takes care of disk management by itself. By using dynamic disks, it has the ability to expand volumes that are associated with protected data sources and manage the spanning procedure of the disks automatically.

There's more...

A DPM server can have up to 120 TB of storage attached to it. To avoid performance issues, never use a disk larger than 15 TB.

Growing volumes automatically in the DPM disk pool

This recipe covers the way to enable System Center Data Protection Manager to automatically grow the volumes for protected data sources.

Getting ready

System Center Data Protection Manager has three auto-protect features, one of which is **Automatically grow the volumes**. This feature relies on the dynamic disk architecture and this is why DPM needs the disks in the DPM disk pool to be dynamic disks.

How to do it...

During the initial configuration of a protection group, you have the ability to set up some unique features, one of them being **Automatically grow the volumes,** also known as **Auto Grow**. This is done in the **Review Disk Allocation** step in the **Protection Group Wizard**.

You can also enable this feature after you have created the protection group. To enable the **Auto Grow** feature, right click a protection group and choose **Modify disk allocation...** and the **Modify Disk Allocation** wizard appears. At the bottom of the window, there is a check box that says **Automatically grow the volumes**. Check the checkbox and click **OK** to enable the **Auto Grow** feature.

How it works...

When the replica volume or the recovery point volume in the DPM disk pool reaches 90 percent of allocation, the auto grow feature will allocate 10 GB more disk space or 25 percent more disk space, whichever is larger.

There's more...

It is important to keep track of how much disk space is allocated in the DPM disk pool. A good way to get an initial forecast is to use the **Disk Utilization report,** that is found under **Reports** in the DPM console.

Creating a replica manually

This recipe will explain how to create a replica manually and the different scenarios that it is applicable to.

Getting ready

Internet Service Providers or ISPs around the world have a challenge in delivering high speed internet connections to all corners of the world. This well-known fact also makes it more convenient for you to be able to create a replica manually if you don't have the bandwidth to create a replica automatically or via the scheduled feature in the DPM.

Creating a manual replica is divided into three steps:

1. Create a copy of the data that you want the DPM to protect.
2. Configure protection in the DPM for the data source.
3. Import the data into the DPM disk pool.

How to do it...

The first step is to get a copy of your data and place it on a mobile media device like a USB disk or similar. When you have a good copy of your data, you are ready to move on to the DPM server and configure a new protection group, or modify an existing one.

 Before you start configuring the DPM server, you must have a DPM agent installed and attached for the server managing the data sources that you would like to protect.

In the **Protection Group Wizard**, there is a step called **Choose Replica Creation Method**. Here, you can choose to create a replica using three different options:

► **Now**
► **Later**
► **Manually**

 For more information regarding the other steps in the **Protection Group Wizard**, please read this chapter that corresponds to the workload you would like to protect.

Choose to create your replica **Manually** and finish configuring the protection group. If you expand the protected data source in the DPM console **Protection** view, you will see the informational text **Manual replica creation pending,** as shown in the following screenshot:

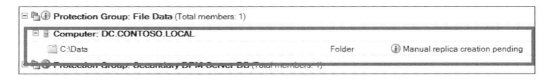

Now you must find out what GUID ID the data source replica is associated with. Do this by clicking on the data source and click on the link present in the information pane at the bottom.

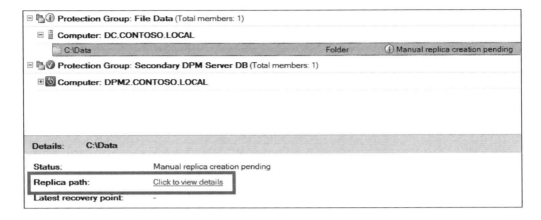

In the window that appears, right-click and choose **Copy**.

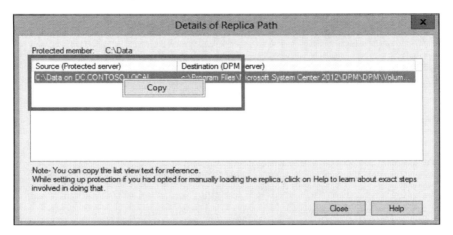

Close the window and open notepad. Paste the previously copied text into notepad.

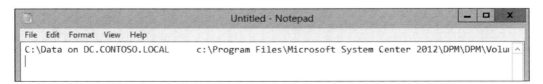

Keep this information for later use. Now, open an elevated command prompt and type the following command:

```
mountvol
```

 You can also pipe the command to a text file if you have a large number of already protected data sources as follows:

```
mountvol > dump.txt
```

Next, find your data source associated GUID. In this example, the following applies:

You have now identified the GUID that is associated with the data source that you have enabled for manual replica creation. Next, you must mount its replica volume within the DPM disk pool.

Mount the volume `\\?\Volume{c70ee8b9-8888-11e2-93fd-00155d0a7b0d}\` by using the `mountvol` command with the following syntax:

```
mountvol R: \\?\Volume{c70ee8b9-8888-11e2-93fd-00155d0a7b0d}\
```

If you open the file explorer, you will now have a hard disk drive called `R:` that is mapped to the GUID of the data source.

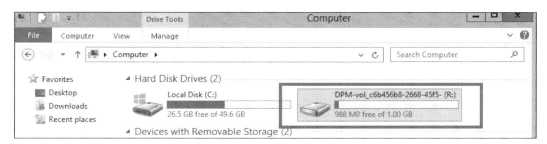

Open `R:` and open all the sub-catalogues `R:\{id}\Full`. Please note that in this example, we are protecting a folder named `Data`. Copy the data from your removable disk.

After the copying process has successfully finished, go to the DPM console and right-click the data source for which you have created a manual replica. From the drop-down list, choose **Perform consistency check...** to trigger a consistency check that will verify the data.

When the consistency check has finished, dismount the `R:` volume by using the syntax `mountvol R:\ /d` from an elevated command prompt.

How it works...

If you have a poor network connection to your branch offices or remote locations where you want to protect company data, you would benefit from creating your replica manually and also enabling DPM agent throttling, which will be covered in the *Configuring DPM agent throttling* recipe in this chapter.

When you have copied the data from your removable media to the DPM disk pool, System Center Data Protection Manager verifies the data consistency by running a consistency check and synchronizing any block-level changed data.

There's more...

If you need to dedicate specific volumes for a specific storage, you can use **Custom Volumes**. The downside of using **Custom Volumes** in DPM is that you need to keep track of the data growth and expand the volumes yourself. This could be automated by using System Center Orchestrator or Service Management Automation. For this, refer to the following website:

`https://technet.microsoft.com/en-us/library/jj627986.aspx`

Installing the DPM agent via the DPM console

This recipe will cover the installation of a DPM agent via the DPM console.

Getting ready

Before you can start protecting a workload within your data center, you must install a DPM agent on the server hosting the workload that you would like to protect. Finish the configuration by attaching it to the DPM console or via the DPM PowerShell CMDLET.

How to do it...

Open the DPM console, go to **Management** and click on **Agents**. At the top left corner of the console, click on the **Install** button to start the **Protection Agent Installation Wizard**.

Under the **Select Agent Deployment Method**, click **Install** agents, followed by the **Next >** button.

The next step is **Select Computers**. DPM will list all computers that are members of the same domain as that of the DPM server. Add the computers that you would like to install the DPM agent to. Click **Next >** to continue.

Enter Credentials is the next step and now you must enter an account that has administrative rights on the server that you would like to install the DPM agent to. If you have selected a node within a cluster, the DPM will then prompt you with the option to install DPM agents to other cluster members. Once you have entered the credentials, click on **Next >** to continue.

In the **Choose Restart Method** step, you choose whether the server can restart once the DPM agent has been installed.

 It is not mandatory to restart your server to be able to protect your workloads in your data center. The reason that this step exists is that the DPM installation process can provide a planned restart, once the installation of the DPM agent is done.

Choose an appropriate option and click on **Next >** to continue.

In the **Summary** step, you can verify the information and then click on **Install** to initialize the installation and configuration process of the DPM agent.

How it works...

The DPM agent is the core component for the DPM to be able to provide restore capabilities for your data center. The DPM relies on the DCOM object of the protected server which is mapped to the DPMRA service so that the SQL job on the DPM server starts. System Center Data Protection Manager stores all protection group configurations as SQL jobs and the SQL Server Agent initializes the DPM agent to start creating snapshots, using the underlying architecture of the Volume Shadow Copy Services, within the operating system.

There's more...

System Center Data Protection Manager manages data replication and provides management of the DPM agents using two different TCP ports:

- ▶ 5718
- ▶ 5719

The TCP port 5718 is used for data replication and the TCP port 5719 is used by the DPM agent coordinator. The **coordinator** is the function within the DPM agent architecture that manages installation, updates, and uninstallation of the DPM agent. For more information regarding firewall ports and configuration, please read the *Firewall configuration* recipe in *Chapter 1, Pre-installation Tasks*.

Installing the DPM agent manually

This recipe covers the manual installation of the DPM agent, it's configuration and attachment to the DPM server console.

Getting ready

There are some scenarios where you will not able to perform a push installation of the DPM agent to the server hosting the workload that you would like to protect. On the DPM server are the executables for the DPM agent that you can share or download to a removable media. The DPM agent is also available on the DPM installation media. There are two different executables:

- ▶ DpmAgentInstaller.exe
- ▶ DpmAgentInstaller_AMD64.exe

The DpmAgentInstaller.exe is for 32-bits operating systems while the DpmAgentInstaller_AMD64.exe is for 64-bits operating systems. Both are applicable for Windows server and Windows client operating systems.

How to do it...

You can perform a manual installation in two different ways:

- ▶ By providing the FQDN of the DPM server when running the DpmAgentInstaller executable
- ▶ By providing the NetBIOS name of the DPM server using setdpmserver.exe if the DPM agent is already installed but not configured

If you do not have a DPM agent installed, run the appropriate DpmAgentInstaller executable from the `%Program Files%\Microsoft DPM\DPM\ProtectionAgents\ RA\3.0.<build number>.0\amd64` catalogue of the DPM server. The easiest way is to perform a UNC path for the catalog or map a drive letter using the `net use` command.

Before installing the DPM agent manually using the `DpmAgentInstaller`, you must configure the local windows firewall to allow the DPM agent to communicate with the DPM server. Open an elevated command prompt and type the following syntax: `netsh advfirewall firewall add rule name="Allow DPM Remote Agent Push" dir=in action=allow service=any enable=yes profile=any remoteip=<IPAddress>` where `IPAddress` is the IP address of your DPM server.

Open an elevated command prompt and go to the UNC path from where the location of the DPM agent installer is executable. Run `DpmAgentInstaller_AMD64.exe` and provide the FQDN for the DPM server. The DPM agent should report to as follows:

DpmAgentInstaller_AMD64 DPM1.contoso.com

The `DpmAgentInstaller` does not configure the firewall for the DPM agent, only the `SetDpmServer.exe` executable does that.

If the DPM agent is already installed, you should run the `setdpmserver.exe` executable with the `-dpmservername` switch to configure the DPM server that the DPM agent should report to as:

Setdpmserver -dpmservername DPM1

When using the `SetDpmServer` executable, you only need the NetBIOS name of the DPM server.

The DPM agent has now been configured and the appropriate firewall exceptions have been made in the domain profile of the Windows firewall. Now you must attach the DPM agent to the DPM server.

Open the DPM console and go to **Management**. Click on **Agents** and at the top left corner of the console, click on the **Install** button to start the **Protection Agent Installation Wizard**.

Under **Select Agent Deployment Method**, click **Attach agents** followed by **Computer on a trusted domain**. Click the **Next >** button to continue.

If you want to attach a DPM agent in an untrusted domain, please refer to *Chapter 10, Workgroup Protection and CBA*.

In the **Select Computers** step, choose the server that you would like to attach to the DPM server and click on **Next >** to continue.

 You can also provide a list of servers that you would like to have attached. The list should have all the FQDN of every server per row in a simple text file. Click on the **Add From File** button to insert the files' data.

The next step is the **Enter Credentials** step where you enter the credentials that should be used to execute this process. Keep in mind that the credentials you provide must have administrative rights on the server that you are trying to attach. Provide the credentials and click on **Next >** to continue.

Under **Summary**, verify the configuration and click on **Attach** to start.

The **Agents** will appear in the DPM console and report **OK** within a short time.

How it works...

The `setdpmserver.exe` executable has the ability to configure the DPM agent to set which DPM server the DPM agent reports to. It also provides the configuration needed for the local Windows firewall, so that the DPM agent can start reporting to the DPM server.

There is more...

There are, of course, more installation scenarios that you could use for deploying a DPM agent. A solid recommendation is to take advantage of System Center Configuration Manager (SCCM) to provide a deployment scenario of the DPM agents.

You can also use the DPM PowerShell PS1 script called `attached-productionserver.PS1` to do the same.

Upgrading the DPM agents

This recipe covers the way to upgrade DPM agents from the DPM console and also provides information about other scenarios.

Getting ready

Microsoft releases updates that are critical for you to apply since they contain the newly updated bits that will provide you with optimization of the DPM software and also enable new restore capability features for your data center.

How to do it...

After you have upgraded the DPM server you must upgrade all the DPM agents that are attached to the DPM server.

 Read the *Applying update rollups (UR) to the DPM server* recipe in this chapter regarding the application of update rollups to a DPM server.

Open the DPM console, select **Management** and on the left-hand side of the console, click on **Agents**. In the display pane, you will see DPM agents reporting **Update Available**. Right-click the agents that you want to update and choose **Update** from the drop-down list.

How it works...

The DPM agent coordinator is the function within the DPM agent architecture that provides you with the ability to upgrade your DPM agents via the DPM console.

 Some update rollups demand a restart if the file filter drivers, or any DLL in the change tracking process has been updated. It is a good idea to read the release note for the update before applying it to the production environment.

There's more...

You can also apply the updates manually via Microsoft Update, your local WSUS or System Center Configuration Manager.

Configuring DPM agent throttling

This recipe will cover how to configure the DPM agent throttling, so you can have control over the network bandwidth consumption during specific hours of the day.

Getting ready

Being able to not let your internet connection choke your remote locations or branch offices are of key importance when you are providing a restore capability to the workloads present in that location.

System Center Data Protection Manager relies on the QoS Packet Scheduler for creating the DPM agent throttling scenario. If the QoS Packet Scheduler is not enabled, you need to enable it both on the DPM server as well as the servers hosting the workloads that you want to protect.

How to do it...

In the DPM console, go to **Management** and click on **Agent** on the left-hand side of the console. Right-click the DPM agent that you would like to configure throttling for and choose **Throttling** from the drop-down menu. The **Throttle** window will present the different configurations possible regarding this specific DPM agent.

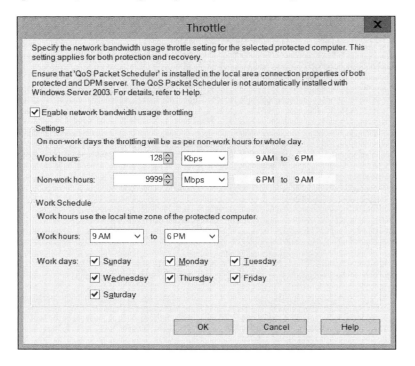

By checking the checkbox **Enable network bandwidth usage throttling**, you enable the throttling feature on the DPM agent. Under **Settings**, define the bandwidth limits for **Work hours** and **Non-work hours** for the DPM agent. The default limit of 128 Kbps is actually too low; it is recommended to not go below 512 Kbps.

Under **Work Schedule**, define **Work hours** and **Work days**, apply the right configuration, and click the **OK** button to confirm the changes made. The throttle information will now be displayed in the **Agents** display pane.

How it works...

The DPM agent relies on the underlying architecture of the Windows operating system, in this case, the QoS Packet Scheduler. If the feature is not enabled on the DPM server or the operating system that hosts the protected workload, throttling will not be possible.

There's more...

Keep in mind that making changes to the DPM database (DPMDB) is not a supported scenario. If you make any changes to DPMDB without any help from Microsoft support engineers, you will end up with an unsupported DPM solution.

If you want to enable a large scale of DPM agents, you should use the DPM server PowerShell management shell, instead of making changes in the DPMDB manually.

Understanding DPM Protection Groups

This recipe explains what a protection group is in System Center Data Protection Manager and the different configurable options that it can contain.

Getting ready

When you have come to the point in your DPM deployment where you have your DPM servers up and running and the agents deployed and attached, you are ready to create your definition of protection that will reflect the restore plan for your company's services. The definition of how you should protect something is defined in something called a **Protection Group**.

A protection group can be seen as a container that you fill with additional information to reflect the actual need for a backup. You define whether you want the protected data to be stored on disk, tape, or in azure; this is what Microsoft calls recovery goals. There are two types of recovery goals:

- ▶ Short-Term recovery goals
- ▶ Long-Term recovery goals

Short-Term recovery goals are disk based backups and as the name suggests, the data is stored only for a few weeks before it is archived to a long-term recovery goal media. The **Long-Term recovery goals** are tapes, virtual tape libraries, or the Azure service called the backup vault.

Building a solid restore scenario comes from knowing your data service dependencies, DPM is all about how you design your protection groups and how you scale the number of DPM servers to your BaaS (Backup as a Service), RaaS (Restore as a Service) or DRaaS (Disaster Recovery as a Service). Don't be afraid to mix up the different technologies, so that you have an optimal plan that fits your company's initial alignments.

Within the protection group configuration, you define the recovery goals. A recovery goal is the definition of how you should protect the file data and applications that are members of that protection group. There are three major categories:

- Retention range
- Synchronization frequency
- Recovery point schedule

Retention range is the number of days, weeks, months, or years that the protected data should be kept on disk, tape, or within Azure.

Synchronization frequency is how often the DPM agent should initialize a change tracking process using Volume Shadow copy Services (VSS) and replicate those block level changes to the DPM server.

 Only Files, SQL and Exchange workload have 15 minutes synchronization frequency.

The recovery point schedule is how often the Express-Full job should be initialized that consists of synchronizing the block level changes, replicating those to the DPM server and, if possible, merge them with previously synchronized data to again merge them to a recovery point.

The protection group also creates the configuration needed in the DPM disk pool to allocate the storage for the workload protection. System Center Data Protection Manager will make an initial calculation for the required disk space; you can also provide the exact number yourself when you have calculated the size needed for protection. The formulas that you should use are available on this DPM blog:

```
http://robertanddpm.blogspot.se/2010/10/how-much-will-workloads-
allocate-in-my.html
```

As part of the protection group configuration, you must also provide information regarding tape and library details for your long-term recovery goals. System Center Data Protection Manager is compatible with a majority of available tape library hardware in the market. For more information, please read *Chapter 13, Tape Management*.

When creating protection for a workload within your data center, you also provide information of how the initial replica creation should take place. System Center Data Protection Manager can create a replica:

- **Now**
- **Later**
- **Manually**

If you choose the option **Now**, DPM will, once the protection group wizard has finished, start an initial replica creation of the workload and copy the data to the replica volume that is associated with the protected data source. However, if you want to schedule the replica creation process, you should choose the option **Later**. For many companies, there could be a challenge with ISP's bandwidth to different remote locations or branch offices. If you don't want to flood the internet access, you can create your replica **Manually**. Please read *Creating a replica manually* and *Configuring DPM Agent throttling* recipes in this chapter, regarding how to manually create your replica and how to configure DPM agent throttling respectively.

How to do it...

In the DPM console, create a new protection group by clicking on the **New** button in the top left corner in the **Protection** area of the DPM console.

For designing an optimal protection group design, refer to the next recipe to get an insight on what you should consider for a specific workload.

How it works...

The recovery goal schedule is transformed into SQL jobs that will execute or initialize the DPM agent on the server that hosts the workload that you want to protect. The most critical part of a DPM server design is the SQL setup. Providing an optimal environment for SQL is of major importance.

There's more...

System Center Data Protection Manager provides a complete solution regarding restore scenarios for a modern data center. The most important fact still remains that the knowledge of how you set up the DPM server software so that your design meets the company's demand and business continuity plan.

Optimizing the Protection Group

This recipe will cover how to optimize a protection group configuration so it fits the organization's data center.

Getting ready

When you have set up a protection group that defines the backup settings for a protected data source that maps to your restore plans, you may find the need of optimizing the protection group configuration.

How to do it...

There are five important configuration methods to optimize a protection group:

- ▶ Enable network throttling
- ▶ Enable data compression
- ▶ Provide staggering
- ▶ Create your replica manually
- ▶ Alter the Express-Full schedule

The network throttling, manual replica creation, and altering the Express-Full schedule methods are covered in corresponding recipes in this chapter.

How it works...

If you modify a protection group or create a new one, you have the ability to optimize the protection group in two ways:

- ▶ Via the Protection Group Wizard
- ▶ Via the DPM console

Open the **Protection** view of the DPM console, and simply click the protection group that you want to optimize. At the top of the console, you will see a button called **Optimize performance** that is a part of the tools ribbon; click on it.

In the **Network** tab, **enable on-the-wire** compression that will compress the data before transferring it to the DPM server. This will take very few resources on the protected server's CPU, yet is important to mention. In the **Network** tab, you also find the staggering function. The staggering function defines an offset to the protection group Express-Full schedule. It is important to keep in mind that the maximum allowed value for the offset is the same as the synchronization frequency.

There's more...

For more information regarding protection group optimization and other information regarding System Center Data Protection Manager, please read and follow this blog:
http://robertanddpm.blogspot.com

DPMDB optimization

This recipe covers how to optimize the DPM database also known as DPMDB.

Getting ready

In larger deployments of System Center Data Protection Manager, it is important to keep track if DPM and its underlying architectural dependencies are functioning optimally. This can be done by levering the possibilities of proactive monitoring using System Center Operations Manager and corresponding management packs.

If you don't have System Center Operations Manager installed, consider implementing it as soon as possible in order to enable a proactive monitoring for your data center that is adaptive and optimized for the Microsoft product stack.

To determine whether or not the DPMDB needs to be optimized, perform a search in the **Recovery** view of the DPM console. Search for Exchange and or SharePoint data. If the time for search takes very long, you should consider optimizing the DPMDB.

How to do it...

Optimizing the DPMDB is all about two things:

- ▶ Rebuilding indexes
- ▶ Reorganizing indexes

The optimization is done in the SQL Management Studio and can be done on five different tables in the DPMDB:

- ▶ tbl_RM_SharePointRecoverableObject
- ▶ tbl_RM_RecoverySource
- ▶ tbl_RM_DatasetROMap
- ▶ tbl_RM_RecoverableObject
- ▶ tbl_RM_RecoverySource

The first two are tables for SharePoint and the last three are tables for Exchange. The queries that you should execute in the SQL Server Management Studio are:

```
USE DPMDB GO ALTER INDEX ALL ON <tableName> REBUILD GO
USE DPMDB GO ALTER INDEX ALL ON <tableName> REORGANIZE GO
```

The first query is for rebuilding the index and the last one is for reorganizing the index.

How it works...

The DPM database, also known as DPMDB, is one of the critical points for System Center Data Protection Manager, the other being the DPM disk pool. If the DPMDB is facing a need for optimization it is crucial that this is taken care of, since the DPM functions depend very heavily on SQL.

There's more...

Keep in mind that your DPM server will never be better than the recovery design implemented in your business continuity plan. Regardless of your backup product of choice, you should keep in mind that there is no product on the market that will suit or fix all the challenges you have within your data center. The key to success is seeing the whole picture and providing a services-based solution that is built up from one vendor, Microsoft.

Report management

This recipe will cover how to get started with the reports in DPM.

Getting ready

Being able to provide a forecast and present the current status or historical information for a service is of great importance for many companies. System Center Data Protection Manager has six standard reports that you can use to get started with the forecast and historical views.

How to do it...

Under **Reporting** in the DPM console, you will find the six standard reports in DPM. The reports are:

- **Disk Utilization**
- **Recovery**
- **Recovery Point Status**
- **Status**
- **Tape Management**
- **Tape Utilization**

The **Disk Utilization** report provides you with information regarding disk capacity, disk allocation, and disk usage in the DPM storage pool. The **Recovery** report provides you with details about recovery items and statistics of the recovery jobs. The **Recovery Point Status** report informs you if there is a recovery point present or not within the defined time window also known as retention time. The **Status** report provides the status of all recovery points for a specific time period. The **Tape Management** report provides details for managing tape rotation. The **Tape Utilization** report provides information on the trends for the tape utilization and capacity planning.

In the **Reporting** view of the DPM console, you can not only view the DPM reports, but also set up subscriptions for all or a selected number of reports. The reports could be sent to you in three different formats:

- HTML
- PDF
- Excel

For DPM to be able to send the reports to you, the DPM server must have an SMTP configuration defined. For information on how to set up the SMTP configuration for DPM, please read the *Configuring e-mail notifications* recipe in this chapter.

How it works...

The reporting part of System Center Data Protection Manager is built up from the SQL Server Reporting Services or SSRS; it is one of the prerequisites for DPM.

There's more...

Using the Report Builder, you will be able to create your own DPM reports. Keep in mind that all the information you need is stored in the DPMDB and it is always a supported scenario if you read information from the DPMDB using SSRS technologies or PowerShell.

Configuring a dedicated backup network

This recipe will explain what a backup network is, why you may need it, and how to set it up.

Getting ready

The majority of the data centers that are built up using the modern data center approach are committed to both redundancy and smart designs in terms of providing uptime for the hosted services.

Providing a dedicated backup network, which the backup traffic can use and rely on, is a good strategy since it will offload the primary network architecture and not be dependent on the network hardware that builds up the production network.

How to do it...

There are some prerequisites for enabling a backup network:

- ▶ Secondary network card
- ▶ Enabling name resolution
- ▶ Verifying network connectivity

The configuration for setting up a backup network is made via PowerShell, but first you must have a secondary network card installed that is configured with an IP address that is a member of the backup network subnet.

The next step is to verify name resolution, alter the HOST file on both the production server and also the DPM server and enter the NetBIOS name for the servers involved.

Verify that you can ping the IP address for the backup network on the DPM server from the production environment and also via NetBIOS name.

To configure the backup network, you open the **DPM Management Shell** and use the PowerShell CMDLET called `Add-BackupNetworkAddress`.

To configure the DPM server to use the dedicated network of 10.1.1.0/24, enter the following syntax: `Add-BackupNetworkAddress –Address 10.1.1.0/24 –DPMServer DPM1 – SequenceNumber 1`.

The three switches are:

- ▶ `Address`
- ▶ `DPMServer`
- ▶ `SequenceNumber`

The Address switch provides the address for the backup network. The `DPMServer` provides the NetBIOS name for the DPM server. With the `SequenceNumber` switch, you provide the primary backup network and also the failover backup network.

How it works...

The DPM agent will verify its XML configuration and understand what network it should use as its primary backup network. Normal communication between the DPM agent and the DPM server will still travel over the production network.

There's more...

If the backup network connectivity fails, the DPM agent can be set up using a secondary backup network that will be a failover network for that traffic. The failover network is something that you must configure for it to work.

Configuring e-mail notifications

This recipe will cover how to configure your DPM server e-mail notifications.

Getting ready

Providing information regarding the current status or historical information with DPM reports, is very important to companies and organizations. System Center Data Protection Manager has the ability to provide this, but it is not recommended to forward DPM alerts to an e-mail recipient, since DPM will send a large number of e-mails.

If you want to have a proactive monitoring or an extended reporting experience, you should install System Center Operations Manager, since this is a Microsoft tool that will fit this need.

How to do it...

In the DPM console, click on **Options** to open the options window for the DPM server. You have six different tabs for options:

- ▶ **Notifications**
- ▶ **Alert Publishing**
- ▶ **Customer Feedback**
- ▶ **End-user Recovery**
- ▶ **Auto Discovery**
- ▶ **SMTP Server**

Click on the tab **SMTP Server** and specify the SMTP server settings. Enter the following information:

- ▶ **SMTP server name**
- ▶ **SMTP server port**
- ▶ **"From" address**

 You must have a valid e-mail address on the SMTP server you specify in the DPM options.

If your SMTP server needs the DPM server to authenticate using a service account, simply provide the credentials in the **Authenticated SMTP server** area.

Now the DPM server is able to send reports according to the subscription which you can define in the **Reporting** view of the DPM console. If you want to know more about DPM reports, please read the *Report management* recipe in this chapter.

To be able to send alerts to a subscriber, click on the **Notifications** tab in the **Options** window. You have three different categories for alerts in DPM:

> ► **Critical alerts**
> ► **Warning alerts**
> ► **Informational alerts**

The setup for **Notifications** for DPM is very easy; simply check the alerts that you would like to be distributed and in the **Recipients** area, then provide e-mail addresses that are separated by commas.

If you want to provide more intelligence behind the alert distribution, simply use the System Center Operations Manager.

How it works...

The DPM server will interact with the specified SMTP server to send information regarding the current status in terms of active alerts and historical reports for identifying trends.

There is more...

Having a coordination between the majority of the System Center stack and Azure in place for your data center will provide you with a high level of solutions for your hosted services. It is recommended that you start thinking of services instead of single products and see the possibilities of the System Center family cooperation for building a new type of data center for your organization.

Applying update rollups (UR) to the DPM server

This recipe will cover the points to keep in mind before, during, and after you apply an update rollup to your DPM server.

Getting ready

Microsoft is continuously improving their products making them more optimal, covering more features or enabling new supported scenarios. This is the main reason that you need to keep up with applying the update rollups that Microsoft creates for you.

There are, however, some considerations that you must keep in mind before you start to apply an update rollup:

▸ Verify that all data sources are reporting healthy

▸ Verify that all DPM agents are reporting OK

▸ Have a rollback plan

▸ Plan the installation of the update rollup

When you upgrade a System Center family member, it is always critical that your database is backed up. Update rollups will alter the configuration of your DPMDB and therefore, it is critical that you either backup the DPMDB by using another DPM server or dump the DPMDB using the DPMBackup executable.

Working with a DPM-DPM-DR setup, also known as primary and secondary DPM server. it is important to upgrade the DPM servers in an order that fits your company's needs. There are some recommendations from Microsoft, but it is your approach to an upgrade that fits your need that will work. Most of the DPM administrators use this upgrade schedule:

▸ Primary DPM servers

▸ DPM agents on the primary DPM server

▸ Secondary DPM server

How to do it...

Take a backup of the DPMDB using a secondary DPM server or the DPMBackup executable.

Run the update rollup MSI on the DPM server and when the update has been applied, it is always a good thing to reboot your DPM server. Verify the version of the DPM server by opening the DPM console and on the top right part, click on the **About DPM** button.

Now it is time to upgrade the DPM agents. Go to the **Management** view and click on **Agents...** on the left-hand side of the DPM console. You will see that all DPM agents are reporting **Update Available...**. Right-click all the agents and choose **Update**.

How it works...

When upgrading the DPM server, the DPM agents' binaries will also be updated. When the DPM server comes back online it will establish a connection to the DPM agents to verify their version of the DPM agent. The DPM agent will report back and will be seeking an upgrade. You can upgrade via the DPM console, manually or via System Center Configurations Manager.

There is more...

Having a rollback plan is always important, that is why you must always have a backup of the DPMDB. Microsoft provides an update rollup uninstallation process that does not need you to uninstall the DPM server. For more information on how to uninstall DPM to enable it to be rolled back, please read the following article:

http://technet.microsoft.com/en-us/library/hh848284.aspx

Working with filters

This recipe covers what filters are and why are they important.

Getting ready

Providing information regarding the current status is always a critical fact for all administrators. Out of the box DPM has four default filters:

- ► All jobs
- ► All jobs in progress
- ► Failed jobs for yesterday and today
- ► Today's job

These filters are nothing more than SQL queries that provide the result via a GUI, the **Monitoring** view in the DPM console.

You can also define your own filters; those are present under **Custom Filter** in the DPM console.

How to do it...

In the Monitoring view of the DPM console, click on the **All jobs** filter, then on **Create filter** and the **Filter** window opens. Enter a **Filter name** followed by the time span that should apply to your filter by defining **Time from** and **Time to**.

Next you should define the parameters that the filter should consist of. You can choose from **Jobs**, **Protection,** or **Other**.

Combining the different types and status will make it possible for you to build up a logic that will extract the information you acquire and present it in the DPM console.

How it works...

Building filters is more or less building SQL queries via a GUI; the logic that you build up from creating a new filter is really complex SQL queries made easy.

There's more...

For more information regarding System Center Data Protection Manager, please visit the DPM blog http://robertanddpm.blogspot.com.

4

File Server Protection

In this chapter, we will cover the protection of file server data using System Center 2012 R2 Data Protection Manager.

We also will provide you with the information you need to understand the different protection configurations that apply to the file server workload.

In this chapter, we will learn the following topics:

- Understanding the prerequisites for supported file server protection
- Protecting file shares, volumes, and catalogs
- Restoring file data to its original location
- Restoring file data to an alternative location
- Copying protected data to tape
- Restoring file data from tape
- Restoring file data from Azure
- Protecting file server clusters
- Understanding file server maintenance and management tasks
- Creating recovery points manually
- Using Migrate-Datasource.ps1

Introduction

The most common workload in any data center is the file server workload. This was the original data type protected by the first version of **Data Protection Manager** (**DPM**), and will continue to be present in most data centers for many years to come.

System Center Data Protection Manager 2012 R2 will provide a versatile data source protection solution for the file server workload, combining fast restoration scenarios and fully optimized and supported backup scenarios.

Understanding the prerequisites for supported file server protection

This section will cover the prerequisites for a supported file server protection scenario. The following list provides the supported versions for the file server workload:

- ► Windows Server 2003 R2 with SP2 (after applying UR2)
- ► Windows Server 2008 (after applying UR2)
- ► Windows Server 2008 R2 with SP1
- ► Windows Server 2012
- ► Windows Server 2012 R2

For System Center Data Protection Manager to be able to protect a volume of data, it must be formatted with NTFS or ReFS and be at least 1 GB in size. This is due to the fact that VSS will only provide a snapshot if the volume is greater than 1 GB and still be able to maintain 64 snapshots of the protected data.

For System Center Data Protection Manager to be able to protect and restore deduplicated volumes or data, the server role for data deduplication must be installed on the DPM server; this is installed by default when you install the DPM server software.

File server protection relies on the underlying technology within the Windows server operating system called **Volume Shadow Copy Services (VSS)**. For more information regarding how the VSS filesystem operates and works, please read the *Change tracking process* recipe in *Chapter 1, Pre-installation Tasks*.

.

In the initial release of System Center 2012 R2 Data Protection Manager, Microsoft removed the support to backup and restore Windows Server 2003. Many voices were raised from the community and MVPs, so Microsoft decided to include Windows Server 2003 in the DPM workload gallery. The support for Windows Server 2003 was restored after applying UR2, which was published in April 2014. For more information, please visit the web page at `http://support.microsoft.com/kb/2958100`.

Protecting file shares, volumes, and catalogs

This recipe will cover how you configure file server protection by protecting the shares or catalogs that reside on NTFS, ReFS, or deduplicated volumes.

Getting ready

Before you are able to start creating the protection group that holds the actual configuration for the protection, you need to have fulfilled the following prerequisites:

► The file server you would like to protect is a supported version for DPM protection

► A DPM agent is installed on all the servers that hold the data sources that you would like to protect

► The DPM agent reports **OK** in the DPM console management workspace

How to do it...

Go to **Protection** and click on **New** in the DPM console, as shown in the following screenshot:

In the **Create New Protection Group Wizard Welcome** step, click on **Next >** to continue. On the **Select Protection Group Type** window, choose **Servers** and click on **Next >** to continue. In the **Select Group Members** window, you should select the file share, volume, or catalog that you would like to protect with DPM, as shown in this screenshot:

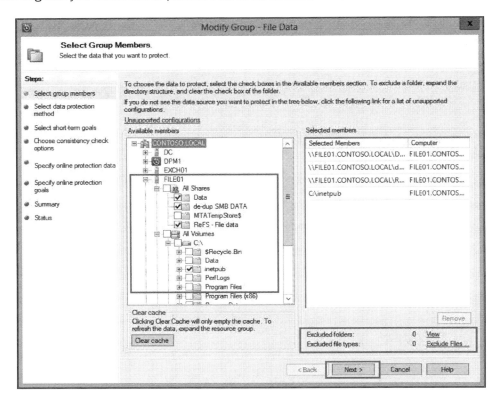

Expand your file server and you will find **All Shares**, which lists all the shares present on the file server. Check the checkbox next to the share you would like to protect, and then an information box will present the information that you should consider when protecting your system state data. You can also expand **All Volumes** and check either an entire volume to protect or a specific folder or folders from that volume.

If you would like to exclude specific file types, you can click on the **Exclude Files...** link at the bottom right-hand side of the window (as shown in the preceding screenshot).

 When you protect a file share, you cannot exclude folders. This can only be done by protecting the volume or a catalog containing subcatalogs.

When you have finished your configuration, click on **Next >** to continue.

On the **Select Data Protection Method** window, you can decide what type of protection you would like to select to protect your file data and specify a value in the **Protection group name** field, as shown in the following screenshot. For DPM to be able to protect your file server workload using Azure or tape, this must be configured before you create or modify the protection group.

 You can use Tape for your short-term protection but this will disable the possibilities for online protection. Using Tape for your short-term protection does not mean that you don't need a DPM disk pool.

Check the checkboxes that you would like to use and click on **Next >** to continue:

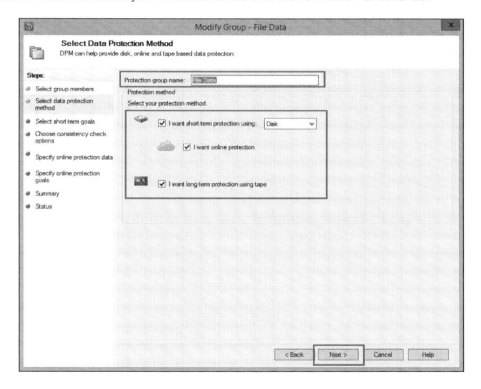

In the **Specify Short-Term Goals** step, you will specify **Retention range**, that is, the number of days you would like to keep the protected data in the DPM disk pool.

Next, you should configure the **Synchronization frequency** value, which tells you how often the DPM agent should replicate the block level changes from the protected data source. You can synchronize it to every **15 minutes** or select the **Just before a recovery point** radio button.

In the **File recovery points** section, you can specify when to create a recovery point for the protected data sources. Clicking on **Modify...** will open a window where you can choose the time of the day and also specific weekdays for recovery point creation. Click on **OK** to get back to the **Select Short-Term Goals** step.

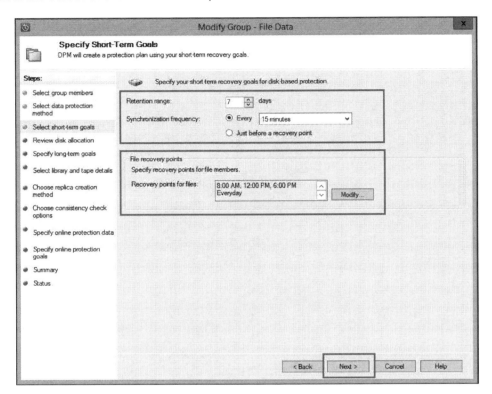

 Keep in mind that the VSS file can keep 64 snapshots, which could be a limitation, but this resides in the actual operating system and not in the DPM product.

When you are finished with your configuration, click on **Next >** to continue the **Review Disk Allocation** step.

In the **Review Disk Allocation** step, you can configure and review the disk space allocated for the protection group. Two specific volumes are created for all protected data sources that the DPM server is protecting: replica and recovery point volumes. One of the auto-heal functions within DPM is the **Automatically grow the volumes** option (as shown in the following screenshot). This feature will expand the volume when the threshold is reached; for more detailed information regarding the **Automatically grow the volumes** function, please read the *Growing volumes automatically in the DPM disk pool* recipe in *Chapter 3, Post-installation Tasks*.

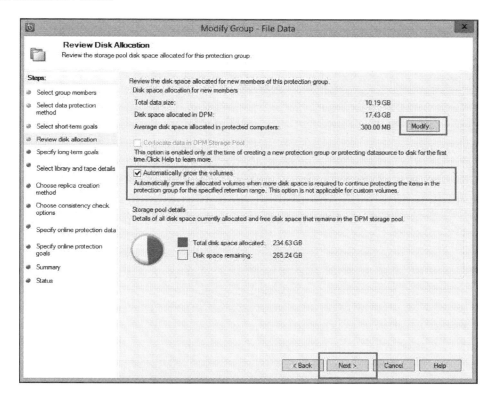

When protecting file server data, you are able to recalculate the size of the volumes that the DPM has allocated and also configure the shadow copy storage that the DPM server should use. This is done by clicking on the **Modify...** button. For more information regarding the **Automatically grow the volumes** function and the modification of the disk space allocation, please read the *Growing volumes automatically in the DPM disk pool* recipe in *Chapter 3, Post-installation Tasks*.

Click on **Next >** to continue to the **Specify Long-Term Goals** step.

In the **Specify Long-Term Goals** step, you can configure the tape settings for the protection group. In the **Recovery goals** section, you can specify the **Retention range** and the **Frequency of the backup** values. DPM will provide you with its default settings for **Recovery goals**, but these can easily be changed by clicking on the **Customize** button. If you want to change the backup schedule, click on the **Modify...** button, as shown here:

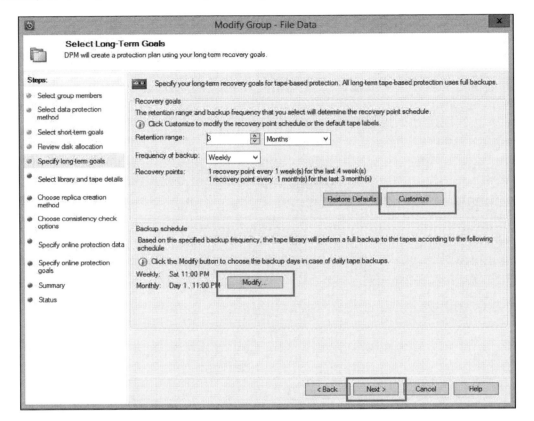

In the **Customize Recovery Goal** window, you can enable up to three different recovery goals by clicking the checkboxes, as shown in the following screenshot. You can choose to make daily, weekly, monthly, or yearly backups to tape.

You can also choose to define a tape label that DPM should use to present the tape in the DPM console. Within this configuration, you can also provide the number of backup copies (as shown in the following screenshot), though, by default, the number is one.

If the different recovery goals should occur on the same day, the DPM administrator has two choices:

- ▸ Make two different backups
- ▸ Make one backup a higher priority than the other

For more information regarding tape management, please read *Chapter 13, Tape management*.

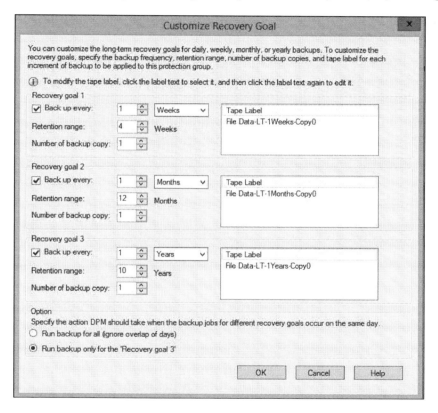

In the **Modify Long-Term Backup Schedule** window, you can define the backup schedules for your recovery goals in the protection group. When you have configured your backup schedules, click on **OK** to return to the **Specify Long-Term Goals** step:

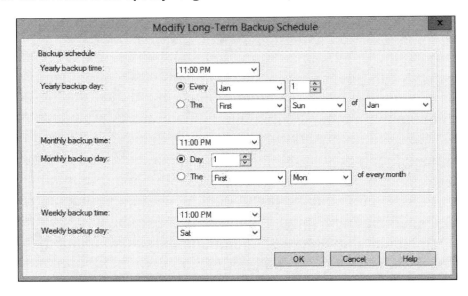

In the **Specify Long-Term Goals** step, click on **Next >** to continue to the **Select Library and Tape Details** step.

In this protection group wizard step, you can configure your primary tape library and if it is present, your copy library as well. You can also define the actual numbers of tape drives that the DPM server should use for this protection group. After the backup to tape has occurred, you can make the DPM server check the backup for data integrity; please note that this is a time-consuming operation.

The DPM server can also either compress or encrypt the data copied to tape; you cannot perform both operations. To continue, click on **Next >**, as shown in this screenshot:

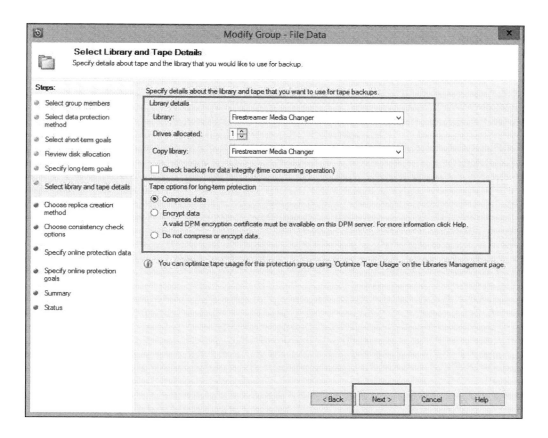

In the **Choose Replica Creation Method** step, you can define how the DPM sever should create the replica of the protected data source. You can create the replica as and when the configuration of the protection group is finished or you can schedule the creation of the replica. You can also create the replica manually; this is covered in the *Creating a replica manually* recipe of *Chapter 3, Post-installation Tasks*. Click on **Next >** to continue, as shown here:

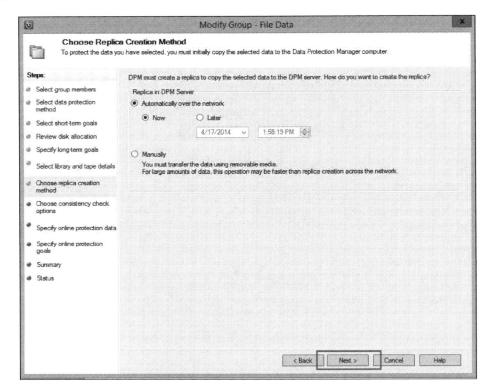

In the **Consistency check options** step, you can specify whether DPM should run a consistency check if a replica becomes inconsistent; this is an auto-heal function within the DPM server technology. You can also specify whether you want it to run a daily consistency check, where you set the start time and the maximum number of hours the task should run for. To continue to the next step, click on **Next >**, as shown here:

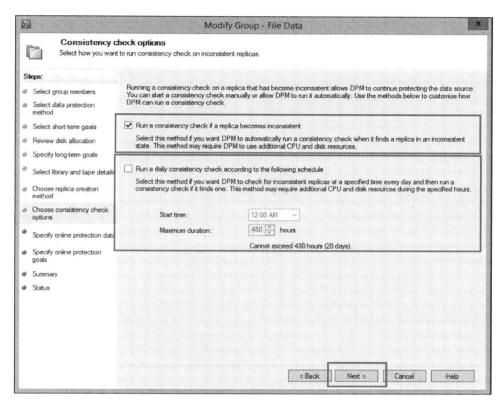

In the **Specify Online Protection Data** step of your protection group wizard, you can specify the protected data source that you will include for online protection.

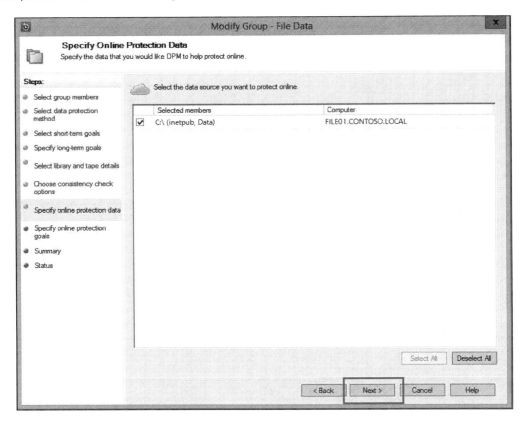

The next step in the configuration is **Specify Online Protection Goals**, where you have two important options for your online protection: daily or weekly synchronization frequencies:

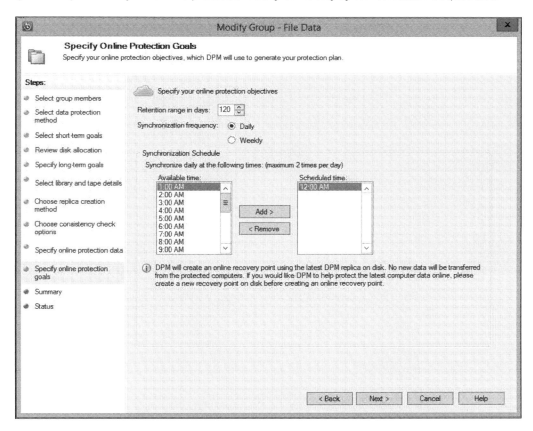

If you place a recovery point every month, you will be able to store data up to 3360 days in Azure. For more information regarding the Azure backup vault retention time configurations, please visit `http://technet.microsoft.com/en-us/library/jj728747.aspx`. Mark the time for online protection in **Available time** and click on **Add >**, as shown in the preceding screenshot.

Choose the **Weekly** synchronization frequency option if you would like to use online protection only on specific weekdays.

Click on **Next >** to continue to the last step, that is, the **Summary** step. Review the summary for the protection group and click on the **Create Group** button to create the protection group.

In the **Status** step, you can see the actual status of the protection group creation.

How it works...

The protection group holds the actual configuration for your backup schedule, protected data sources, and specific configurations, such as on-the-wire-compression. The DPM server will call the DPM agents, which are members of the protection group, to initialize the backup job; this is the VSS request procedure that starts the VSS snapshot process on the protected server.

There's more...

For more information regarding how the DPM server operates, it's recommended that you read all the recipes in *Chapter 1, Pre-installation Tasks*.

Restoring file data to its original location

The most common recovery operation that a DPM administrator performs is the recovery of protected file data. This recipe will provide you with the steps to restore your protected file data to its original location.

Getting ready

Before you start the recovery, you should always verify that the targeted data source is accessible and that the DPM agent is reporting **OK** in the DPM console.

How to do it...

1. In the DPM console, go to **Recovery** and choose the data source you would like to recover.

 For file, exchange, and SharePoint, you can use the search function that is available in the **Restore** pane.

Mark the data source and choose the data and time for the recovery. Right-click on the data source and choose **Recover...** to start the **Recovery** wizard.

2. In the **Review Recovery Selection** step, review the data source that is chosen for recovery and click on **Next >** to continue.

3. In the **Select Recovery Type** step, choose **Recover to the original location** and click on **Next >**.

4. In the **Specify Recovery Options** step, you can configure the specific options for the recovery.

5. In the **Existing version recovery behavior** section, you can define what DPM should do if the data source exists in the targeted location. **Create copy** will create a copy if the data source you are recovering already exists, **Skip** will skip restoring the data source if it already exists, and **Overwrite** will overwrite the data source if it already exists in the targeted location.

6. In the **Restore security** section, you can define how the restored data source should apply the security setting in the targeted location to itself. The restored data could either keep its security settings that are present in the recovery point version, or apply the security settings of the targeted location.

7. If the recovery restores data over a poor WAN link, you can click on the **Modify...** link in the **Network bandwidth usage throttling** part to define how much bandwidth the restore job should consume.

8. If you have VSS hardware providers installed on the DPM sever and a **Logical Unit Number** (**LUN**) presented for the SAN storage of the protected data source, you can perform a SAN-based recovery by checking the checkbox in the **SAN Recovery** part.

9. When the restore job has finished, you can send an e-mail to a specific addressed user or users, notifying them that the restore job has finished. This is enabled by checking the checkbox in the **Notification** section. Click on **Next >** to continue.

 In order to be able to send e-mails, your DPM sever needs to have an SMTP server configured in the DPM options. Please read the *Configuring e-mail notifications* recipe in *Chapter 3, Post-installation Tasks*.

10. In the **Summary** step, verify the recovery configuration and click on **Recover** to start the recovery.

11. In the **Recovery Status** window, you will be able to see the current state of the recovery. This could also be monitored in the **Monitoring** part of the DPM console.

How it works...

When DPM initializes the recovery job, it will rely on the VSS architecture that is a part of the server operating system architecture. For more information regarding how DPM works, please read all the recipes in *Chapter 1, Pre-installation Tasks*.

If the recovery job fails, you should be able to read the alert that the DPM server will raise, which tells you what has happened and gives you a guide to how you might achieve a possible scenario for a successful recovery.

Restoring file data to an alternative location

This recipe will provide you with the steps to restore your protected file data to an alternative location, that is, a different server, drive, and folder path from the location where the backup occurred.

Getting ready

Before you start the recovery, you should always verify that the targeted data source is accessible and that the DPM agent is reporting **OK** in the DPM console.

How to do it...

1. In the DPM console, go to **Recovery** and choose the data source you would like to recover.

    For file, exchange, and SharePoint, you can use the search function.

2. Mark the data source and choose the data and time for the recovery. Right-click on the data source and choose **Recover...** to start the **Recovery** wizard.

3. In the **Review Recovery Selection** step, review the data source that is chosen for recovery and click on **Next >** to continue.

4. In the **Select recovery type** step, choose **Recover to an alternate original location** and click on **Browse...** to choose a server that should be the target for the restoration.

[Keep in mind that you must have a DPM agent installed on the targeted server that is connected to the DPM server.]

5. In the **Specify Alternate Recovery Destination** window, choose the restore target and click on **OK** to return to the **Select Recovery Type** step in the **Recovery** wizard. Back in the **Select Recovery Type** step, click on **Next >** to continue.

6. In the **Specify Recovery Options** step, you can configure the specific options for the recovery.

7. In the **Existing version recovery behavior** part, you can define what DPM should do if the data source exists in the targeted location. **Create copy** will create a copy if the data source you are recovering already exists, **Skip** will skip restoring the data source if it already exists, and **Overwrite** will overwrite the data source if it already exists in the targeted location.

8. In the **Restore security** part, you can define how the restored data source should apply the security setting in the targeted location. The restored data could either keep its security settings that are present in the recovery point version, or apply the security settings of the targeted location.

9. If the recovery restores data over a poor WAN link, you can click on the **Modify...** link in the **Network bandwidth usage throttling** part to define how much bandwidth the restore job should consume.

10. If you have VSS hardware providers installed on the DPM sever and a LUN presented for the SAN storage of the protected data source, you can perform a SAN-based recovery by checking the checkbox in **SAN Recovery**.

11. When the restore job has finished, you can send an e-mail to a specific addressed user or users, notifying them that the restore job has finished. This is enabled by checking the checkbox in the **Notification** part. Click on **Next >** to continue.

 To be able to send e-mails, your DPM sever needs to have an SMTP server configured in the DPM options. Please read the _Configuring e-mail notifications_ recipe in _Chapter 3, Post-installation Tasks_.

12. In the **Summary** step, verify the recovery configuration and click on **Recover** to start the recovery.

13. In the **Recovery Status** window, you will be able to see the current state of the recovery. This could also be monitored in the **Monitoring** part of the DPM console.

How it works...

In all the restore processes, DPM will rely on the VSS architecture present both in the operating system and on the application layer for a successful restore that is both optimal and fully supported.

There's more...

Keeping track of the restore process can be done either via the **Monitoring** pane in the DPM console or by verifying the final result in System Center 2012 R2 Operations Manager.

Copying protected data to tape

There may be occasions where you may want to _export_ backup data to tape to archive, for portability, or other reasons. This recipe will provide you with the steps to teach you how to copy protected data to tape.

Getting ready

Before you start a recovery, verify that your tape library does not report any errors and that you have a valid recovery point to restore to.

How to do it...

1. In the DPM console, go to **Recovery** and choose the data source you would like to recover.

 For file, exchange, and SharePoint data, you can use the search function if you don't know where the file or object you want to restore could be found.

2. Mark the data source and choose the data and time for the recovery. Right-click on the data source and choose **Recover...** to start the **Recovery** wizard.

3. In the **Review Recovery Selection** step, review the data source that is chosen for recovery and click on **Next >** to continue.

4. In the **Select recovery type** step, choose **Copy to tape** and click on **Next >** to continue.

5. In the **Specify Library** step, you can define which tape library you should use for **Primary library** and **Copy library** if you have multiple libraries present in your DPM server. In the **Tape options** section, you are able to specify a custom Tape label that could provide an easier way to determine the actual contents of the tape.

6. By marking the **Compress** option, you are able to compress the data that is written to the tape. You can also encrypt the data by choosing **Encrypt** or you can chose to do neither by choosing **Do not compress or encrypt**. Click on **Next >** to continue.

 You cannot both encrypt the data written to the tape and also compress it.

7. In the **Specify Recovery Options** step, you can specify the options that should apply to the recovery. If you have the prerequisites for a SAN-based recovery, you are able to check the checkbox in the **SAN Recovery** section to enable this feature.

8. When a recovery job is finished, an e-mail could be send to recipients if the DPM server has an SMTP server configured. For more information on how to configure an SMTP server, please read the *Configuring e-mail notifications* recipe in *Chapter 3, Post-installation Tasks*. Click on **Next >** to continue.

9. In the **Summary** step, you can verify the recovery configuration and if it looks accurate, click on **Recover** to start the process of copying it to tape.

10. In the **Recovery Status** step, you can follow the progress of the job; you can also follow the progress in the **Monitoring** part of the DPM console.

How it works...

All restore processes depend on the cooperation of multiple architectural technologies within both the server operating system and the actual application being restored.

There's more...

If the job fails, you will be able to retry by clicking on the recommend action link that is raised by the alert in the **Monitoring** pane of the DPM console.

Restoring file data from tape

A scenario that backup administrators may meet with is when you must restore data from an archiving media—like tape. This recipe will provide you with the steps to recover protected data from tape.

Getting ready

Make sure that your library is online and does not report any errors; this can be done by verifying the alerts in the **Monitoring** section of the DPM console or in the **Libraries** section of the **Management** part of the DPM console.

How to do it...

1. In the DPM console, go to **Recovery** and choose the data source you would like to recover.

 For file, exchange, and SharePoint data, you can use the search function if you don't know where the file or object you want to restore can be found.

2. Mark the data source and choose the data and time for the restore. Right-click on the data source and choose **Recover...** to start the **Recovery** wizard.

3. In the **Review Recovery Selection** step, review the items that you have chosen for recovery. To continue, click on **Next >**.

4. In the **Select Recovery Type** step, you will choose how to recover your data. When you recover file data from tape you can:

   ❑ Recover it to the original location

   ❑ Recover it to an alternative location

   ❑ Copy it to tape

5. If you select **Recover to an alternate location**, you need to have a DPM agent deployed and a data source that is protected by the DPM server, in order for the server to be listed as a recovery target.

6. If you choose **Copy to tape**, you must have a standalone library or virtual tape drive configured on the DPM server.

 You can restore data from a deduplicated volume or ReFS volume to a standard NTFS volume and the other way around.

7. In this recipe, we will cover how to recover tape data to its original location. Mark the **Recover to the original location** option and click on **Next >** to continue.

8. In the **Specify Recovery Options** step, you can configure specific options for the recovery.

9. The first thing to verify is the **Recovery library** section. It is important to choose the library that hosts all the tapes that are needed for the recovery.

10. In the **Existing version recovery behavior** part, you can define what DPM should do if the data source exists in the targeted location. **Create copy** will create a copy if the data source you are recovering already exists, **Skip** will skip restoring the data source if it already exists, and **Overwrite** will overwrite the data source if it already exists in the targeted location.

11. In the **Restore security** section, you can define how the restored data source should apply the security setting in the targeted location. The restored data should either keep its security settings that are present in the recovery point version, or apply the security settings of the targeted location.

12. If the recovery restores data over a poor WAN link, you can click on the **Modify...** link in the **Network bandwidth usage throttling** part to define how much bandwidth the restore job should consume.

13. If you have VSS hardware providers installed on the DPM sever and a LUN presented for the SAN storage of the protected data source, you can perform a SAN-based recovery by checking the checkbox in the **SAN Recovery** section.

14. When the restore job has finished, you can send an e-mail to a specific addressed user or users, notifying them that the restore job has finished. This is enabled by checking the checkbox in the **Notification** part. Click on **Next >** to continue.

To be able to send e-mails, your DPM sever needs to have an SMTP server configured in the DPM options. Please read the *Configuring e-mail notifications* recipe in *Chapter 3, Post-installation Tasks*.

15. When you have verified and configured your options, click on **Next >** to continue to the **Summary** step of the **Recovery** wizard.

16. In the **Summary** step, verify the recovery setting and start the recovery by clicking on the **Recover** button.

17. In the **Recovery Status** step, you can follow the progress of the recovery; you can also follow the progress in the **Monitoring** part of the DPM console.

How it works...

When you restore data from a tape, DPM uses a scratch before it provides the data to the selected data source. It is very important that your DPM `%systemdrive%` server has more than 10 GB of free space.

Restoring file data from Azure

System Center 2012 R2 Data Protection Manager can interact seamlessly with Microsoft Azure, providing an online protection for file, SQL, and Hyper-V workloads. This recipe will cover how you restore file data from the Microsoft Azure recovery service backup vault.

Getting ready

To be able to recover data from the recovery service backup vault in your Microsoft Azure technology portal, you must have Internet connectivity and a valid recovery point that resides in Microsoft Azure. For more information regarding Azure integration with DPM and the backup vault recovery service, read *Chapter 11, Azure integration*.

How to do it...

1. In the DPM console, go to **Recovery** and find the data source you would like to recover.

2. Mark the data source and choose the data and time for the recovery. Right-click on the data source and choose **Recover...** to start the **Recovery** wizard.

3. In the **Review Recovery Selection** step, review the items that you have chosen for recovery. To continue, click on **Next >**.

4. In the **Select Recovery Type** step, you will need to choose how to recover your data. When you recover file data from Azure you can:

   ❑ Recover it to the original location

   ❑ Recover it to an alternative location

5. If you select **Recover to an alternate location**, you need to have a DPM agent deployed and configured on this location.

> You can restore data from a deduplicated volume or ReFS volume to a standard NTFS volume and the other way around.

6. In this recipe, we will cover how to restore data from Azure to its original location, so mark the **Recover to the original location** option and click on **Next >** to continue.

7. In the **Specify Recovery Options** step, you can configure specific options for the recovery.

8. In the **Existing version recovery behavior** section, you can define what DPM should do if the data source exists in the targeted location. **Create copy** will create a copy if the data source you are recovering already exists, **Skip** will skip restoring the data source if it already exists, and **Overwrite** will overwrite the data source if it already exists in the targeted location.

9. In the **Restore security** part, you can define how the restored data source should apply the security setting in the targeted location. The restored data could either keep its security settings that are present in the recovery point version or apply the security settings of the targeted location.

10. If the recovery restores data over a poor WAN link, you can click on the **Modify...** link in the **Network bandwidth usage throttling** part to define how much bandwidth the restore job should consume.

11. If you have VSS hardware providers installed on the DPM sever and LUN presented for the SAN storage of the protected data source, you can perform a SAN-based recovery by checking the checkbox in the **SAN Recovery** section.

12. When the restore job has finished, you can send an e-mail to a specific addressed user or users, notifying them that the restore job has finished. This is enabled by checking the checkbox in the **Notification** part. Click on **Next >** to continue.

> To be able to send e-mails, your DPM sever needs to have an SMTP server configured in the DPM options. Please read the *Configuring e-mail notifications* recipe in *Chapter 3, Post-installation Tasks*.

13. In the **Summary** step, you can verify the recovery configuration, and if it looks accurate, click on **Recover** to start the recovery process.

14. In the **Recovery Status** step, you will be able to see the current state of the restore job. This job status can also be monitored in the **Monitoring** part of the DPM console.

How it works...

The restore process for Azure Backup Vault data differentiates itself from a standard restore process. The data that should be restored from Azure to your production setup must first be restored on the DPM server and then copied to the production targeted data source.

There's more...

Keeping track of the restore jobs that are initiated is critical. The easiest way is to view the **Monitoring** pane in the DPM console or by using System Center Operations Manager with the management pack for DPM.

Protecting file server clusters

Any modern data center has one or several server clusters to provide a high availability service for its hosted data. This recipe will provide help you with the requirements that are needed before you protect your clustered file servers.

Getting ready

A clustered file server resource relies on resource groups that will host the data, enabled for high availability. There are some considerations that the DPM administrator must keep in mind, while both setting up the protection and adapting the DPM server technology to the cluster maintenance or management tasks.

It is important to understand how DPM interacts with and sees the actual clustered resources; this is particularly important in the case of different failover scenarios. In the case of a planned failover of a cluster, DPM will continue to protect the data source. In the case of an unplanned failover, DPM issues an alert that a consistency check is required.

For DPM to be able to start protecting a clustered resource, DPM agents must be deployed and configured for all servers that are the members of the cluster. If you install a DPM agent to only one cluster node, DPM will prompt you in the installation wizard that you need to deploy the DPM agent to the other cluster members. DPM will also provide you with a list of the cluster members and also with the option of installing the DPM agents now or skipping the installation.

If the cluster administrator decides to decommission a node in a cluster, DPM will raise an alert that the former cluster node member is no longer a part of the cluster. The DPM agent interacts with the clustering services and understands this management task very well when a cluster node is no longer is part of the cluster.

How to do it...

1. To start protecting your file server's clustered resources, you must create a new protection group in the **Protection** section of the DPM console.

2. Click on **New** to open the **Protection group** wizard.

> Remember that you must install DPM agents to all cluster members before you start to protect the cluster.

3. In the **Select Group Members** step of the wizard, you will see all the cluster nodes presented as Windows servers. The cluster and its resources will be present under the resource group name followed by **(cluster)** at the top of the **Available members** section. Expand the resource group name and you will be able to see your clustered resources available for DPM protection.

4. Mark the clustered resources and finish the wizard to enable DPM protection.

How it works...

System Center 2012 R2 Data Protection Manager will understand the cluster configuration and avoid any unwanted configurations by providing the necessary alterations of the DPM server's configuration.

There's more...

The most important part regarding protecting clustered services, such as a clustered file server, is to keep track of the actual real-time health of the clustered servers. This is accomplished by using System Center Operations Manager with the corresponding management packs.

Understanding file server maintenance and management tasks

In all data centers, it is normal to perform maintenance and management tasks on the file servers. DPM will understand and adapt to the maintenance tasks performed on the file server; more importantly, DPM also understands the management tasks of the file server workload. This recipe will provide you with an understanding of how DPM interacts with common file server maintenance and management tasks.

Getting ready

With the introduction of this recipe, we will list the possible scenarios for a file server workload's management tasks. They are:

- Changing the path of a data source
- Moving file servers between domains
- Renaming a file server
- Changing the time zone of a file server
- Changing the members of a file cluster
- Changing resource groups on clustered file servers

How to do it...

When performing any of the following management tasks, it will interrupt the DPM protection for the workload in some manner.

If you change the path of a protected data source, the DPM protection will fail. To get it up and running again, you need to stop the protection within the DPM console and re-enable it by making it a member of the protection group again so that it is able to continue protecting the data source. The reason for this that the path to the shared folder includes the logical path on the volume.

In a scenario where you would like to change the domain membership of a file server, you will need to stop the protection and uninstall the DPM agent. After the file server has been moved and joined the new domain, you could choose to protect the now untrusted file server using workgroup protection or if you prefer a high-security approach, you should use **Certificate Based Authentication** (**CBA**).

A scenario that could occur is the need to rename a protected file server, if the administrator just renames the server, the DPM protection will fail. To be able to perform a seamless transition, you need to stop the protection, uninstall the DPM agent, install the DPM agent on the renamed file server, and add the protection back to the protection group.

 DPM will not reuse the previously protected data since the renamed file server is seen as a new protectable data source.

If the administrator changes the time zone of a protected file server, the protection will fail. During the installation of the DPM agent, DPM identifies the current time zone of the server that hosts the protectable data sources. To be able to restore the protection for the updated time zone workload, the DPM administrator needs to update the **DPM database** (**DPMDB**). This is easily done via the DPM console by refreshing the DPM agent status in the **Management** section of the console. DPM will then raise an error and asks if you would like to remove this record from the DPM database. After doing so, reinstall the DPM agent and perform a consistency check to get the protection back in order.

When the cluster administrator adds a new node to the cluster, DPM will raise an alert saying that it needs to install a DPM agent on that newly added cluster node member.

For a file cluster, the cluster administrator may change the file cluster members or the name of the resource group; this will interrupt the DPM protection. To get the protection operational again, you should reinitialize the protection; this is done by stopping the protection and making it a member of a protection group again. If the cluster administrator changes the name of the resource group, the DPM administrator needs to stop the protection and re-enable the protection under the new resource group name.

Creating recovery points manually

This recipe will cover how you can manually create a recovery point from the DPM console. It is an important task to make sure you have a current backup of the protected data before performing any major changes or implementations that could have a negative impact on the data.

Getting ready

Before you create a recovery point manually, you need to verify that the data source that should be provided with an extra recovery point is in a healthy state and is reporting **OK** in the DPM console. You must also verify that the DPM agent for the server that is hosting the data source also is reporting **OK** in the DPM console **Management** part.

How to do it...

1. In the **Protection** section of the DPM console, you will be able to see all your protected data sources as members of a protection group. Right-click on the data source and choose **Create recovery point...** from the menu, as shown here:

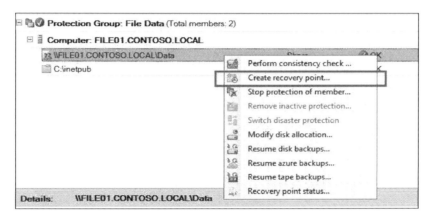

2. In the **Create recovery point** window, you can choose how you would like to create your recovery point:

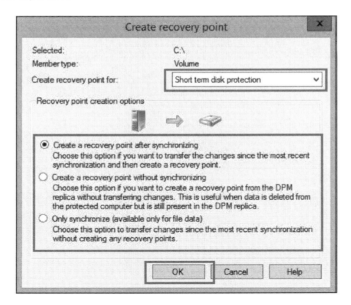

3. If you want to create your recovery point to disk, you have the following three options:

    ❑   Creating a recovery point after synchronization

    ❑   Creating a recovery point without synchronization

    ❑   Only synchronization

    For the first option, DPM will create a recovery point after the DPM agent has replicated the identified block-level changes on the server hosting the protected data source and synchronized them with the DPM sever.

    For the second option, DPM will create a recovery point using only the synchronized data in the DPM disk pool.

    If you select the third option, the DPM server will only synchronize the block-level changes from the server that hosts the protected data source. There is no recovery point created when choosing this option.

[The option to only synchronize is available only for the file data workload.]

4. In the drop-down menu, you are able to create recovery points manually to tape and also to Microsoft Azure. Keep in mind that you must have these configured for them to be selectable:

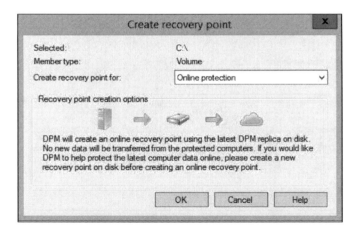

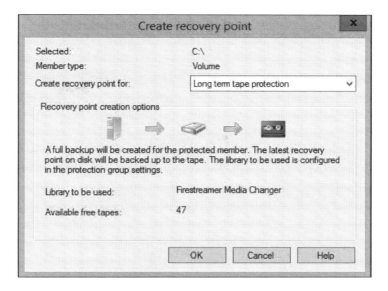

How it works...

When the DPM administrator initializes a manual recovery point creation, the DPM server will create a VSS request via the DPM agent on the protected data source server and start to create the recovery point or just synchronize the block-level changes.

There's more...

If the backup job fails, you will be able to get further recommended actions in the alerts raised by the DPM server. In all the DPM alerts, you will find decent information regarding the failure and also a recommended action that you can try to solve the error.

Using Migrate-Datasource.ps1

This recipe will explain the purpose of the `Migrate-Datasource.ps1` (PowerShell) script and how to use it. It is important to keep in mind that the `Migrate-Datasource.ps1` script only applies to the file server workload.

Getting ready

In the scenario where the protected data source has been migrated to another volume, the DPM protection will fail due to the new GUID information of the volume where the data source resides. By using the `Migrate-Datasource.ps1` script, you will be able to continue protecting a data source (file, folder, volume, or share) to the same replica volume.

 Even if you keep the same drive letters for the volume, you still need to run the `Migrate-Datasource.ps1` script since DPM identifies the volumes by the GUID.

There are two important options for the PowerShell script:

- Auto
- Manual

The auto option will search the production server for changes and make the necessary updates in the DPMDB so that it is able to continue to protect the data source. If you choose the manual switch, you must migrate each data source individually. The script will provide you with a list of volumes that are protected by DPM and a list of volumes that are unprotected. With the manual switch, you must perform the migration for each volume that you would like to migrate; this gives you a more controlled migration process but it can also be time consuming.

 Before any changes are made, it is important that you have a recently backed up DPMDB.

How to do it...

From an elevated PowerShell DPM Management Shell, type `Migrate-Datasource.ps1`. Next, type the NETBIOS name for the DPM server, followed by the migration option (**auto** or **manual**). If you have chosen to use the `auto` option, you only need to provide the FQDN for the production server, shown as follows:

```
DPM Management Shell                                    _ □ X

PS C:\Program Files\Microsoft System Center 2012 R2\DPM\DPM\bin> .\Migrate-DataS
ource.ps1
DPMServer: DPM1
WARNING: Connecting to DPM server: DPM1
   auto for AUTO SEARCH for matching volume letters
   manual for MANUAL INPUT of 'from' and 'to' Volumes, to be migrated
option( auto or manual): auto
PSName: FILE01.CONTOSO.LOCAL
Running inquiry on the PS
Finished running inquiry
Could not find any volumes for migrating automatically

PS C:\Program Files\Microsoft System Center 2012 R2\DPM\DPM\bin>
```

If you have set up a DPM-DPM-DR protection scenario for the protected data source, you also need to run the `Migrate-Datasource.ps1` script on the secondary DPM severs.

There's more...

It is very important that the `Migrate-Datasource.ps1` script is used properly. You need to keep in mind the following:

- The `Migrate-Datasource.ps1` script is used only for the migration of file system data resources, such as volumes.
- DPM does not support migration from a volume on a drive to a mounted volume.
- You should migrate volumes only if you have reformatted them or if the volume GUID associated with the volume has changed.
- After the migration of a volume, you will not be able to restore the recovery points created before the migration to the original locations. You can still restore the recovery points to an alternative location.

5
SQL Protection

In this chapter, we will cover how System Center 2012 R2 Data Protection Manager can protect the SQL Server workloads within your datacenter.

We will cover the following topics:

- ▸ Understanding SQL Server's protection considerations
- ▸ Configuring your SQL Server 2012 for DPM protection
- ▸ Understanding the SQL Server management tasks from a DPM perspective
- ▸ Protecting SQL Server 2012 AlwaysOn
- ▸ Protecting an availability group using SQL Server's AlwaysOn configuration
- ▸ Protecting your SQL Server databases
- ▸ Enabling parallel backups
- ▸ Configuring the auto-protection feature
- ▸ Configuring online protection
- ▸ Restoring a SQL Server database to its original location
- ▸ Restoring a SQL Server database to an alternative location
- ▸ Restoring a SQL Server database and renaming the database
- ▸ Restoring a SQL Server database to a network location
- ▸ Restoring a SQL Server database from Azure
- ▸ Restoring a SQL Server database from tape
- ▸ Restoring a SQL databases using the Latest feature

Introduction

One of the most important Microsoft workloads present in a modern datacenter is the SQL Server due to the majority of Microsoft-based enterprise applications that use its functionality. An important Microsoft application needs to have optimal protection to be able to restore services following a data corruption or other malfunctions.

The recipes in this chapter will provide you with important prerequisite information regarding configuration and how to protect your SQL Server workloads. The content of this chapter provides a complete guide to restore and archive your SQL Server workloads.

Understanding SQL Server protection considerations

This section will provide you with the necessary information needed to understand what to consider before enabling a SQL data source for DPM protection.

Before you start to plan your protection for your SQL server workload, it is important that you understand the SQL server protection considerations. For all SQL Server versions, you must consider that SCDPM 2012 R2 does not support the protection of SQL Server data that is located on a remote file share. The protection will fail and generate the error ID 104.

 Never use both SCDPM 2012 R2 and the SQL Management Studio backup feature; the SQL Management Studio backup function will not update the SQL VSS information, so the DPM agent will lose track of the changed blocks, which can results in an inconsistent replica.

The supported SQL Server versions that could be protected using DPM are:

- ▶ SQL Server 2012
- ▶ SQL Server 2008 R2
- ▶ SQL Server 2008
- ▶ SQL Server 2005

 For DPM to protect SQL Server 2005, you must apply the UR2 for DPM 2012 R2.

If you have a nonsupported configuration for your SQL Server protection, you will not be able to receive any support from Microsoft if you face any need to open a support case. Always keep in mind that you should design and implement a fully supported scenario for your SQL Server data sources.

For SQL Server 2012, you must consider the following:

► To be able to protect SQL Server 2012, you must add **NT SERVICE\DPMRA** as a member of the **sysadmin** group on the SQL Server instances

► You cannot protect databases that are located on remote SMB shares

► Ensure that the availability group replicas are configured as read-only

► When you are restoring a partially contained database, you must restore the database to a SQL instance that has the contained database feature enabled

Configuring your SQL Server 2012 for DPM protection

This recipe will cover how you configure your SQL Server 2012 for System Center 2012 R2 Data Protection Manager to be able to protect the SQL Server 2012 databases.

Getting ready

Microsoft took a new security approach with the release of Microsoft SQL Server 2012 and further restricted who actually is granted SA rights. This is a great approach, but it also causes some headaches for some backup administrators who are not familiar with how the SA rights work or operate in SQL Server.

As a DPM administrator, it is important that you implement the right security approach to protect and recover the SQL Server technology. It is not a recommended idea to grant too many rights in a system; instead, provide just the needed security rights so that DPM can operate without causing unnecessary security exposure.

If you don't give DPM the appropriate security rights, your DPM server will generate a critical alert stating **Unable to configure protection**, as shown in the following screenshot:

How to do it...

1. In the DPM console, you will get an alert that states that DPM is unable to configure protection, as shown in the following screenshot:

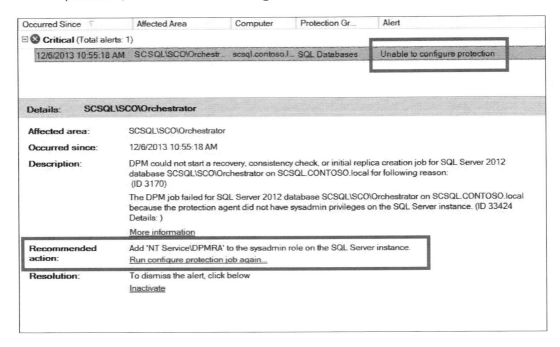

2. Open **Management Studio** and connect to the SQL Server instance that DPM should protect. We should now focus on the **Security** part of the SQL instance configuration, as shown in the following screenshot:

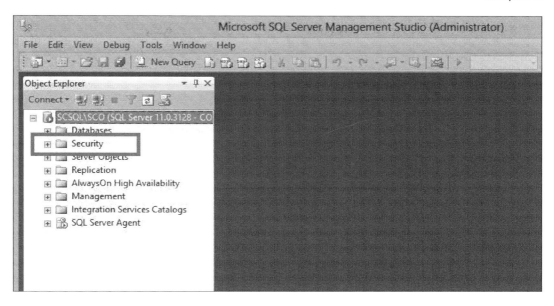

3. Expand **Security** and **Logins**, right-click on **Logins**, and choose **New Login...** to create a new login.

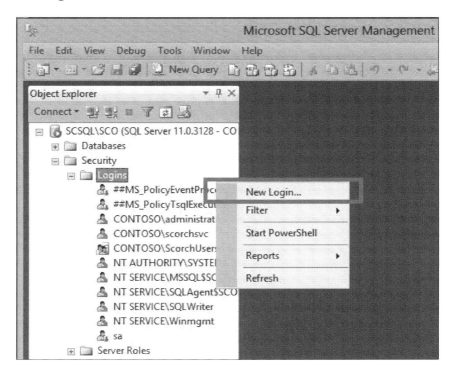

4. It is now important that you grant the SA rights to the **NT SERVICE\DPMRA** service.

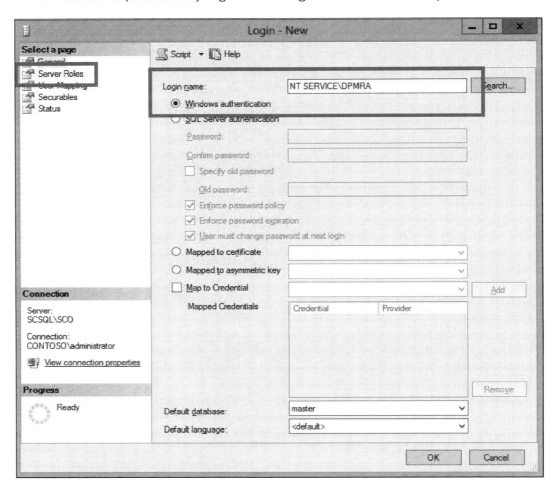

5. Grant the **sysadmin** rights to **NT SERVICE\DPMRA** so that SCDPM 2012 R2 can protect and, of course, recover the SQL Server databases. Use the **Search...** button to find the DPMRA service. Next, click on **Server Roles**:

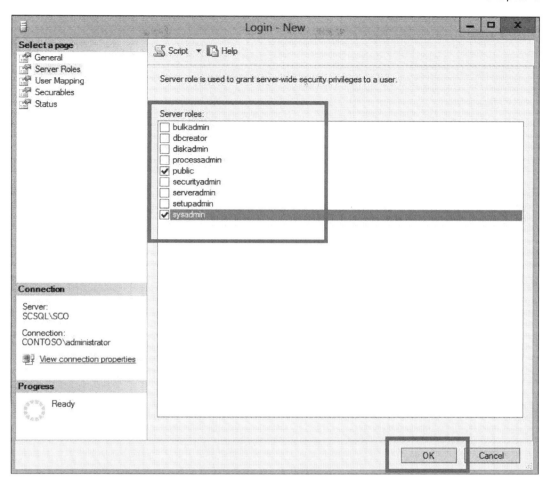

6. Grant the **public** and **sysadmin** security privileges to the DPMRA service. Click on **OK** and you are ready to start protecting your SQL Server 2012 workloads within your datacenter.

How it works...

If the DPM agent does not have the sufficient rights to access the data sources you would like to protect, the VSS request will not be able to get a response from the VSS writer. This will result in the **Unable to configure protection** error message.

There's more...

During the deployment of new SQL Servers, you should consider preconfiguring the necessary security and access configurations to avoid any unwanted misconfigurations for the DPM protection of all your SQL Servers.

Understanding the SQL Server management tasks from a DPM perspective

There are several management tasks that a database administrator must perform; this recipe will cover the most common scenarios and how System Center 2012 R2 Data Protection Manager will cooperate with them.

Getting ready

When the database administrator makes changes to the SQL Server configuration, it could cause the DPM protection to fail.

The most common management tasks for SQL Server are:

- Upgrading SQL Server versions
- Moving SQL Servers to new domains
- Renaming the computer running SQL Server
- Changing the recovery model of a database
- Changing the path of a SQL Server database
- Renaming a SQL Server database

How to do it...

In all the earlier mentioned management tasks, the DPM configuration will not automatically update itself. When the database administrator performs any of the mentioned management tasks, the DPM protection will fail.

To restore the DPM protection, the DPM administrator must stop the protection of the workload and choose to retain the data and reprotect the new or updated SQL Server workload. The old recovery points will be available for recovery even when you change the SQL Server configuration.

How it works...

Since the SQL Server configuration will not update the DPM configuration with the most current information, the changes made by the SQL administrator will cause the protection to fail.

This could easily be avoided by using automation concepts for the SQL Server management task. In the scenario that the SQL administrator needs to perform SQL Server management tasks, he or she starts an automated process that provides the necessary configurations to re-enable to DPM protection.

A very useful component for this purpose is **System Center Orchestrator**. Or, you can also use **Windows Azure Pack** (**WAP**) with the orchestration of **Service Management Automation** (**SMA**).

There's more...

In the scenario that the SQL Server crashes due to a disk failure, it is most important to restore the SQL Server disk with the same drive letter for DPM to continue to protect the SQL Server workload.

If you have a planned migration or upgrade, you must stop the protection and choose to retain the data and reprotect the SQL Server workload under the new configuration or name. You will be able to restore your old recovery points even when you change the SQL Server configuration.

Protecting SQL Server 2012 AlwaysOn

This recipe will cover the information you need before you can start protecting an SQL Server 2012 AlwaysOn-enabled data source.

Getting ready

A great new feature that Microsoft included in the SQL Server 2012 was the **AlwaysOn** feature that makes it possible for DBAs to create a highly available database instance using availability groups that are actually containers for the databases configured for failover.

The **AlwaysOn** feature is really an upgraded, improved version of SQL Server log shipping, and to be able to protect SQL Server 2012 Always-On, you must understand some configuration details.

How to do it...

When System Center 2012 R2 Data Protection Manager protects an SQL Server 2012 with the AlwaysOn feature enabled, it will honor the backup policy for the availability groups, but there are some known limitations:

▶ **Prefer secondary**: The backup should occur on a secondary replica except when the primary replica is the only replica online. In the scenario that there are multiple secondary replicas available, you should back up the node with the highest backup priority due to bandwidth or geographical limitations. In the case that only the primary replica is available, the backup should be done on the primary replica.

▶ **Secondary only**: The backup should not be performed on the primary replica. If the primary replica is the only replica online, the backup should not run.

▶ **Primary**: The backups should always occur on the primary replica.

▶ **Any Replica**: The backups can happen on any of the available replicas in the availability group. The nodes have their backup priorities that will reflect the node that will be backed up.

How it works...

System Center 2012 R2 Data Protection Manager will honor the backup policy for the availability group and it will know how to protect the data sources in an optimal way.

There's more...

There are some configurations details that you must consider before you decide how to protect your AlwaysOn-enabled data sources. The backup can be done from any readable replica, which means primary, synchronous secondary, or asynchronous secondary.

If a replica in your SQL Server AlwaysOn configuration is excluded for backup, then it will not be selected for backup.

In the scenario that there are multiple replicas present in the SQL Server AlwaysOn feature, the replica with the highest backup priority will be chosen for the backup. An important note is that if any of the backups fail on the selected node, the entire backup operation will fail.

The most critical part regarding DPM protecting SQL Server 2012 AlwaysOn is the restore operation. As a DPM admin, you will not be able to restore to the **original location** as this is not a supported scenario from the SQL Server production team.

Protecting an availability group using SQL Server AlwaysOn configuration

This recipe will cover an introduction to how you can start to protect your SQL Server AlwaysOn configuration using DPM.

Getting ready

In your SQL Server 2012 AlwaysOn configuration, you will add your database to something called **Availability Groups**, which are basically containers for your databases that are configured for failover. DPM will protect your databases that are part of your Availability Group.

DPM will detect the Availability Group when you are creating or modifying a new or existing Protection Group. If the database that is a member of the Availability Group fails over, DPM will continue to protect the database. You may encounter the replica for the Availability Group becoming inconsistent and you may need to perform a consistency check.

If you have a multisite cluster configuration for an instance of your SQL Server, DPM will support the protection of the workload.

How to do it...

To start protecting your SQL Server 2012 databases that are also selected members of your configured Availability Groups, you must create a new Protection Group.

On starting the **New** Protection Group wizard, you will find the Availability Groups under the node called **Cluster Group**. You can protect both the entire Availability Group by selecting the group name, or you can protect an explicit database that is a selected member of the Availability Group by expanding the group name and selecting the database.

How it works...

When it comes to System Center 2012 R2 Data Protection Manager, to understand the SQL Server availability group configuration, it will honor the configured backup policy for the availability group and therefore understand how the protection should be configured.

There's more...

If you would like to read more regarding SQL Server 2012 Availability Groups, you should start reading official Microsoft Technet articles at this URL: `http://technet.microsoft.com/en-us/sqlserver/gg490638.aspx`

Protecting your SQL Server databases

This recipe will cover how to configure your protection group to enable DPM protection.

Getting ready

Before you start to protect your SQL Server workloads, you need to have a DPM agent deployed and attached to the DPM server and a disk pool attached for your DPM storage.

How to do it...

1. Go to **Protection** and click on **New** in the DPM console.

2. In the **Welcome** step of the **Create New Protection Group** wizard, click on **Next >** to continue.

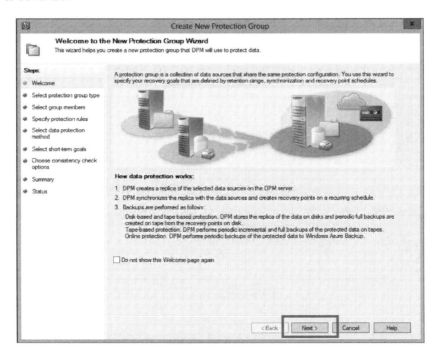

3. In the **Select Protection Group Type** step, choose **Servers** and click on **Next >** to continue.

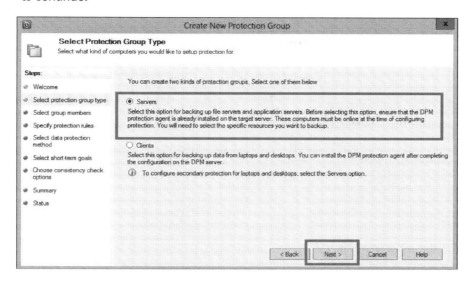

4. In the **Select Group Members** step, select the SQL Server databases that you would like to protect with DPM. Expand your SQL Server and you will find **All SQL Servers** listed. Expand this node and you will see all the instances present on this SQL Server. Select the instance, database, or databases that you would like to add to the protection group and click on **Next >** to continue.

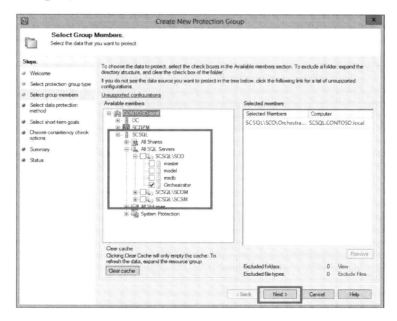

5. In the **Select Data Protection Method** step, you are provided with the different options of how you can protect your SQL Server databases. You can use the following three different protection methods for SQL databases:

❑ Short-time protection using disk or tape

❑ Online protection using Azure

❑ Long-term protection using tape or **Virtual Tape Library** (**VTL**)

 For more information regarding tape management, refer to *Chapter 12, Disaster Recovery.*

6. Enter the **Protection group name** value, choose **Protection method** that applies to your protection group, and click on **Next >** to continue.

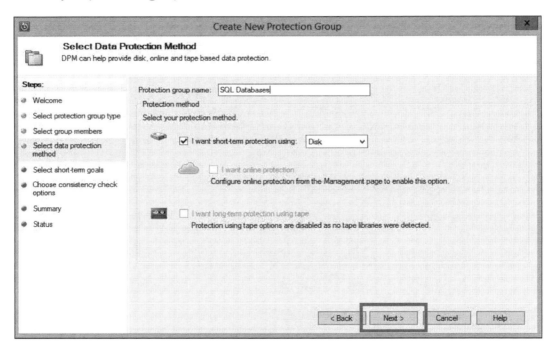

7. In the **Select Short-Term Goals** step, you can define your backup schedule and synchronization frequency. First, set the number of days for **Retention range** followed by **Synchronization frequency**, which is how often you would like to transfer the block level changes from the production environment to your DPM server for protection.

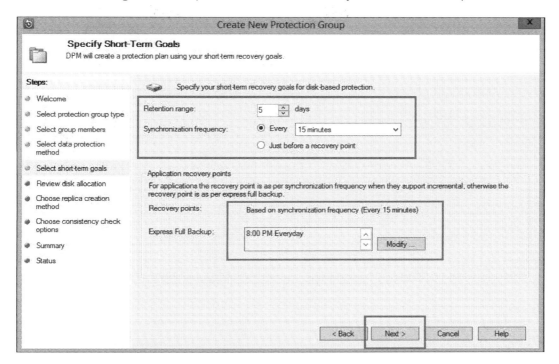

8. You can choose to just synchronize your block level changes at the time of recovery point creation by choosing the **Just before a recovery point** option. You can also define a more frequent synchronization frequency, for SQL databases as frequently as every 15 minutes.

For transactional log systems such as SQL, Exchange, and File workloads, you are able to perform synchronization every 15 minutes. This only applies if the system has any log files that could be synchronized, such as a SQL database with a FULL or BULKED-LOGGED recovery model.

9. Next, you should define **Express Full Backup** by clicking on the **Modify...** button, and a new window will appear.

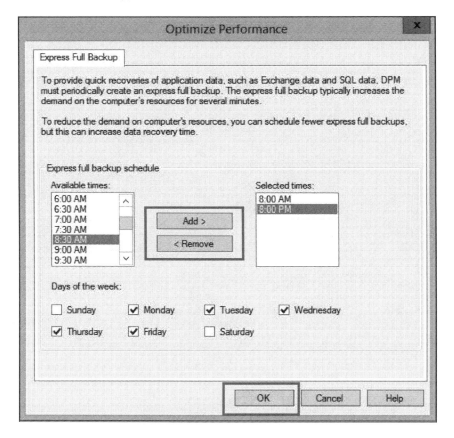

10. In the **Optimize Performance** window, you can define the **Express-Full** backup schedule.

Express-Full is the name for the backup schedule in DPM. There are two functions components in DPM that the **Express-Full** function consists of. The **Express-Full** function is a combination of the synchronization function and the creation of a recovery point function.

11. Choose a time for recovery point creation under **Available times** and click on **Add >** to add the selected time to the backup schedule.

 You can create a recovery point every 30 minutes.

12. After you have selected your time for recovery point creation, you can define the weekdays on which the backup should occur. Check the appropriate checkboxes schedule and click on **OK** to return to the **Specify Short-Term Goals** step; click on **Next >** to continue to the **Review Disk Allocation** step.

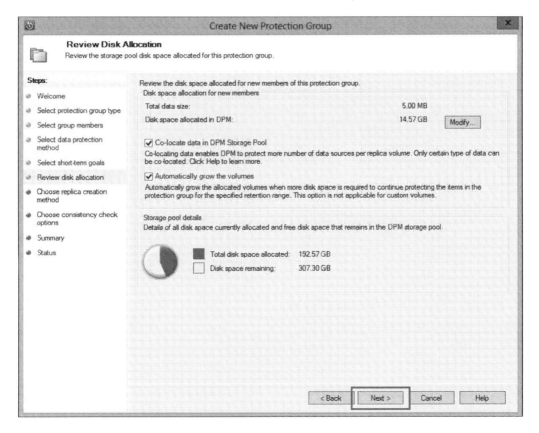

13. In the **Review Disk Allocation** step, you can choose **Automatically grow the volumes** or **Co-locate data in DPM Storage Pool** by ticking the checkboxes. To perform further disk configurations, click on **Modify...** or **Next >** to continue.

14. In the **Review disk allocation** step, you configure and review the disk space allocated for the protection group. Two specific volumes are created for all protected data sources that the DPM server is protecting: replica and recovery point volumes. One of the auto-heal functions within DPM is **Automatically grow the volumes**. This feature will expand the volume when the threshold is reached.

15. The **Co-locate data in DPM Storage Pool** option is a disk optimization feature that will make it possible to store a larger quantity of replica data within the same replica volume. This feature applies to clients, Hyper-V, and SQL databases.

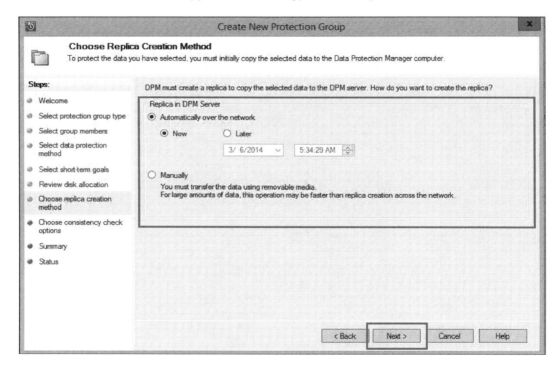

 For more information regarding the auto-grow and co-location function, refer to the *Growing volumes automatically in the DPM disk pool* recipe in *Chapter 3, Post-installation Tasks*.

16. In the **Choose replica creation method** step, you can define how the DPM server should create the replica of the protected data source. You can create the replica as the configuration of the protection group is finished, or you can schedule the replica creation. You can also create the replica manually.

> For more detailed information regarding replica creation, refer to the *Creating a replica manually* recipe in *Chapter 3, Post-installation Tasks*.

17. Click on **Next >** to continue.

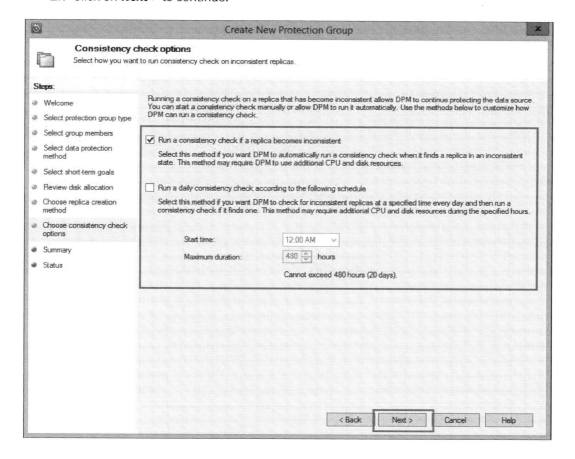

18. In the **Consistency check options** step, you can specify whether the DPM server should run a consistency check if a replica becomes inconsistent; this is an auto-heal function within the DPM server technology. You can also specify how to run a daily consistency check where you specify the start time and how many hours the task should run.

19. To continue to the next step, click on **Next >**.

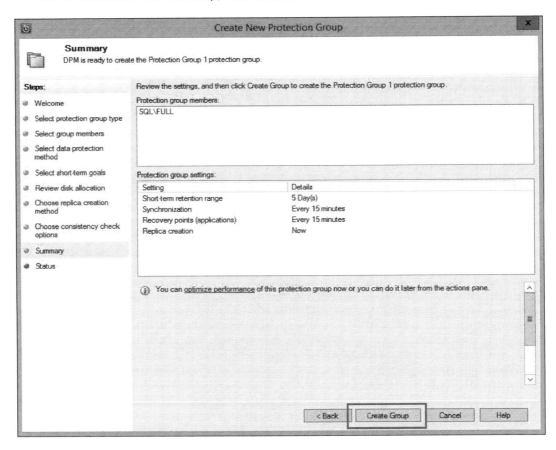

20. The last step is the **Summary** page. Review **Summary** for the protection group and click on the **Create Group** button to create the protection group. In the **Status** step, you can see the actual status of the protection group creation.

21. If you need to optimize the performance for the protection group, you can click on the **optimize performance** link or create the configurations from the DPM console later.

How it works...

The Protection Group holds the actual configuration for your backup schedule, protected data sources, and specific configurations like on-the-wire-compression. The DPM server will call the DPM agents that are members of the Protection Group to initialize the backup job; this is the **VSS Request** procedure that starts the VSS snapshot process on the protected server.

There's more...

For more information regarding how the DPM server operates, it is recommended that you read all the recipes in *Chapter 1, Pre-installation Tasks*.

Enabling parallel backups

For the protection of larger SQL implementations using DPM, it is important to understand how to design the protection in an optimal way to gain the benefits that reside in both products. This recipe will explain the design considerations that must be done to be able to use the parallel backup feature.

Getting ready

The possibility to optimize a SQL database backup is something that is already present within the SQL Server code. The function parallel backup was written in the 2008 version of SQL Server; to be able to use it, you need to set up your DPM protection in a specific way.

How to do it...

When DPM backs up the SQL databases that are present in a SQL instance, the backup will be provided in a serial fashion. If the SQL implementation hosts databases that have a low value of RPO, the SQL team should place the databases in another SQL instance to enable the parallel backup feature.

How it works...

System Center 2012 R2 Data Protection Manger will adapt to the SQL Server configuration and understand how to protect its data sources in the most optimal way for the current Microsoft technology.

Configuring the auto-protection feature

The DPM administrator will rarely be informed by the database administrators that they have deployed new SQL databases that they would like to include in the backup. This recipe will cover how to enable the auto-protection feature for your protected SQL Servers so that new SQL databases are always protected.

Getting ready

One of the most common management tasks from a database administrator perspective is to provide new databases for the organization. DPM has the ability to automatically protect these newly added SQL databases by enabling the **auto-protection** feature. During a nightly scheduled job, the auto-protection feature will add the unprotected SQL databases that are members of the SQL instance that has auto-protection enabled.

How to do it...

When you create or modify a protection group, you can expand your SQL Server name and the **All SQL Servers** nodes will appear. Expand the **All SQL Servers** node and you will be able to see all the SQL instances present on the SQL Server.

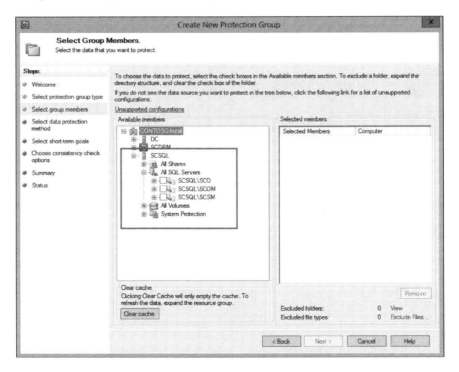

To enable to auto-protection feature, mark the checkbox next to the SQL instance. You can also right-click on the instance name and choose **Turn on auto protection**.

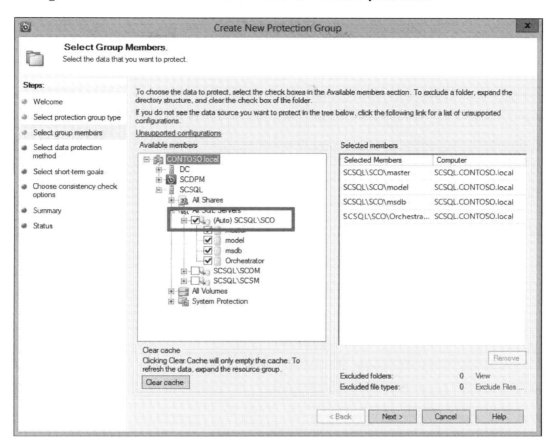

When you select the checkbox, the **(Auto)** text will be displayed.

Finish the protection group configuration by clicking through the protection group configuration wizard and finally, click on the **Update Group** button.

How it works...

Every night, your DPM server will initialize the auto-protection script, which will include all newly added SQL Server databases to the auto-protected SQL Server instance. You can also trigger this script manually, and by empowering the interaction of PowerShell and Windows Server technologies, it's possible to create very powerful automation concepts.

There's more...

If you can't wait for the DPM server to discover the newly added SQL databases, you can always use the `Start-DPMAutoProtection.PS1` PowerShell script from **DPM Management Shell** to force the DPM server to discover new databases and add them to the protection group.

 The auto-protection for SQL instances can fail when the WMI is not properly working on a protected SQL Server.

Configuring online protection

This recipe will describe how you can configure the SQL Server workload for online protection.

Getting ready

SQL Server is one of the workloads that you can configure for online protection, which will give you a cost-effective, cloud-based archiving solution. Before you can enable the online protection for an SQL Server database, you must first configure your DPM server for the Azure recovery service called **Backup Vault**; you can find more information in the *Configuring your DPM server for online protection* recipe in *Chapter 11, Azure Integration*.

How to do it...

1. When you create or modify a protection group, you can enable the online protection in the **Select Data Protection Method** step of the protection group wizard. If your DPM server has successfully registered with the Azure restore service, the Backup Vault service, you will be able to tick the checkbox named **I want online protection**.

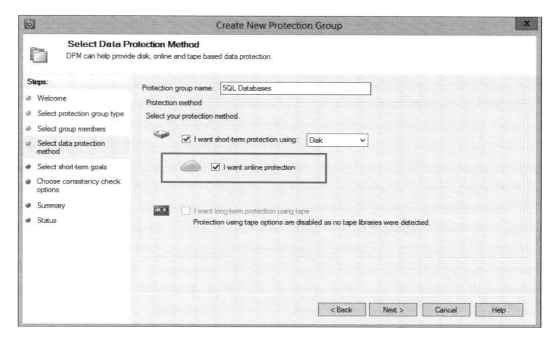

This will provide two further steps for your protection group configuration:

- ❑ Specify the online protection data
- ❑ Specify online protection goals

2. In the **Specify Online Protection Data** step of your protection group wizard, you can specify what protected data source you would want to include for online protection.

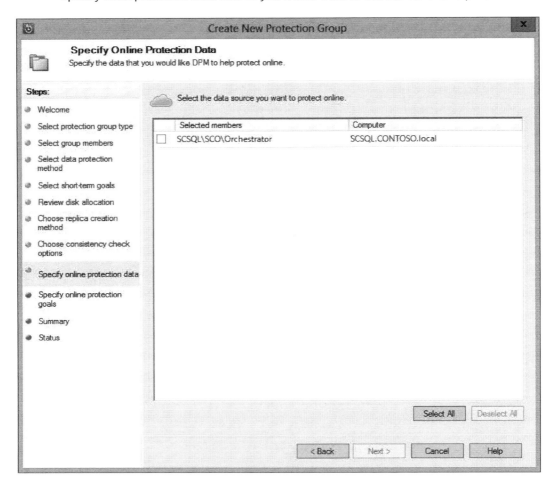

3. The next step in the configuration is the **Specify Online Protection Goals** step, where you have two important options for your online protection, **Daily** or **Weekly** synchronization frequency.

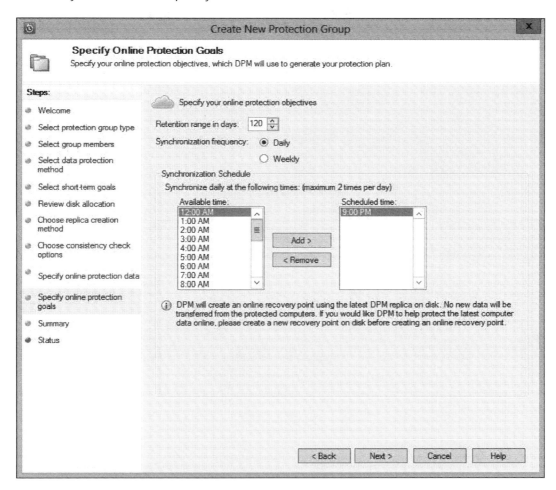

4. With the UR5 for System Center 2012 R2 Data Protection Manager, the Azure integration is provided without limits. If you pay for it, Azure will store it. Mark the time for online protection in **Available time** and click on **Add>**.

5. Choose the **Weekly** option for the synchronization frequency if you would like to use online protection only on specific weekdays.

How it works...

In the Microsoft Azure Management Portal, Microsoft created a service called **Backup Vault** that can easily be connected to both DPM servers and also to the **Windows Server Backup** (**WSB**) feature of Windows 2012 Server 2008R2, 2012, and 2012 R2 releases. Using certificates and explicit passphrases, Microsoft can assure not just a great feature to reduce the tape management for companies, but also a highly secured one. The recipes of *Chapter 11, Azure Integration*, will walk you through the complete configuration of your System Center 2012 R2 Data Protection Manager server.

The steps to get started are:

  ▸ Sign up for Azure services

  ▸ Install an Windows Azure Backup agent

  ▸ Register your DPM server with the Azure service

  ▸ Start protecting your production data

There's more...

For more detailed information regarding how to enable SQL Server databases for online protection, refer to *Chapter 11, Azure Integration*.

Restoring a SQL Server database to its original location

This recipe will cover how to restore a SQL database to its original location. This is one of the most common scenarios that a DPM administrator must be able to perform.

Getting ready

This restore operation is the most common and the easiest to perform. There are some options that you should consider regarding the restore process, and they are explained in this recipe.

How to do it...

1. Open the DPM console and click on **Recovery**. Browse the tree on the left-hand side of the console and click on the SQL database that you want to restore. Choose the date and the recovery point time for restore. Right-click on the database and click on **Recover...** to start **Recovery Wizard**.

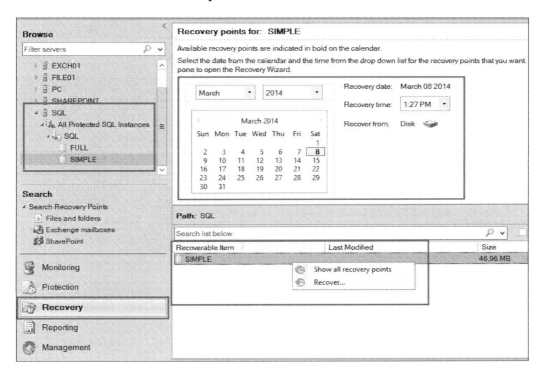

2. In the **Review Recovery Selection** step, verify that you have chosen the right database and click on **Next >** to continue.

3. In the **Select Recovery Type** step, choose **Recover to original instance of SQL Server (Overwrite database)** and click on **Next >**.

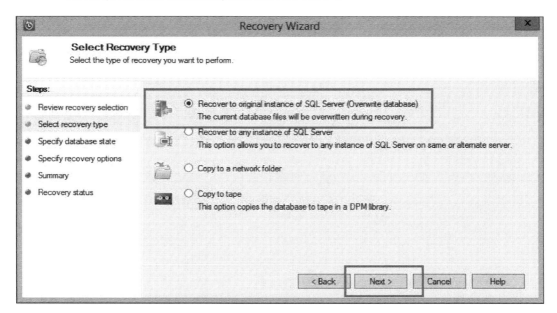

4. In the **Specify Database State** step, you can decide the state in which the database should be left after the restore job is finished. Choose the **Leave database operational** option and click on **Next >** if you want to perform a full recovery and leave the database ready for use.

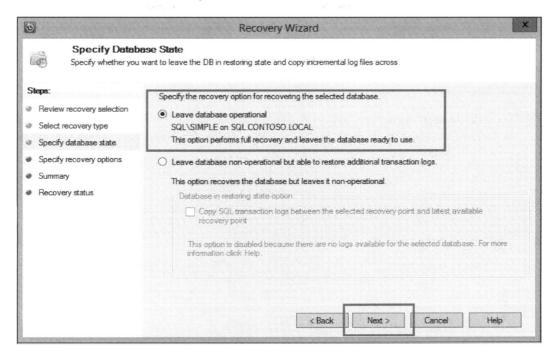

5. In the **Specify Recovery Options** step, you can choose whether you would like to enable **Network bandwidth usage throttling** for the specific restore job; this option will make sure that the restore job does not consume all the bandwidth for the production network.

6. If you have a VSS hardware provider configured for the data source, you can utilize the **SAN Recovery** option for the restore job.

7. When the restore job is finished, you are able to let the DPM server send an e-mail message to the DBA who ordered the restore job; this is done under the **Notification** option. You must configure an SMTP server in your DPM server options for the e-mail notification to work.

8. To continue, click on **Next >**.

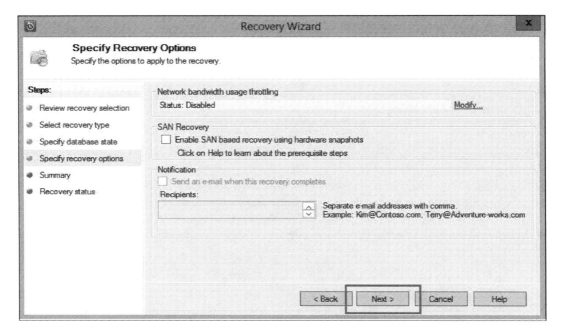

9. Verify the restore job setup in the **Summary** step and click on **Recover** to start the restoration of the SQL database to its original location.

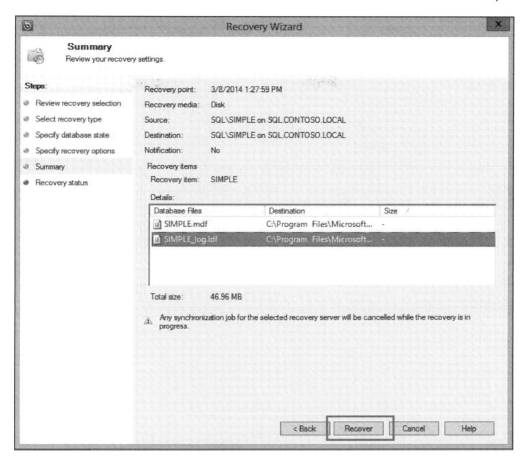

10. You can follow the restore progress in the **Recovery status** step of the wizard or choose **Close** to follow the progress in the **Monitor** view of the DPM console.

How it works...

When DPM initializes the recovery job, it will rely on the VSS architecture that is a part of the server operating system architecture.

There's more...

If the recovery job fails, you should verify the alert that the DPM server will raise to inform you what has happened and guide you on how to create a possible scenario for the recovery to occur.

Restoring a SQL Server database to an alternative location

This recipe will cover how to perform a restore job of a SQL Server database to an alternative location.

Getting ready

System Center 2012 R2 Data Protection Manager provides you with the possibilities to restore an SQL database to an alternative location or SQL Server instance. Before you can restore your SQL databases to an alternative location, you must have a DPM agent installed to the SQL Server that is your target location and have it attached to your DPM server.

How to do it...

1. Open the DPM console and click on **Recovery**. Expand the tree on the left-hand side of the console and click on the SQL database that you want to restore. Choose the date and the recovery point time for the restore. Right-click on the database and click on **Recover...** to start **Recovery Wizard**.

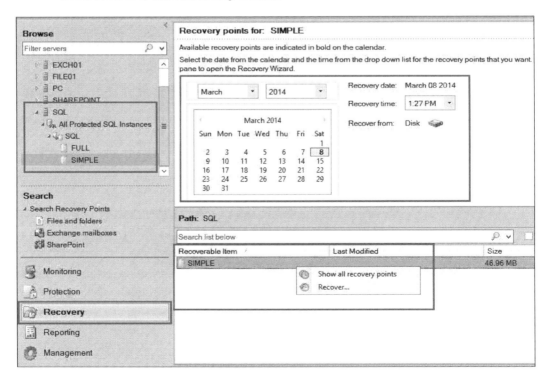

2. In the **Review Recovery Selection** step, verify that you have chosen the right database and click on **Next >** to continue.

In the **Select Recovery Type** step, choose **Recover to any instance of SQL Server**. Click on **Next >** to continue.

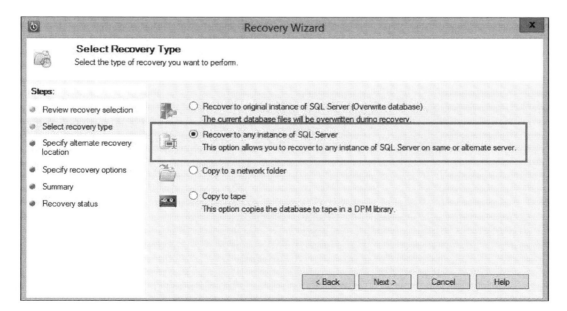

You can also use this recovery type to migrate your SQL databases between SQL Servers or SQL instances as long as you have a DPM agent attached to the targeted SQL Server.

3. The next step is **Specify alternative recovery location**; this is where you decide to restore your SQL database. You can restore the SQL database to another instance on the same SQL Server, or you can choose to restore the SQL database to another SQL Server instance.

4. To be able to restore the SQL database to another SQL Server instance, you must have a DPM agent installed and attached for that SQL Server. To point out the new SQL Server for the targeted restore, click on **Browse...**.

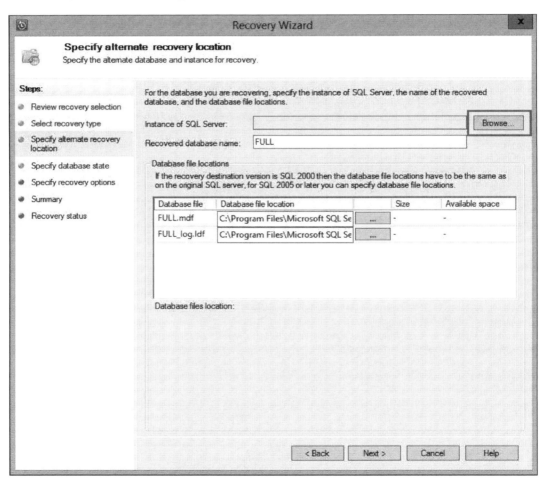

5. Expand the server that you would like to restore your SQL database to, mark the SQL Server instance, and click on **OK** to continue.

6. If you choose to restore the database to another SQL Server, you should point out the location for the database files on the targeted SQL Server by clicking on the **...** button. To continue, click on **Next >**.

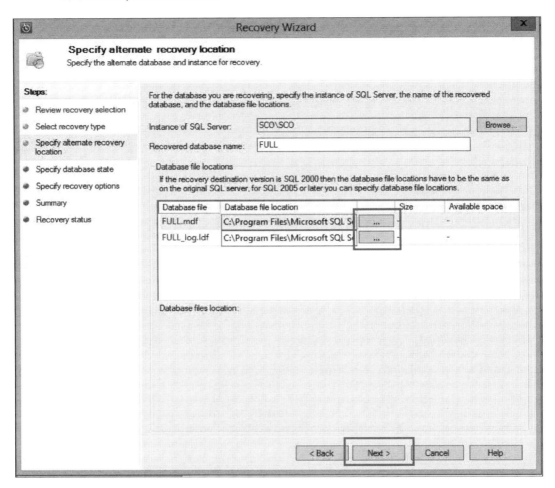

7. In the **Specify Database State** step, you can choose **Leave the database operational** or **Leave database non-operational but able to restore additional transaction logs**. In the latter case, you will be able to restore the database with a non-operational state and specify a destination where you restore your SQL log files. To continue, click on **Next >**.

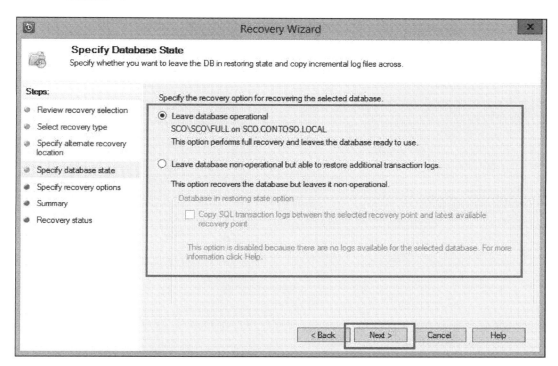

8. In the **Specify Recovery Options** step, you can choose whether you would like to enable **Network bandwidth usage throttling** for the specific restore job; this option will make sure that the restore job does not consume all the bandwidth for the production network.

9. If you have a VSS hardware provider configured for the data source, you can utilize the **SAN Recovery** option for the restore job.

10. When the restore job is finished, you can let the DPM server send an e-mail message to the DBA who ordered the restore job; this is done under the **Notification** option. You must configure an SMTP server in your DPM server options for the e-mail notification to work. Click on **Next >** to continue.

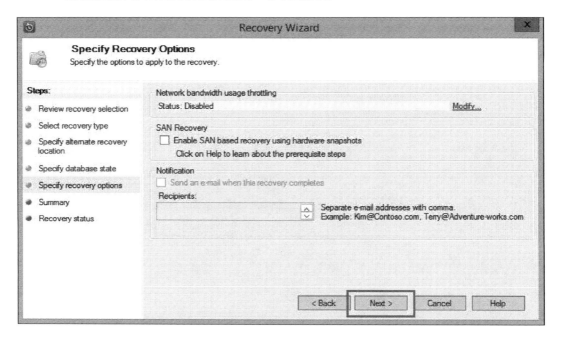

11. Verify the information in the **Summary** step and click on **Recover** to start the restore job.

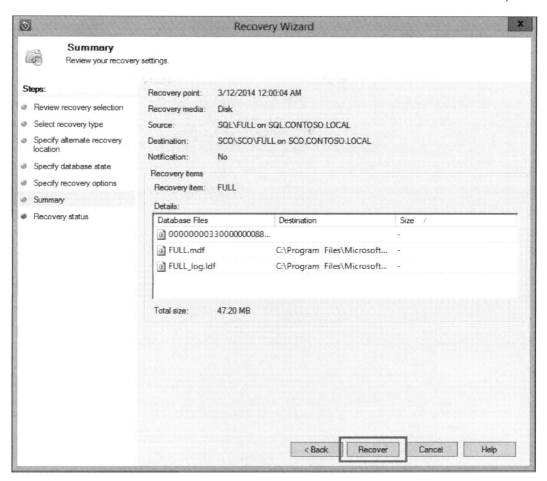

12. You can follow the restore progress in the **Recovery status** step of the wizard or choose **Close** to follow the progress in the **Monitor** view of the DPM console.

How it works...

When DPM initializes the recovery job, it will rely on the VSS architecture that is a part of the server operating system architecture.

There's more...

If the recovery job fails, you should verify the alert that the DPM server will raise to inform you what has happened and guide you to create a possible scenario for the recovery to occur.

Restoring a SQL Server database and renaming the database

This recipe will cover how to recover a SQL database but change the SQL alias for the database. A scenario for this is when you recover a development database to a production environment.

Getting ready

In the scenario that you would like to restore a SQL database with another SQL alias, you must keep in mind that if you restore the SQL database to the same SQL instance that it originates from, you must change the location of the database file and/or the log files for the database, or you cannot perform the restore operation.

If you don't specify an alternate file location, the restore job will fail and DPM will describe it as a VSS error.

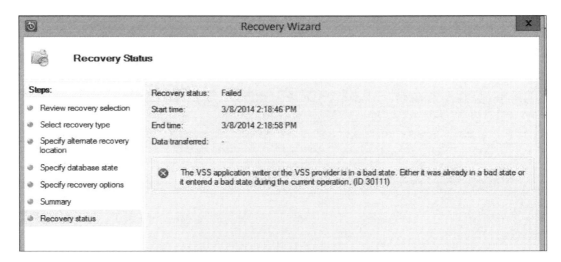

How to do it...

1. Go to **Recovery** and choose the right database, date, and time in the DPM console. Right-click on the database and choose **Recover...** to start **Recovery Wizard**. In the **Review Recovery Selection** step, verify that you have chosen the right database and click on **Next >** to continue.

2. Choose the **Recover to any instance of SQL Server** option and click on **Next >**.

3. In the **Specify alternate recovery location** step, point out the same or another SQL Server that you would like to restore to. You must also change the location of the SQL database files. When both have been taken care of, you click on **Next >** to continue.

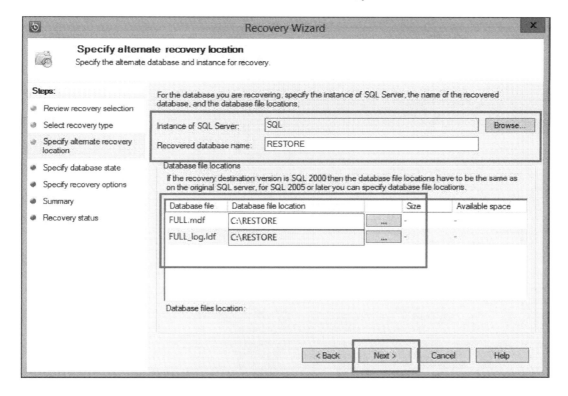

4. Click through **Recovery Wizard** and you will successfully restore your SQL database with another SQL alias.

How it works...

When DPM initializes the recovery job, it will rely on the VSS architecture that is a part of the server operating system architecture.

There's more...

If the recovery job fails, you should verify the alert that the DPM server will raise to inform you what has happened and guides you to create a possible scenario for the recovery to occur.

Restoring a SQL database to a network location

This recipe will cover how to successfully restore a SQL database to a network location.

Getting ready

Before you can restore your SQL database to a network location, you need to have a DPM agent installed and attached to the DPM server.

How to do it...

1. Open the DPM console and click on **Recovery**. Expand the tree on the left-hand side of the console and click on the SQL database that you want to restore. Choose the date and the recovery point time for the restore. Right-click on the database and click on **Recover...** to start **Recovery Wizard**.

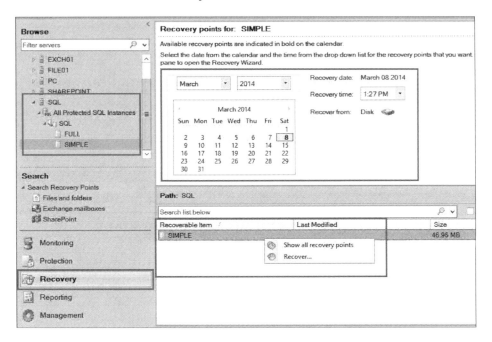

2. In the **Review Recovery Selection** step, verify that you have chosen the right database and click on **Next >** to continue.

3. Choose the **Copy to a network folder** option and click on **Next >**.

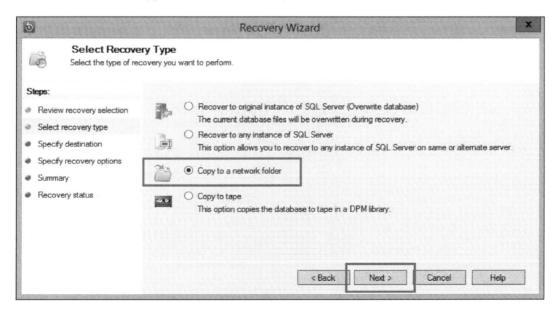

4. In the **Specify Destination** step, click on **Browse...** to point out the destination for your restore.

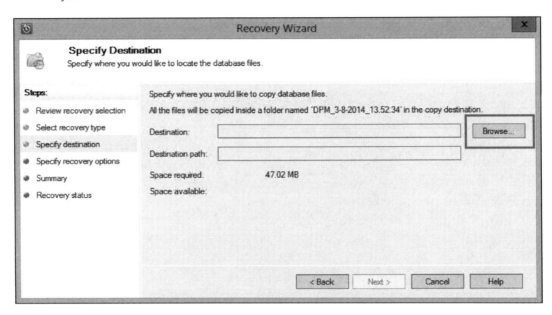

5. Choose the appropriate location for your restore and click on **OK** to continue.

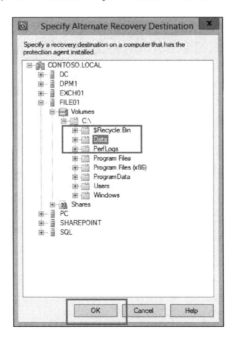

6. Click on **Next >** to continue. In the **Specify Recovery Options** step, you can choose whether you would like to enable **Network bandwidth usage throttling** for the specific restore job; this option will make sure that the restore job does not consume all the bandwidth for the production network.

7. If you have a VSS hardware provider configured for the data source, you can utilize the **SAN Recovery** option for the restore job.

8. When the restore job is finished, you can let the DPM server send an e-mail message to the DBA who ordered the restore job; this is done under the **Notification** option. You must configure an SMTP server in your DPM server options for the e-mail notification to work.

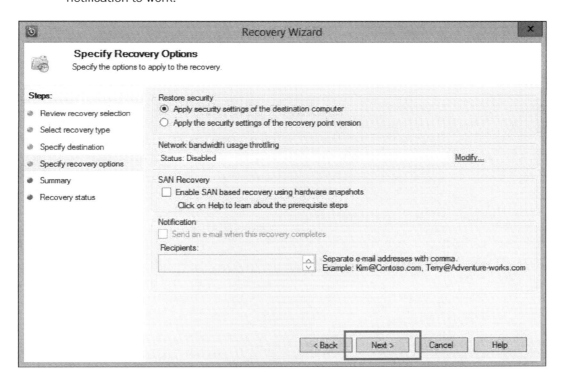

9. Verify the information in the **Summary** step and click on **Recover** to start the restore job.

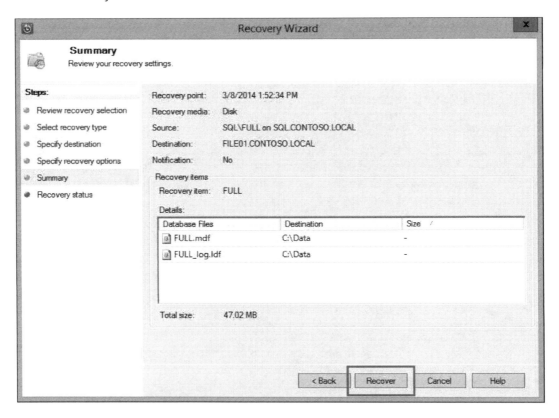

10. You can follow the restore progress in the **Recovery status** step of the wizard or choose **Close** to follow the progress in the **Monitor** view of the DPM console.

How it works...

When DPM initializes the recovery job, it will rely on the VSS architecture that is a part of the server operating system architecture.

There's more...

If the recovery job fails, you should verify the alert that the DPM server will raise to inform you what has happened and guide you on how to create a possible scenario for the recovery to occur.

Restoring a SQL database from Azure

This recipe will cover the scenario where you need to restore your SQL database from your Azure recovery service.

Getting ready

The most important thing regarding the restore operation from Azure is that you have network connectivity. The Azure Backup Vault should never be seen as a disaster recovery function; it is a data recovery function. The difference is that Microsoft Azure depends on an Internet connection.

How to do it...

1. Open the DPM console and click on **Recovery**. Expand the tree on the left-hand side of the console and click on the SQL database that you want to restore. Choose the date and the recovery point time for the restore.

2. The main difference is that you need to choose recovery from an online snapshot; all time for online snapshot will be listed as **Online** in the drop-down time list.

3. Right-click on the database and click on **Recover...** to start **Recovery Wizard**.

4. By restoring from your online backup, you can restore your SQL database to the original instance of SQL Server or an alternative SQL Server instance, or you can copy the database to a network folder.

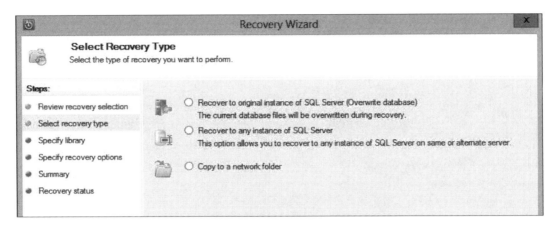

5. Choose the option that fits your restore purpose and follow the **Recovery Wizard** guide.

6. You can follow the restore progress in the **Recovery status** step of the wizard or choose **Close** to follow the progress in the **Monitor** view of the DPM console.

How it works...

When DPM initializes the recovery job, it will rely on the VSS architecture that is a part of the server operating system architecture.

There's more...

If the recovery job fails, you should verify the alert that the DPM server will raise to inform you what has happened and guide you on how to create a possible scenario for the recovery to occur.

Restoring a SQL Server database from tape

This recipe will cover the scenario where you need to restore a SQL database from tape.

Getting ready

The most important thing to remember is that tapes needs to be kept in a healthy state to complete their expected lifetime. Now and then, you should exercise the tapes, which means reading data from them to verify that they are good to restore from; never trust a tape 100 percent.

How to do it...

1. Open the DPM console and click on **Recovery**. Expand the tree on the right-hand side of the console and click on the SQL database that you want to restore. Choose the date and the recovery point time for restore.

2. When you are restoring SQL databases from tape, you need to choose the correct recovery point in time for the restore. In the drop-down menu, the recovery point that is placed on a tape will be listed with **(Tape)**.

3. Right-click on the database and click on **Recover...** to start **Recovery Wizard**.

4. By restoring from the tape, you can restore your SQL database to the original instance of SQL Server or an alternative SQL Server instance/location, or you can copy the database to a network folder.

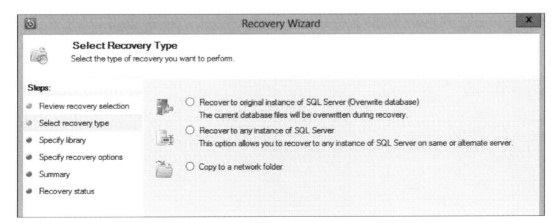

5. Choose the option that fits your restore purpose and follow the **Recovery Wizard** guide.

6. You can follow the restore progress in the **Recovery status** step of the wizard or choose **Close** to follow the progress in the **Monitor** view of the DPM console.

How it works...

When DPM initializes the recovery job, it will rely on the VSS architecture that is a part of the server operating system architecture.

There's more...

If the recovery job fails, you should verify the alert that the DPM server will raise to inform you what has happened and guide you on how to create a possible scenario for the recovery to occur.

Restoring SQL databases using the Latest feature

This recipe will cover the restore scenario of SQL databases using the **Latest** feature technology.

Getting ready

When restoring the SQL database using the latest technology, you are only able to restore the SQL database to its original location. The purpose of the Latest technology is to restore the database and additional log files that are present on the SQL Server and have not yet been synchronized to the DPM server. The restore process will only restore good transactions.

How to do it...

1. Open the DPM console and click on **Recovery**. Expand the tree on the left-hand side of the console and click on the SQL database that you want to restore. Choose the date and the recovery point time for the restore.

2. If the SQL database has a recovery model of full or bulked-logged, you can restore the SQL database using the Latest technology.

3. You choose to restore the SQL database using the Latest technology by choosing **Latest** in the drop-down list.

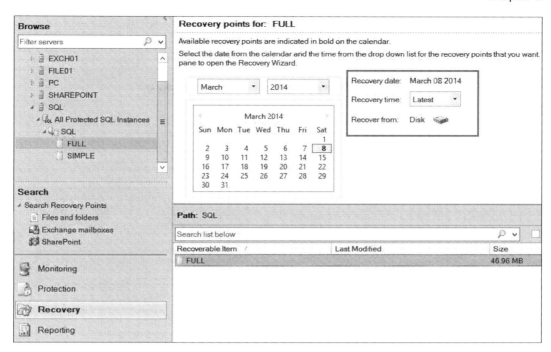

4. You can only restore the SQL database to its original location using the Latest technology; all other options are grayed out.

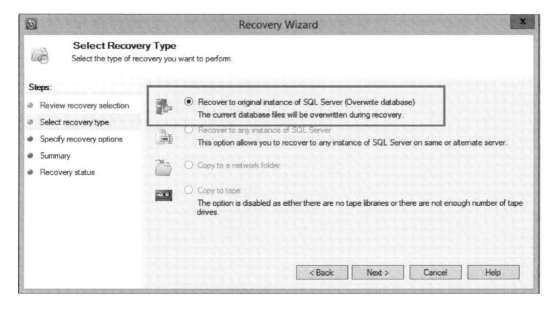

5. Follow the **Recovery Wizard** guide and you can follow the restore progress in the **Recovery status** step of the wizard or choose **Close** to follow the progress in the **Monitor** view of the DPM console.

How it works...

When DPM initializes the recovery job, it will rely on the VSS architecture that is a part of the server operating system architecture.

There's more...

If the recovery job fails, you should verify the alert that the DPM server will raise to inform you what has happened and guide you on how to create a possible scenario for the recovery to occur.

6

Hyper-V Protection

In this chapter, we will cover the following topics:

- ▶ Understanding the prerequisites for Hyper-V protection
- ▶ Understanding the considerations for Hyper-V protection
- ▶ Protecting large-scale Hyper-V environments
- ▶ Protecting System Center Virtual Machine Manager
- ▶ Integrating SCDPM with SCVMM
- ▶ Restoring a Hyper-V virtual machine
- ▶ Restoring a VHD or VHDX
- ▶ Using ILR (Item Level Restore)
- ▶ Understanding Hyper-V management tasks

Introduction

From a modern perspective, a majority of the companies using or provisioning any services should be considered as service providers for other companies. Regardless of whether the company is a hosting company or not, IT must consider this and approach of the new data center that is building services, which they will provide, instead of virtual machines.

With this in mind, the content of this chapter will provide you with the basics regarding a private cloud protection, in terms of what to consider and how to setup DPM as the primary protection for the virtualization that the Microsoft Hyper-V platform provides. Specifically, we will cover how to set up an optimal Hyper-V protection for virtual machine protection. We will also cover the different restore scenarios and also some important configurations regarding protecting large scale implementations.

Understanding the prerequisites for Hyper-V protection

This recipe will cover the prerequisites for Hyper-V protection. Before you are able to provide a restore plan for your virtual machines to recover the services that you are providing in your modern data center, you need to understand the prerequisites for protecting Hyper-V.

The supported versions of Hyper-V that DPM 2012 R2 can protect and restore are:

- Windows Server 2012 R2 - Data center and Standard
- Windows Server 2012 - Data center and Standard
- Windows Server 2008 R2 SP1 - Enterprise and Standard

 System Center Data Protection Manager 2012 R2 can also protect Linux running as a virtual machine in the Hyper-V environment.

The different versions of the Hyper-V role that the Windows Server operating system hosts work similarly but uses different kinds of underlying architecture within the operating system.

The most common approach is the usage of CSVs for storing the VHD files for older versions of Hyper-V. With the 2012 release of the Windows Server operating system, the possibility of empowering the virtual concept by levering the possibilities of **Scale-Out File Servers** (**SOFS**) took Microsoft hypervisor to the next level, and made it a natural competitor in the larger enterprise segment.

System Center Data Protection Manager 2012 R2 honors the empowerments and provides a solid restore functionality for private cloud deployment using the SOFS technology and also adapts and takes advantage of it regarding the deduplication possibilities of the DPM disk pool.

For more information regarding supported versions of Microsoft Hyper-V, please read the following TechNet article:

`http://technet.microsoft.com/en-us/library/jj860400.aspx`

Understanding the considerations for Hyper-V protection

This recipe covers what needs to be considered before providing a solid restore plan for your virtual environments.

One of the key tasks is to be able to provide a restore operation that is based on and delivered through a well thought-out design. A majority of new deployments of a private cloud forget the importance of having a backup and the function it provides, in case of either corruption or accidental deletion of data. For System Center Data Protection Manager 2012 R2 to be able to start sending its VSS queries, it must be able to communicate via its DPM agents. You must deploy DPM agents to all Hyper-V nodes and also to all members of the SOFS cluster and also enable the File Server VSS Agent on all servers that host the SOFS.

System Center Data Protection 2012 R2 will understand the Hyper-V clusters in a fully supported manner. When different virtual machines fail -over from one node in the cluster to another, DPM will seamlessly continue to protect the virtual machines. With the integration of VMM client components, DPM can also adapt to outer-external cluster migration scenarios and provide a seamlessly continuous protection.

In a large scale deployment, it is important to provide a backup for the tenants in the most efficient and cost effective way. Whether your cluster hosts a thousand or just a few hundred tenants, it's still very important to provide a backup solution that is provisioned within the concept of the newly deployed virtual machines or tenants. This also makes a cost effective backup. A key takeaway from managing a large cluster environment is to exclude the page file that every virtual operating system hosts. The page file is not of great interest regarding a normal restore scenario.

Every operating system needs a page file to be able to swap parts of the RAM memory to a flat file. The flat file will contain only temporary data that is important for the operating system's current process and not from a restore perspective.

In the virtual machine template that you are using to deploy new virtual machines, you should provide a dedicated volume that hosts only the page file. System Center Data Protection Manager 2012 R2 will honor a registry key that states that if the page file is hosted by a dedicated volume, it will be excluded from the backup after a global configuration is made, using a DPM PowerShell cmdlet.

To enable System Center Data Protection Manager 2012 R2 to exclude the page files, you must move the page file of every virtual machine to a dedicated volume, and after that, enable the exclusion of the page file data churn by running the `Set-DPMGlobalProperty CMDLET.cmdlet` It is important that you have a standard naming convention for the page file exclusion disks, since you must work with a standardized concept while hosting the virtual machines. Use this syntax to enable the page file exclusion on every DPM server that provides restore capabilities to the Hyper-V environments:

```
Set-DPMGlobalProperty -DPMServerName "Contoso-DPMServer"
-HyperVPagefileExclusions "*_pagefile.vhd"
```

The `Set-DPMGlobalProperty` will exclude all VHD files that has `_pagefile.vhd` in their name.

While the System Center Data Protection Manager 2012 protects a CSV cluster environment hosted by Windows Server 2012 or newer, the CSV code has been changed significantly, compared to the former version. Within the CSV version 2.0, the System Center Data Protection Manager 2012 R2 will be able to make backups both quicker and, more importantly, without the need to query the actual virtual machine for changes that have been made.

The CSV version 2.0, provides the architecture to enable parallel backups of virtual machines. This provides you with a more time-efficient solution regarding meeting the RPO requirement for the organization. By default, the System Center Data Protection Manager 2012 R2 will try to backup three virtual machines simultaneously on Hyper-V node. This could be optimized by modifying the registry key called Microsoft Hyper-V, which is a DWORD that is located in `HKEY_LOCAL_MACHINE\SOFTWARE\Microsoft\Microsoft Data Protection Manager\2.0\Configuration\MaxAllowedParallelBackups`

System Center Data Protection Manager 2012 is able to provide online snapshots of a virtual machine, making it possible to eliminate the scheduled backup windows. For System Center Data Protection Manager 2012 R2 to be able to make a snapshot of the virtual machine, the Hyper-V VSS must be in a stable state and most importantly, the virtual machine must have its own VSS stable. If the virtual machine operating system is facing an internal VSS error, System Center Data Protection Manager will not able to provide a consistent data snapshot and will therefore throw an error message, stating that the virtual machine internal VSS is reporting an error.

Protecting large-scale Hyper-V environments

This recipe covers how to set up a protection for a large scale environment or protecting a private cloud.

Getting started

The challenge that the DPM team met earlier was how to be able to scale the restore capabilities in a large, clustered environment. As a result of hard work, the DPM team released the Scaled-Out Protection feature that makes it possible to protect large, clustered environments.

How to do it...

For every DPM server to provide protection for the Hyper-V clustered environment, simply run the `SetDPMServer` executable from an elevated command prompt. Running the command on every node and SOFS that hosts the Hyper-V service, you must also use the—add switch. The syntax you should run on every Hyper-V node and members of the SOFS is: `SetDPMServer -Add -DPMServerName NETBIOSNAMEOFTHEDPMSERVER`

When every node and SOFS member has been configured, add the Hyper-V node cluster members and the SOFS server to every DPM server that provides the **Backup as a Service** (**BaaS**) and **Restore as a Service** (**RaaS**) services. Once you have added the Hyper-V nodes and the SOFS members, you are ready to set up your Protection Groups.

 A virtual machine can only be protected by one DPM server that is a member of the Scaled-Out Protection configuration. You cannot protect the same virtual machine on multiple members of the Scaled-Out Protection configuration.

How it works...

The Scale-Out Protection simply combines multiple primary DPM servers as a unit, making it possible to provide restore capabilities on a large scale. This adapts to the approach of delivering BaaS or RaaS where the DPM servers should be seen as instances that constitute the BaaS and RaaS service.

 When enabling Scale-Out Protection, you are not able to provide a DR scenario by using the DPM-DPM-DR approach.

See also

► The DPM team has written an article regarding the protection of large scale environments that is an interesting read: `http://blogs.technet.com/b/dpm/archive/2013/07/09/dpm-how-to-plan-for-protecting-vms-in-private-cloud-deployments.aspx`

 Before you can protect Hyper-V servers running over SMB 3.0 on a SOFS, you need to deploy DPM agents to all servers that make up the SOFS service and also enable the File Server VSS Agent Service.

Protecting System Center Virtual Machine Manager

This recipe covers how to protect the System Center Virtual Machine Manager configuration that is stored in an SQL database.

Getting ready

System Center Virtual Machine Manager (**SCVMM**) is a key component in cloud deployment and therefore of major importance to be provided with an optimal restore process.

With System Center Data Protection Manager 2012 R2, you are able to provide restore capabilities using the **Generic Data Source Protection**. This feature was introduced in the 2012 release of System Center Data Protection Manager and is an important standing point component for the development of the DPM software application in many cases. System Center Data Protection Manager 2012 R2 provides a restore function that is targeted to the **Original location** and the **Copy As File** option for the SCVMM host.

How to do it...

To enable System Center Data Protection Manager to start protecting SCVMM, simply install and attach a DPM agent on the virtual machine manager server and create a protection group.

When creating or modifying a protection group, expand your SCVMM server and mark the checkbox next to the **VMM Express Writer**.

How it works...

Every VSS has its own identifier that DPM can register via the PowerShell command script called `Modify-RegisteredWriters.ps1`. It allows you to register or remove the VSS writer ID that is registered with the DPM server.

There's more...

System Center Data Protection Manager 2012 R2 protects the SCVMM 2012 R2 by using the functions of Generic Data Source Protection. DPM provides a snapshot via the Express-Full technique; using incremental backup via the synchronization engine is not possible.

Integrating SCDPM with SCVMM

This recipe covers how to integrate System Center Data Protection Manager 2012 R2 with System Center Virtual Machine Manager 2012 R2.

Getting ready

A common scenario in a modern data center is to provide the ability of outer external cluster migration where virtual machines are migrated to other clusters or standalone Hyper-V hosts. System Center Data Protection Manager has the ability to interact with the SCVMM client component to understand where the protected virtual machine was migrated to.

 You will not need any integration with SCVMM if you only perform inter-cluster migration scenarios. System Center Data Protection Manager 2012 R2 understands and adapts to this, since the storage is not changed.

There are some important facts that must be considered before SCVMM integration and protection can occur:

- ▶ DPM protection for live migration is only available on servers that are running Windows Server 2012 and Windows Server 2012 R2.
- ▶ Live migration protection does not support the backup of data to tape, disk-to-tape, or disk-to-tape-to-tape.
- ▶ DPM performs a one-time consistency check for all live migrations that include storage migration.
- ▶ When live migration of storage occurs, Hyper-V reorganizes the virtual hard disk (VHD) or VHDX) and, therefore, there is a one-time spike in the size of DPM backup data.
- ▶ Turn on auto-mount on the virtual machine host to enable virtual protection.
- ▶ Disable the feature TCP Chimney Offload.

How to do it...

There are three prerequisites that are needed for you to be able to ensure the continuous protection of your virtual machines:

- ▶ The virtual machines are managed in a cloud that is configured on a **VMM** management server that is running System Center 2012 SP1 at the least.
- ▶ The DPM servers are connected to the **VMM** management server on which the private cloud is located.
- ▶ All servers that are running Hyper-V are connected to all DPM servers.

When the three prerequisites are in place, the System Center Data Protection Manager 2012 R2 communicates with VMM to understand where the virtual machine is currently running.

To set up the VMM integration, you need to perform the following steps:

1. Verify that the DPM servers, VMM management servers, and servers that are running Hyper-V are located in the same domain.

2. Deploy the DPM protection agent on all computers that are to host the virtual machines.

3. Install the VMM console as the VMM client component on all DPM servers to enable the DPM server to communicate with and track the VMM management server.

4. The DPMMachineName$ account should be a read-only administrator account on the VMM management server.

5. Ensure that the VMM console is the same version as the VMM management server that is used in the deployment.

6. Set the Global Property value for the KnownVMMServerName using PowerShell.

The syntax for the KnownVMMServerName is:

```
Set-DPMGlobalProperty -dpmservername <dpmservername> -knownvmmservers
<vmmservername>
```

How it works...

Since System Center Data Protection Manager 2012 R2 can integrate with the System Center Virtual Machine Manager via the Virtual Machine Manager client components, it understands any outer-cluster scenarios, even when a live migration triggers a storage migration.

There's more...

Enable the DPM VMM communication first. All virtual machines on servers that are running Hyper-V should be discovered before configuring the protection groups. Otherwise, live migration does not work as expected. To correct this situation, you have to stop the protection of data with **Retain Data** option, and then reconfigure protection for the same computer.

Restoring a Hyper-V virtual machine

This recipe covers how to restore a virtual machine, and also the different locations you are able to point the restore operation to.

Getting ready

When you want to restore a virtual machine, you open the DPM console and go to **Recovery**.

How to do it

In the **Recovery** section of the DPM console, choose your virtual machine in the **Browse** area. Expand the **SCVMM "SERVERNAME"** and on the right- hand side of the DPM console, select the desired date in the calendar and desired time in the drop-down list next to **Recovery time**. Under **Recoverable items**, right- click the server and choose **Recover...**; this will trigger the **Recovery Wizard**.

In the first step called **Review recovery selection**, you are provided with the information regarding what to restore. Verify the information and click on **Next >** to continue.

The next step is the **Select recovery type**, where you are able to choose where to restore the virtual machine. You can restore the virtual machine to:

▸ **Recover to original location**

▸ **Recover as virtual machine to any host**

▸ **Copy to a network folder**

Choose the **Recover to original location** option and click on **Next >** to continue.

In the **Specify Recovery Options** step, configure the specific options for the recovery.

If the recovery will be restoring data over a poor WAN link, you can click the **Modify...** link in the **Network bandwidth usage throttling** part to define how much bandwidth the restore job should consume.

If you have VSS hardware providers installed on the DPM server and a LUN presented for the SAN storage of the protected data source, perform a SAN based recovery by checking the checkbox in the **SAN Recovery** part.

When the restore job has finished, you can send an e-mail to a specific user or users, notifying them that the restore job has finished. This is enabled by checking the checkbox in the **Notification** part. Click on **Next>** to continue.

 To be able to send e-mails, your DPM server needs to have an SMTP server configured in the DPM options. Please read the *Configuring e-mail notifications* recipe in *Chapter 3, Post-installation Tasks*.

In the **Summary** step, verify the recovery configuration and click on Recover.

In the **Recovery Status**, you will be able to see the current state of the recovery. The status could also be monitored in the **Monitoring** part of the DPM console.

How it works...

When DPM initializes the recovery job, it relies on the VSS architecture that is part of the server's operating system architecture.

There's more...

If the recovery job should fail, verify the alert that the DPM server will raise to inform you about what has happened. It also gives you a guide to create a possible scenario for the recovery to occur.

Restoring a VHD or VHDX

This recipe covers the restore process of a VHD or VHDX virtual hard disk file.

Getting ready

In a scenario where a virtual machine has lost its volume or the data has been corrupted, the most optimal restore scenario is to recover the VHD or VHDX file that hosts the volume. System Center Data Protection Manager 2012 R2 makes that possible.

How to do it...

When you want to restore a virtual machine, open the DPM console and go to **Recovery**. In the **Recovery** section of the DPM console, choose your virtual machine in the **Browse** area. Expand the **SCVMM "SERVERNAME"** and scroll down to the very end, to find your virtual machine disks. On the right-hand side of the DPM console, choose the desired date in the calendar and desired time in the drop-down list next to **Recovery time**. Under **Recoverable items**, right click the VHD or VHDX file and choose **Recover...**; this will trigger the **Recovery Wizard**.

In the first step, called **Review recovery selection**, you are provided with the information regarding what to restore; verify the information and click on **Next >** to continue.

The next step is the **Select recovery type**. The only option you have here is to restore the VHD or VHDX file to a network location, using the **Copy to a network location** option.

Next, define the **Destination** and the **Destination path** in the **Specify destination** step. Click on **Browse...** button to point out the location.

In the **Specify Alternate Recovery Destination**, expand the server that should host the recovered VHD or VHDX file and click on **OK** to go back to **Specify destination** step, click on **Next >** to continue.

In the **Specify Recovery Options** step, configure the specific options for recovery.

In the **Restore security** part, define how the restored data source should apply to the security settings in the targeted location. The restored data can either keep the security settings that are present in the recovery point version or apply the security settings of the targeted location.

If the recovery will be restoring data over a poor WAN link, you can click the **Modify...** link in the **Network bandwidth usage throttling** part to define how much bandwidth the restore job should consume.

If you have VSS hardware providers installed on the DPM server and a LUN presented for the SAN storage of the protected data source, perform a SAN based recovery by checking the checkbox in the **SAN Recovery** part.

When the restore job has finished, send an e-mail to a specific user or users, notifying them that the restore job has finished. This is enabled by checking the checkbox in the **Notification** part. Click on **Next>** to continue.

 To be able to send e-mails, your DPM server needs to have an SMTP server configured in the DPM options. Please read the *Configuring e-mail notifications* recipe in *Chapter 3, Post-installation Tasks*.

In the **Summary** step, verify the recovery configuration and click on **Recover** to start the recovery.

In the **Recovery Status**, you will be able to see the current state of recovery. The status could also be monitored in the **Monitoring** part of the DPM console.

How it works...

When DPM initializes the recovery job, it relies on the VSS architecture that is part of the server's operating system architecture.

There's more...

If the recovery job fails, verify the alert that the DPM server will raise to inform you about what has happened. It also gives you a guide to create a possible scenario for the recovery to occur.

Using ILR (Item Level Restore)

This recipe covers how to restore a single flat file from a protected virtual machine.

Getting ready

The most common scenario in a private cloud deployment is to protect the tenants and offer the possibility to restore flat files from within the protected virtual machine. This restore scenario does not demand any additional configuration since it is present as an out-of-the-box feature.

How to do it...

When you want to restore a flat file from within a virtual machine, open the DPM console and go to **Recovery**. In the **Recovery section** of the DPM console, choose your virtual machine in the **Browse** area. Expand the **SCVMM "SERVERNAME"** and scroll down to the very end, till you find your virtual machine disks. On the right-hand side of the DPM console, choose the desired date in the calendar and desired time in the drop-down list next to **Recovery time**. Under **Recoverable items**, double-click the VHD or VHDX file and right-click the flat file that you would like to recover. Choose **Recover...**; this will trigger the **Recovery Wizard**.

In the first step called **Review recovery selection**, you are provided with the information regarding what to restore; verify the information and click on **Next >** to continue.

The next step is the **Select recovery type**, where the only option you have is to **Copy to a network folder**; click on **Next >** to continue.

Next, define the **Destination** and the **Destination path** in the **Specify destination** step. Click on the **Browse...** button to point out the location.

In the **Specify Alternate Recovery Destination** tab, expand the server that should host the recovered VHD or VHDX file and click on **OK** to go back to **Specify destination** step. Click on **Next >** to continue.

In the **Specify Recovery Options** step, configure the specific options for recovery.

In the **Restore security** part, define how the restored data source should apply to the security setting in the targeted location. The restored data can either keep the security settings that are present in the recovery point version or apply the security settings of the targeted location.

If the recovery will be restoring data over a poor WAN link, click the **Modify...** link in the **Network bandwidth usage throttling** part to define how much bandwidth the restore job should consume.

If you have VSS hardware providers installed on the DPM server and a LUN presented for the SAN storage of the protected data source, perform a SAN based recovery by checking the checkbox in the **SAN Recovery** part.

When the restore job has finished, send an e-mail to a specific user or users notifying them that the restore job has finished. This is enabled by checking the checkbox in the **Notification** part. Click on **Next>** to continue.

 To be able to send e-mails, your DPM server needs to have an SMTP server configured in the DPM options. Please read the *Configuring e-mail notifications* recipe in *Chapter 3, Post-installation Tasks*.

In the **Summary** step, verify the recovery configuration and click on **Recover** to start recovery.

In the **Recovery Status**, you will be able to see the current state of recovery. The status could also be monitored in the **Monitoring** part of the DPM console.

How it works...

System Center Data Protection Manager will virtually mount the VHD or VHDX file to provide the DPM administrator with the ability to restore a flat file; the restore process consists of several steps using scratch areas.

There's more...

It is an important fact that the restore process using the ILR feature is only applicable for flat files. If you would like to recover other workloads besides file and folder, you need to deploy a DPM agent into the virtual machine and use the VSS that is supported for providing a consistent data snapshot.

Understanding Hyper-V management tasks

Expanding the data center's capabilities is a common scenario in a modern data center, other than reducing or replacing different data center capabilities. Understanding how this impacts the protection provided by the System Center Data Protection Manager 2012 R2 is crucial.

The most common management tasks for a Hyper-V environment are:

- ▸ Adding nodes to a Hyper-V cluster
- ▸ Removing nodes from a Hyper-V cluster
- ▸ Changing the name of a protected virtual machine

When you add a new Hyper-V node to a cluster hosting protected virtual machines, System Center Data Protection Manager raises an alert saying that there is a new node cluster member that needs to have the DPM agent installed.

If you remove a Hyper-V cluster node, DPM raises an alert stating that the server is no longer a member of the cluster.

In the scenario that you need to change a virtual machine's name, you cannot do so without causing interruption to the DPM protection, since System Center Data Protection Manager 2012 R2 uses the name as a unique identifier for replicas, recovery points, DPM database entries, and reporting database entries. To be able to protect the virtual machine under its new name, you need to stop the protection and choose to retain the data. Then, enable the protection again by adding the virtual machine under its new name to a protection group.

All management tasks should be planned and well communicated. This is, unfortunately, rare in industries today. A lack in providing important information to other parties can have a devastating effect. Using a ticketing system like the System Center Service Manager, is the recommended solution.

7

SharePoint Protection

In this chapter, we will cover protecting a SharePoint server using System Center 2012 R2 Data Protection Manager.

We will cover the following topics:

- ▶ Understanding the prerequisites for supported SharePoint server protection
- ▶ Configuring the SharePoint VSS
- ▶ Protecting a SharePoint farm
- ▶ Protecting a SharePoint search
- ▶ Protecting a SharePoint farm that uses SQL aliases
- ▶ Restoring a SharePoint farm
- ▶ Restoring individual objects (Item-level Recovery)
- ▶ Understanding SharePoint maintenance tasks
- ▶ Understanding SharePoint management tasks

Introduction

Since Microsoft introduced the first SharePoint server to the market, it has grown in popularity and more companies are realizing its potential. SharePoint has rapidly become a line-of-business application that companies rely on and, therefore, they also realize the importance of designing and building an optimal SharePoint server restore scenario. System Center 2012 R2 Data Protection Manager will meet this demand in an optimal and fully supported way.

SharePoint is an advanced and complex technology that has many dependencies between different Microsoft components. It is crucial to have a decent SharePoint design which does not go beyond the scope that is supported by Microsoft; you must always verify that your customization is within the supported scenario.

There are several third-party solutions in the market that claim they support backing up SharePoint server technology; however, since a backup is useful only if it can be restored, Microsoft can be proud to be one of the few service providers in the market that actually can perform a **restore** of a backed up SharePoint farm. The recipes in this chapter will provide you with the foundation you need to get started with the design and deployment of your restore scenario for SharePoint.

Understanding the prerequisites for supported SharePoint server protection

This recipe will cover the information that you need to understand the prerequisites for a supported SharePoint server protection scenario.

These supported versions are used for the SharePoint server workload for DPM protection:

- SharePoint 2013
- SharePoint 2010
- SharePoint 2007
- Windows SharePoint Server 3.0

If your SharePoint version is not listed in the preceding list, you should consider upgrading your SharePoint farm if you want to be able to recover it using System Center 2012 R2 Data Protection Manager.

SharePoint server protection relies on an underlying technology within the Windows Server operating system called **Volume Shadow Copy Services (VSS)**. For more information on how a VSS file operates and works, please read the *Change tracking process* recipe in *Chapter 1, Pre-installation Tasks*.

If the SQL Server that is hosting the content databases for the SharePoint farm using **Always-On**, the protection is, unfortunately, out of scope of the supported protection scenario.

 If your SQL Server that hosts the databases for the SharePoint farm is configured to use an SQL alias, you must configure your SharePoint protection in a specific way. For more information on this topic, please read the *Protecting a SharePoint farm that uses SQL aliases* recipe.

Configuring the SharePoint VSS

This recipe will teach you how to enable the SharePoint VSS, so that System Center 2012 R2 Data Protection Manager can start protecting your SharePoint farm.

Getting ready

The core component that System Center Data Protection Manager relies on is **VSS**. The SharePoint VSS is not enabled by default and must be enabled for DPM so that it is able to start protecting your SharePoint farm.

Before you can enable the SharePoint VSS, you must install the DPM agent on one of your frontend web servers. When the DPM agent is installed, you will run the DPM agent specific executable called `ConfigureSharePoint.exe`.

How to do it...

On one of your SharePoint frontend web servers, open an elevated command prompt and go to the `bin` catalog for the DPM agent catalog structure at `C:Program files\ Microsoft Data Protection Manager\DPM\bin`. Run the executable with this syntax: `ConfigureSharePoint -EnableSharePointProtection`, and press *Enter*.

You will now be prompted to enter a username and password. You should enter the username in the `username@domain.xyz` format, as shown in this screenshot:

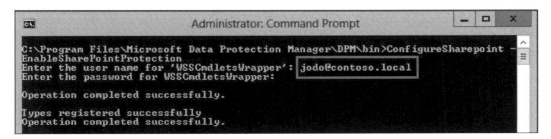

The account that you are using must have the security privileges of a **farm administrator**. If the account you are providing has insufficient rights, it will lead to VSS errors during the backup process and cataloging errors for the backed up SharePoint data.

 Note that if you change the farm administrator account, you must update the configuration for the SharePoint VSS. The change in the configuration is not directly replicated to the VSS configuration.

How it works...

The `ConfigureSharePoint.exe` executable provides a lot of functions for the DPM protection with regard to the SharePoint workload. When you run the executable, it registers the `WSSCmdletsWrapper` DCOM object and enables the SharePoint VSS writer. The credentials provided during the configuration process will be used for the cataloging job on the protected data. The same credentials will also be used to continue to protect your SharePoint farm.

There's more...

If you forget to enable the VSS writer for your SharePoint farm, it will not be listed as a selectable data source when you create or modify a protection group in DPM.

If you provide credentials that have insufficient rights during the initialization phase, you will be prompted with an error. If the credentials have some rights in the SharePoint farm but are not sufficient, the DPM server will raise an alert saying that the cataloging job has failed for the protected SharePoint farm data.

Protecting a SharePoint farm

This recipe will cover the information that you need to understand the prerequisites for a supported SharePoint server protection scenario.

Getting ready

Before you start creating the protection group that holds the actual configuration for the protected data sources, you have to fulfil the following prerequisites:

- The SharePoint Server you would like to protect should be a supported version for DPM protection
- A DPM agent should be installed on all the servers that are members of the SharePoint farm
- The DPM agent should report **OK** in the DPM console management workspace

How to do it...

1. Go to **Protection** and click on **New** in the DPM console.

2. In the **Welcome** step of the **Create New Protection Group** wizard, click on **Next >** to continue. In the **Select Protection Group Type** step, choose **Servers** and click on **Next >** to continue.

3. In the **Select Group Members** step, you should expand you frontend web server and check the checkbox next to your SharePoint farm. Click on **Next >** to continue, as shown here:

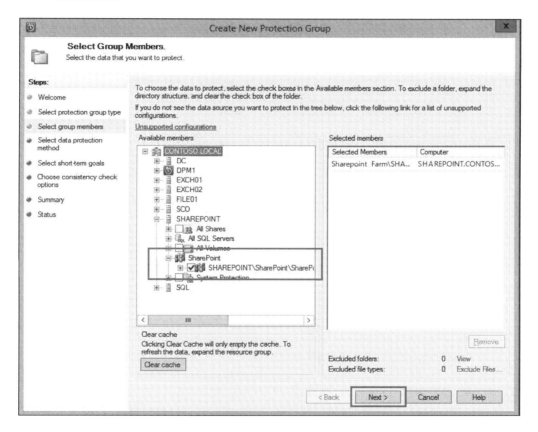

4. In the next **Select Data Protection Method** step, you can choose what **Protection method** you would like to use and provide **Protection group name**. The supported protection methods are **short-term using Disk** and **long-term using tape**:

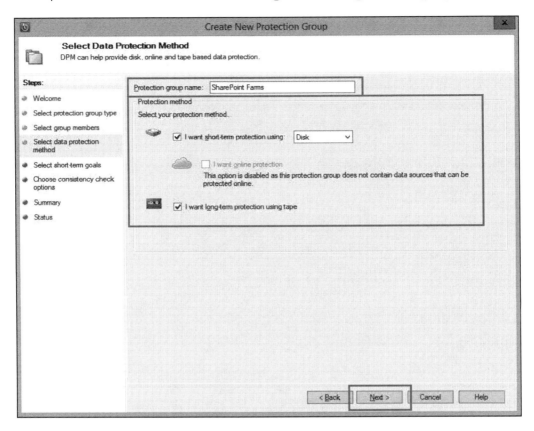

5. Choose that **Protection method** that suits your recovery plans and click on **Next >** to continue.

6. In the **Select Short-Term Goals** step, you can define **Retention range** for the protection followed by **Application recovery points**. To modify the backup schedule for the protection group, simply click on the **Modify...** button and configure your days and hours for a recovery point creation:

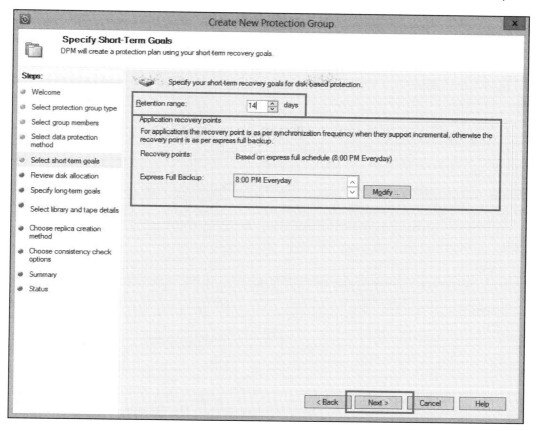

7. To continue, click on **Next >**.

8. In the **Review Disk Allocation** step, you can configure and review the disk space allocated for the protection group. Two specific volumes are created for all the protected data sources that the DPM server is protecting: replica- and recovery-point volume. One of the auto-heal functions within DPM is **Automatically grow the volumes**. This feature will expand the volume when the threshold is reached. For more detailed information regarding the **Automatically grow the volumes** function, please read the *Growing volumes automatically in the DPM disk pool* recipe in *Chapter 3, Post-installation Tasks*.

9. Click on **Next >** to continue to the **Select Long-Term Goals** steps.

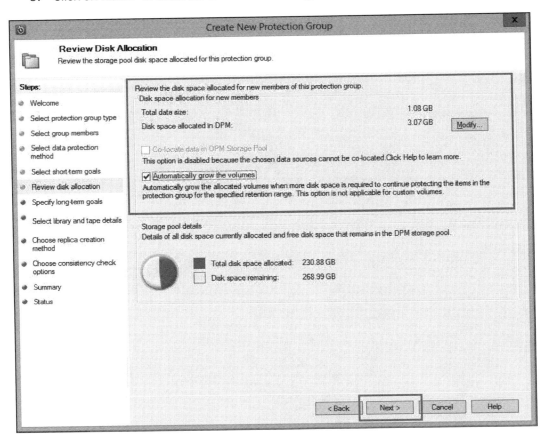

10. In the **Select Long-Term Goals** step, you can configure the tape settings for the protection group. In the **Recovery goals** section, you can specify the **Retention range** value and the **Frequency of backup** value. DPM will provide you with its default settings for **Recovery goals**, but this can easily be changed by clicking on the **Customize** button. If you want to change the backup schedule, click on the **Modify...** button:

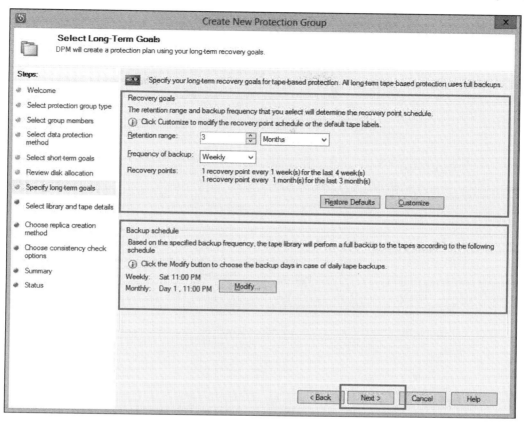

11. In the **Customize Recovery Goal** window, you can enable up to three different recovery goals by clicking on the checkboxes. You can choose to make daily, weekly, monthly, or yearly backups to the tape.

 You can only make a biweekly tape backup in the **Select Long-Term Goals** step.

12. You can also choose to define a tape label that DPM should use to present the tape in the DPM console. Within the configuration, you can also provide the **Number of backup copy** value; by default the number is one.

13. If the different recovery goals should occur on the same day, the DPM administrator has two choices:

   ❏ Making two different backups

   ❏ Making one backup that has a higher priority than the others

For more information regarding tape management, please read *Chapter 13, Tape Management*.

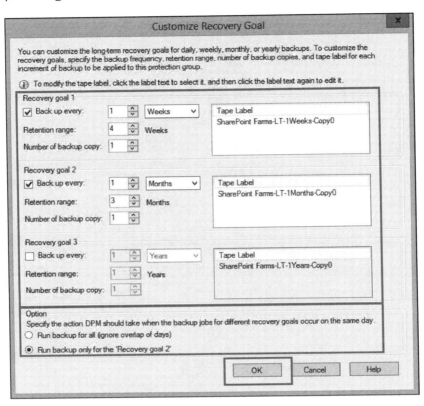

14. In the **Modify Long-Term Backup Schedule** step, you can define the backup schedules for your recovery goals of the protection group, as shown in the following screenshot. When you have configured your backup schedules, click on **OK** to return to the **Select Long-Term Goals** step.

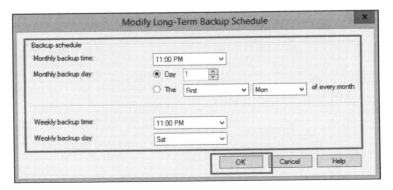

15. In the **Select Long-Term Goals** step, click on **Next >** to continue to the **Select Library and Tape Details** step.

16. In this protection group wizard step, you can configure your primary tape library and if present, your copy library. You can also define the actual numbers of tape drives the DPM server should use for this protection group. After the backup to tape has occurred, you can make the DPM server check the backup for data integrity; please note that this is a time consuming operation.

17. The DPM server can either compress or encrypt the data copied to tape, you cannot perform both operations. To continue, click on **Next >**, as shown in the following screenshot:

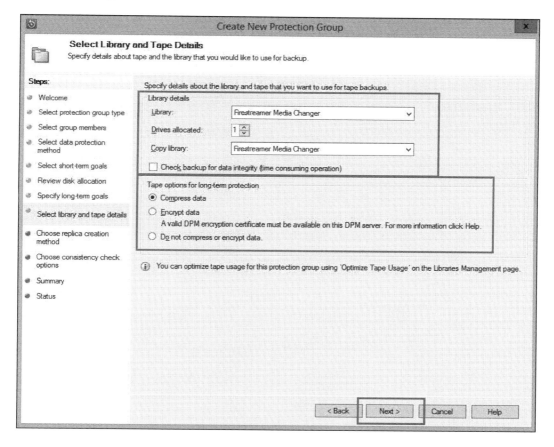

18. In the **Choose Replica Creation Method** wizard, you can define how the DPM sever should create the replica of the protected data source. You can create the replica after the configuration of the protection group is finished or you can schedule the creation of the replica. You can also create the replica manually; this is covered in the *Creating a replica manually* recipe of *Chapter 3, Post-installation Task.*

19. Click on **Next >** to continue, as shown in the following screenshot:

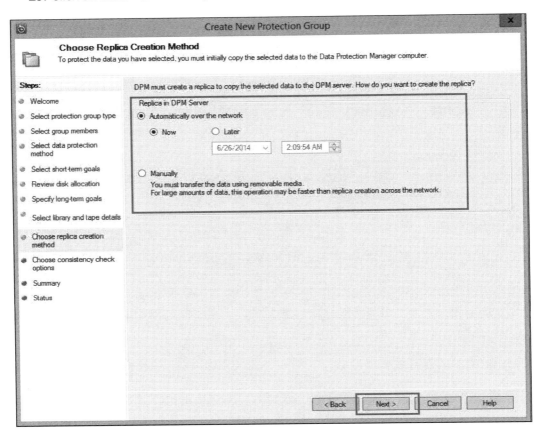

20. In the **Consistency check options** step, you can specify if the DPM should run a consistency check if a replica becomes inconsistent;, this is an auto-heal function within the DPM server technology. You can also specify running a daily consistency check where you specify the start time and how many hours the task should run for.

21. To continue to the next step, click on **Next >**:

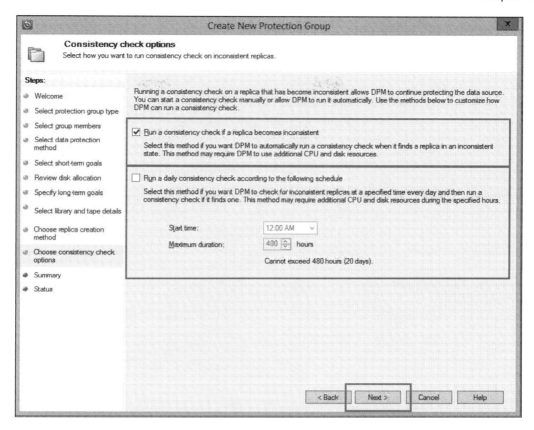

22. Click on **Next >** to continue to the last step, that is, the **Summary** step. Review the summary for the protection group and click on the **Create Group** button to create the protection group. In the **Status** step, you can see the actual status of the protection group creation.

How it works...

The protection group holds the actual configuration for your backup schedule, protected data sources, and specific configurations, such as **on-the-wire-compression**. The DPM server will call the DPM agents that are members of the protection group, to initialize the backup job; this is the VSS request procedure that starts the VSS snapshot process on the protected server.

See also

For more information regarding how the DPM server operates, it is recommended that you read all the recipes in *Chapter 1, Pre-installation Tasks*.

Protecting a SharePoint search

This recipe will cover the information that you need to start and protect the SharePoint search.

Getting ready

By default, the SharePoint search is not included in the SharePoint protection and, therefore, needs to be enabled for protection. The configuration uses the same executable that is required when you enable the SharePoint VSS.

How to do it...

On one of your SharePoint frontend web servers, open an elevated command prompt and go to the `bin` catalog for the DPM agent catalog structure at `C:\Program files\ Microsoft Data Protection Manager\DPM\bin`. Run the executable with the `ConfigureSharePoint -EnableSPSearchProtection` syntax and press *Enter*.

You will now be prompted to enter a username and password. You should enter the username in the `username@domain.xyz` format

How it works...

The account that you use must have the security privileges of a **farm administrator**. If the account you provide has insufficient rights, it will lead to VSS and initialization errors during the backup process.

There's more...

The protection for a search is only applicable for Microsoft Office SharePoint Server 2007.

Protecting a SharePoint farm that uses SQL aliases

This recipe will cover the information that you need to understand how to protect a SharePoint farm that is configured with SQL aliases.

Getting ready

The purpose of having a SharePoint farm using SQL aliases is that it makes it possible to provide a name for SQL that the SharePoint servers query, instead of the actual SQL server NetBIOS name. This makes the SQL server hardware easy to change as well as making it easy to replace virtual SQL Servers during the expansion of the SharePoint farm.

How to do it...

To make the protection of the SharePoint farm operational, it is important that the SQL alias has some specific configurations, as listed here:

- ▸ You must only use TCP/IP aliases
- ▸ You must configure SQL server aliases and define all SQL aliases in the farm on the frontend web server

The configuration is performed in two steps. First, you must install the components of the SQL server client connectivity on the frontend web server.

The second step is to resolve all the SQL aliases from the DPM server; this is done by using the `ConfigureSharePoint` executable with the `-ResolveAllSqlAliases` switch.

On your DPM server, open an elevated command prompt and go to the `bin` catalog in the DPM server catalog structure at `C:\Program files\Microsoft Data Protection Manager\DPM\bin`. Run the executable with the `ConfigureSharePoint - ResolveAllSqlAliases` syntax and press *Enter*.

You will see your DPM server resolving all the SQL aliases and your DPM server will now be able to protect your SharePoint farm.

How it works...

The resolved aliases will provide a layer of function between the DPM server and the SQL aliases, making name resolving possible and, therefore, listing all the SharePoint databases that reside on the backend SQL Servers.

See also

For more information on how to enable your SharePoint farm for the usage of SQL aliases, please refer to `http://blogs.msdn.com/b/sowmyancs/archive/2012/08/06/install-amp-configure-sharepoint-2013-with-sql-client-alias.aspx`

Restoring a SharePoint farm

This recipe will cover the information that you need to understand the prerequisites for a supported SharePoint server recovery scenario.

Getting ready

Before you start the recovery, you should always verify that the targeted data source is accessible and that the DPM agent is reporting **OK** in the DPM console.

How to do it...

1. In the DPM console, go to **Recovery** and choose the SharePoint farm you would like to recover.

 For File, Exchange, and SharePoint, you can use the **Search** function.

2. Mark the SharePoint farm and choose the date and time for the recovery. Right-click on the data source and choose **Recover...** to start the **Recovery Wizard**:

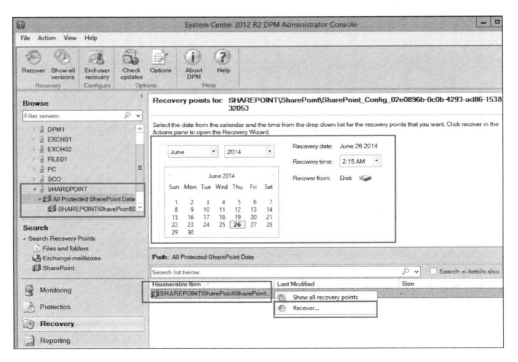

3. In the **Review Recovery Selection** step, review the data source that is chosen for recovery and click on **Next >** to continue:

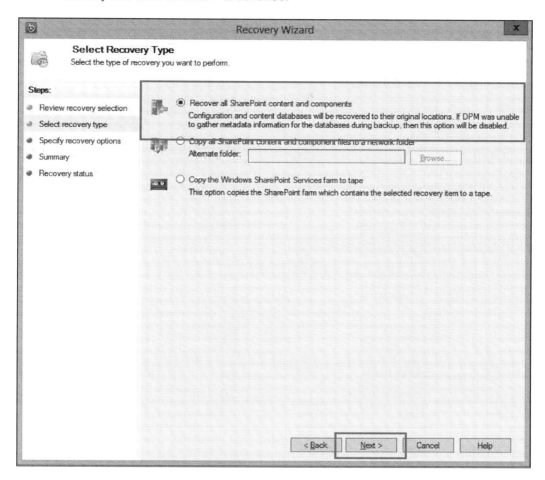

4. In the **Specify Recovery Options** step, you configure the specific options for the recovery.

5. If the recovery restores data over a poor WAN link, you can click on the **Modify...** link in the **Network bandwidth usage throttling** part to define how much bandwidth the restore job should consume.

6. If you have VSS hardware providers installed on the DPM sever and a LUN presented for the SAN storage of the protected data source, you can perform a SAN-based recovery by checking the checkbox in the **SAN Recovery** part.

7. When the restore job has finished, you can send an e-mail to a specific addressed user or users, notifying them that the restore job has finished. This is enabled by checking the checkbox in the **Notification** part. Click on **Next >** to continue.

 To be able to send e-mails, your DPM sever needs to have an SMTP server configured in the DPM options. Please read the *Configuring e-mail notifications* recipe in *Chapter 3, Post-installation Tasks*.

8. In the **Summary** step, verify the recovery configuration and click on **Recover** to start the recovery.

9. In the **Recovery Status** step, you will be able to see the current state of the recovery. This could also be monitored in the **Monitoring** part of the DPM console.

How it works...

When DPM initializes the recovery job, it will rely on the VSS architecture that is a part of the server operating system architecture.

There's more...

If your SharePoint server is configured to use SQL aliases, it is important for the configuration present in the SharePoint farm to correspond with the configuration at the time of the recovery.

Restoring individual objects (Item-level recovery)

This recipe will cover the information that you need to understand the supported SharePoint server recovery scenario for a single object.

Getting ready

Before you start the recovery, you should always verify that the targeted data source is accessible and that the DPM agent is reporting **OK** in the DPM console.

With System Center 2012 R2 Data Protection Manager, you can recover SharePoint items. Items are defined as:

- Sites
- Site collections
- Documents
- Document libraries

- ▸ Lists
- ▸ List items

You can recover a SharePoint item from a DPM recovery point to the original site or you can restore the item at an alternate site.

 Documents that were checked out during the recovery point creation will not be available for recovery from the recovery point.

How to do it..

1. In the DPM console, go to **Recovery** and choose the SharePoint farm you would like to recover.

 For File, Exchange, and SharePoint, you can use the **Search** function.

2. You can either drill down to the SharePoint item that you would like to restore or you can use the **Search** function. Mark the SharePoint farm item and choose the date and time for the recovery. Right-click on the SharePoint item and choose **Recover...** to start the **Recovery Wizard**:

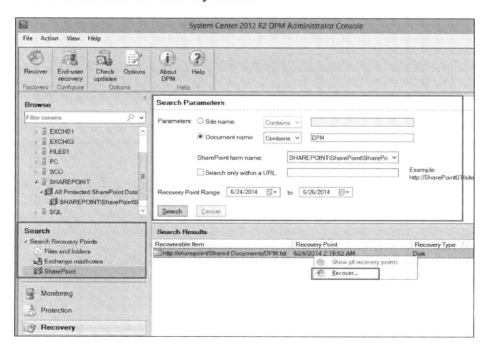

3. In the **Review Recovery Selection** step, review the data source that is chosen for recovery and click on **Next >** to continue.

4. For the **Select Recovery Type** step, you choose where you would like to restore your SharePoint item. You can choose from:

 ❑ **Recover to original site**

 ❑ **Recover to an alternate site**

 ❑ **Copy the Windows SharePoint Services farm to tape**

 For the tape option to be available, you must have configured a tape library for your DPM server.

5. If you would like to restore the SharePoint item to another SharePoint farm, choose **Recover to an alternate site**. To recover the SharePoint item to the original site, choose **Recover to original site** and click on **Next >** to continue.

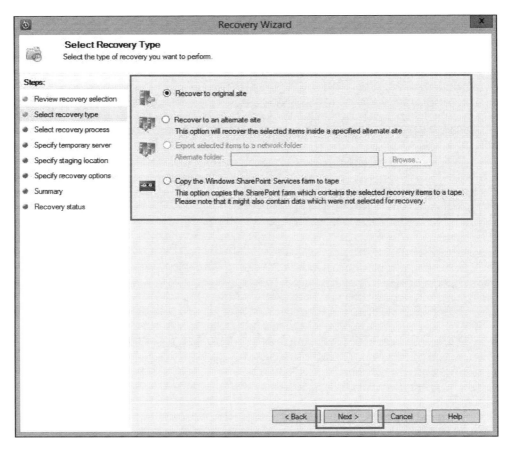

6. In the **Select Recovery Process** step, you can specify if you want to restore the SharePoint item via a recovery farm or not.

 For MOSS 2007 servers, you should use a recovery farm. From a SharePoint server 2010 and newer versions, you can restore SharePoint items without using a recovery farm.

7. Choose **Recover without using a recovery farm** and click on **Next >** to continue.

8. In the **Specify Temporary Server** step, point out an instance of an SQL S\server that you would like to use to temporarily stage the content database. This is done by clicking on the **Browse...** button next to the **SQL instance** field. Next, you should specify a location where database files can be copied. Click on the **Browse...** button next to the **Database file location** field.

 The database file location must reside on the same server as the temporary SQL server.

9. Click on **Next >** to continue.

10. The next step is the **Specify Staging Location** step, where you specify a temporary location on your frontend web server in the SharePoint farm that you want to recover the SharePoint item to. Click on **Browse...**, choose a temporary location on the SharePoint frontend web server, and click on **OK** to return to the **Specify staging location** step. Click on **Next >** to continue.

11. In the **Specify Recovery Options** step, you can configure the specific options for the recovery.

12. In the **Restore security** part, you can define how the restored data source should apply to the security settings in the targeted location. The restored data could either keep its security settings that are present in the recovery point version, or apply the security settings of the targeted location.

13. If the recovery will restore data over a poor WAN link, you can click on the **Modify...** link in the **Network bandwidth usage throttling** part to define how much bandwidth the restore job should consume.

14. If you have VSS hardware providers installed on the DPM sever and a LUN presented for the SAN storage of the protected data source, you can perform a SAN-based recovery by checking the checkbox in the **SAN Recovery** part.

15. When the restore job has finished, you can send an e-mail to a specific addressed user or users, notifying them that the restore job has finished. This is enabled by checking the checkbox in the **Notification** part. Click on **Next >** to continue.

To be able to send e-mails, your DPM sever needs to have an SMTP server configured in the DPM options. Please read the *Configuring e-mail notifications* recipe in *Chapter 3, Post-installation Tasks*.

16. In the **Summary** step, verify the recovery configuration and click on **Recover** to start the recovery.

17. In the **Recovery Status** step, you will be able to see the current state of the recovery. This could also be monitored in the **Monitoring** part of the DPM console.

How it works...

When you initiate a recovery job for a SharePoint item for SharePoint 2010 or newer versions, DPM restores the database to a temporary instance of a SQL server. The next step is to extract the item from the content database and then import it to the targeted farm.

There's more...

The files that were put in the temporary location during the staging process will be deleted when the recovery job has finished.

Regarding recovery jobs for MOSS 2007 servers, you must use a recovery farm since the MOSS server will use it as a staging area and filter out the individual object when preparing it for recovery.

In some cases, when you search for an individual item, it will not be listed; this can be caused by one of two different scenarios:

▶ The SharePoint item that you would like to restore was checked out during the recovery point creation process

▶ The catalog task has not run and indexed the items that have been backed up

The catalog task for the backed up SharePoint data is triggered once a day, three hours after the first successful recovery point. The time frame can be changed by using the PowerShell `Set-DPMProtectionJobStartTime` command from the DPM management shell.

If you need to trigger a SharePoint catalog task manually, you can execute this syntax from the DPM management shell:

```
Get-ProtectionGroup DPMSERVERNAME | get-datasource | where-object
  {$_.type -like "*sharepoint*"} | start-createcatalog
```

The `DPMSERVERNAME` term should be replaced with the NetBIOS name if your DPM server.

See also

For a detailed description of how to trigger the catalog task manually, please read `http://robertanddpm.blogspot.se/2010/11/cant-perform-item-level-restore-on.html`

Understanding SharePoint maintenance tasks

This recipe will cover the information that you need to understand the SharePoint maintenance tasks.

Getting ready

As a SharePoint administrator, it is important to perform different maintenance tasks on the SharePoint farm, SQL Server, and the Windows server operating systems that host the SharePoint farm, so as to keep it in a state of optimal performance.

How to do it...

When maintenance tasks are being performed on a SharePoint farm, it is important that no backup job is running. This can easily be controlled since you can easily disable the DPM agent via the DPM console.

Go to **Management** and click on **Agent**; right-click on the DPM agent and choose **Disable protection**. An information box will inform you that you can't perform any recovery job for the data sources that reside on the server on which the DPM agent is installed during the time it is disabled. Click on **Yes** to confirm that you would like to set the DPM agent to a disable mode.

How it works...

When a DPM agent is put into disabled mode, all backup jobs will still be present in the backup schedule. Since the backup job still resides in the scheduled backup, the job will fail.

See also

For more information regarding post-installation tasks, please read *Chapter 3, Post-installation Tasks*.

Understanding SharePoint management tasks

This recipe will cover the information that you need to understand the SharePoint management tasks.

The most common management tasks for SharePoint are:

- ▶ Changing the SharePoint farm administrator password
- ▶ Adding databases to the SharePoint farm
- ▶ Removing databases from the SharePoint farm
- ▶ Switching frontend web servers

How to do it...

It is important to have a decent password security policy within a company or organization. When the password of the SharePoint farm administrator is changed, it will reflect negatively on the DPM protection. You need to rerun the `ConfigureSharePoint.exe` executable that is described in *Configuring the SharePoint VSS* recipe of this chapter. When the password for the SharePoint farm administrator is changed, DPM will not be able to discover any changes in the SharePoint farm or update the URL that points to the SharePoint items, and the recovery of the entire SharePoint farm cannot be initialized from the DPM server. The easiest way to discover that the password of the SharePoint farm administrator has changed is to look for an alert that says **BackupMetaDataEnumeration failed**.

When a SharePoint farm administrator adds a new database, it will be included in the DPM protection after midnight. If DPM tries to create a recovery point before the database has been automatically included in the DPM protection, the alert **Farm configuration changed** will be raised. You can either wait till the next day or modify the protection group by unchecking the SharePoint farm and rechecking it, clicking through the protection group, and finally clicking on the **Update Group** button.

In a scenario where the SharePoint farm administrator removes a database, the DPM protection needs to be stopped and reinitialized. It is important for you to **retain your data**, so that you don't lose your backup history.

When the SharePoint farm administrator switches the frontend web servers, you need to make DPM protect the SharePoint farm using the other frontend web server. For more information, follow the instructions on this TechNet article, available at `http://technet.microsoft.com/en-us/library/hh758181.aspx`.

How it works...

Since System Center Data Protection Manager will highly depend on the server technologies that it is protecting, it cannot just remove deleted databases from the DPM protection or adapt to any changes, since the responsibility to do this lies in the hands of the administrators. It is important that there is a plan or process that will aid the administrators internally, so important data does get omitted from a backup due to a lack of internal communication.

There's more...

For more information regarding an optimal DPM server deployment, please refer to the *Chapter 1, Pre-installation Tasks*, *Chapter 2, Installation and Upgrade*, and *Chapter 3, Post-installation Tasks*.

8
Exchange Server Protection

In this chapter, we will cover the following recipes:

- ▶ Understanding the prerequisites of supported Exchange server protections
- ▶ Configuring Exchange server protection
- ▶ Understanding how to adapt DPM to Exchange server management tasks
- ▶ Understanding how to adapt DPM to Exchange server maintenance tasks
- ▶ Protecting a single Exchange mailbox database
- ▶ Understanding how DPM protects DAG configurations
- ▶ Understanding how DPM can verify data integrity using ESEUTIL
- ▶ Restoring an Exchange mailbox database to its original location
- ▶ Restoring an Exchange mailbox database to an alternative location
- ▶ Restoring an Exchange mailbox database to an Exchange Recovery Database
- ▶ Restoring an Exchange mailbox database to a network folder
- ▶ Copying the Exchange mailbox database to tape

Introduction

Many companies are migrating their e-mail functions to different hosted mail solutions from service providers or different cloud services, such as O365 from Microsoft. However, there are still companies that have their Exchange server technology on premises; service providers or companies that have not begun their cloud journey are two examples.

For companies that still have their Exchange server technologies on premises, they ask themselves why they should back up a DAG-enabled Exchange server solution. The answer is simple:

- Disaster Recovery
- Application errors
- Logical corruption
- Security breaches
- Malware

Creating a restore scenario for Exchange is more about empowering the possibilities in both the Exchange DAG configuration and the restore operations provide by DPM. A combination of DAG and DPM will give you:

- Less complicated point-in-time restore
- Fewer Exchange servers
- Offsite backup and recovery
- Longer retention time on DPM compared to a lagged recovery in the DAG configuration

As a service provider, it is critical that you focus on the restore scenarios instead of the backup jobs. Providing and designing a decent restore scenario that can be mapped to a corresponding SLA should be the primary focus instead of focusing on the backup as the primary approach. Restore jobs should primarily be done from the DAG and point-in-time restores beyond the 14 day limit should be done from the DPM server.

System Center Data Protection Manger 2012 R2 will provide you with the possibilities of searching and restoring a single mailbox to only its original location. However, with this recovery job, the entire mailbox database needs to be restored, and this will put some pressure on the Exchange administrators to also consider the different restore scenarios for the Exchange server workload.

In this chapter, we will cover the protection for Exchange server data using System Center Data Protection Manager 2012 R2.

We also will provide you with the information you need to understand the different protection configurations that apply to the Exchange server workload.

Understanding the prerequisites for supported Exchange server protection

This recipe will cover the information that you need to understand the prerequisites for a supported scenario of Exchange server protection.

The following list provides the supported versions for the Exchange server workload:

- Exchange Server 2013
- Exchange Server 2010
- Exchange Server 2007

For System Center Data Protection Manager 2012 R2 to be able to protect the Exchange server workload, a DPM agent must be installed on the Exchange server and attached to the corresponding DPM server.

If the Exchange server is installed in an environment where limited storage capability is an issue, the Exchange administrator can enable circular logging in the Exchange configuration.

All Exchange server protection relies on the underlying technology within the Windows server operating system called **Volume Shadow Copy Services** (**VSS**). For more information regarding how the file VSS operates and works, read the *Change tracking process* recipe in *Chapter 1, Pre-installation Tasks*.

System Center Data Protection Manager 2012 R2 will understand the clustered configuration within Exchange 2007, such as:

- **Local Continuous Replication** (**LCR**)
- **Cluster Continuous Replication** (**CCR**)
- **Standby Continuous Replication** (**SCR**)

In the Exchange 2010 release, Microsoft presented a new feature called **Database Availability Group** (**DAG**). This feature will enable mailbox databases for a high-availability scenario by making a mailbox database member of a DAG group. System Center Data Protection Manager 2012 R2 will protect a DAG-enabled Exchange environment, but the DPM administrator needs to disable the circular logging feature and also install and attach a DPM agent on all the DAG members.

However, there are some design considerations that need to be discussed, which will reflect some features installed on the DPM server.

 For information on how System Center Data Protection Manager 2012 R2 protects large-scale Exchange environments, read the *Configuring Exchange server protection* recipe.

Configuring Exchange server protection

This recipe will cover the pre- and post-configuration steps needed to protect the Exchange server workload in an optimal way.

Getting ready

For System Center Data Protection Manager 2012 R2 to be able to start protecting the Exchange server workload, you must disable circular logging on the Exchange server and install DPM agents on every member of the DAG mailbox servers or the standalone mailbox server.

You can also make DPM 2012 R2 verify the data integrity for the Exchange server workload in a more advanced manner by installing the Exchange Server Management Tools on the DPM server.

How to do it...

System Center Data Protection Manager 2012 R2 uses the underlying technology called VSS, to identify the block-level changes made by the workload's VSS writer. If the DPM agent loses track of the changed block, the replica will become inconsistent and an alert will be raised in the DPM console. For DPM to successfully protect the Exchange Server workload, the circular logging feature must be disabled, as this will not update the VSS information for the Exchange VSS writer.

> ► For System Center Data Protection Manager 2012 R2 to understand the Exchange Server technology more deeply, the DPM administrator needs to install the Exchange Server management tools on the DPM server. This will install the ESEUTIL.EXE and ESE.DLL files that will provide the data integrity checks for the backed up data. You can also copy ESEUTIL.EXE and ESE.DLL directly from the Exchange server. Keep in mind that you should keep the versions of the files consistent between the Exchange server and the DPM server. If you update the files on the Exchange server, you must also update the files on the DPM server. For more information on how to enable data integrity, check the Exchange server workload in DPM. Refer to the *Understanding how DPM can verify data integrity using ESEUTIL* recipe.

How it works...

System Center Data Protection Manager 2012 R2 will depend on the already present architecture within the Microsoft workload and only use supported operations in the backup and restore process. This gives the DPM administrator the positive aspect of the backup and restore jobs always operating from a supported and optimized scenario.

If the DPM administrator does not disable the circular logging feature on the Exchange server, System Center Data Protection Manager 2012 R2 will have a challenge in understanding the different changes made to the blocks owned by the Exchange VSS writer.

There's more...

In the scenario that System Center Data Protection Manager 2012 R2 should protect a large scale Exchange DAG environment, the DPM agents need to be installed in a different manner.

DPM can protect 80 TB of Exchange data per DPM server, but this does not mean that you cannot combine multiple DPM servers to provide a DPM protection for a large-scale DAG environment. If the DAG consists of six nodes, DPM agents from the first DPM server will be installed on the nodes 1,2, and 3, and DPM agents from the second DPM server will install its DPM agents on nodes 4, 5, and 6. During the deployment of the DPM agents, DPM will raise a warning saying "You cannot protect cluster data in the selected nodes without installing agents on the other nodes"; this is a warning and it will not reflect negatively on the DPM protection or the restore capabilities of DPM.

 Exchange 2013 supports up to eight parallel backups. This gives the DPM administrators the opportunity to have eight DPM servers protecting large Exchange environments.

Understanding how to adapt DPM to Exchange server management tasks

This section will explain how System Center Data Protection Manager 2012 R2 will adapt to Exchange server management tasks and what is important to know as a DPM administrator.

As an Exchange administrator, you need to either expand or adjust your Exchange server environment to fit the changing company needs. From a DPM perspective, there are some important considerations that you need to keep in mind as to how DPM identifies data sources within a workload.

The most common Exchange server management tasks are:

- ▶ Adding storage groups and databases
- ▶ Dismounting a database
- ▶ Changing the path of a database or a log file
- ▶ Renaming storage groups
- ▶ Moving databases between storage groups

In the scenario that you as an Exchange server administrator add storage groups, the DPM administrator must add them manually in DPM. This is however not a negative thing; think of this question: do you really want to add all of your Exchange server storage groups automatically to the DPM protection? I believe your answer is no, as different storage groups will be of different importance to the company or organization. You could, however, create an automated scenario using the combined power of the System Center family and make a service offering in System Center Service Manager that will use System Center Orchestrator to automate the setup of the new Exchange storage group and include it in the DPM protection.

> If you move an Exchange server from one domain to another, you must set up two-way transitive trust between the domains or deploy a new DPM server in the other domain and start protecting the Exchange server all over again.

If the Exchange administrator needs to dismount a database, DPM will not be able to protect it and the log files will not be truncated at the Exchange server side. It is very important from an Exchange perspective that the log files do not grow too big, as this will cause problems in the Exchange environment. If the Exchange administrator does not need the database, it is better to remove it than keep it dismounted.

When the Exchange environment has grown and the Exchange administrator needs to add more disks to the Exchange server boxes, the DPM protection will fail. The DPM administrator needs to modify the protection group to update the information where the data source files reside at the protected Exchange server. However, if the databases or log files are moved to a volume that contains data that is protected by DPM 2012 R2, the protection will continue without failing. Keeping this in mind, you can easily create optimal scenarios when moving protected Exchange server data sources.

If the Exchange admin changes the name of a storage group, the protection will fail. The DPM administrator must stop the protection and reprotect the storage group under the new name.

In the scenario that you move a database that is a member of a protected storage group to another storage group that is also protected using the same DPM server, the protection will continue. If you choose to move the database from a protected storage group to a nonprotected storage group, DPM will stop the protection of that database;, this is resolved by running a consistency check for the protected storage group after the move.

System Center Data Protection Manager 2012 R2 will identify data sources using the VSS technology and **Global Unique Identifiers** (**GUIDs**). In some cases, this will force the DPM administrator to stop the protection of a data source and reprotect it. It's important to keep in mind that the majority of these scenarios could be automated using the combined power of System Center to minimize the support overhead.

System Center Data Protection Manager 2012 R2's most important component is the DPM database called DPMDB. The DPMDB will grow with time and, in some cases, become slower regarding searches, but this could, of course, be optimized by rebuilding and reorganizing indexes, as the DPMDB becomes more fragmented over time.

For more information regarding how to do this, read the *DPMDB optimization* recipe in *Chapter 3, Post-installation Tasks*.

Understanding how to adapt DPM to Exchange server maintenance tasks

This section will cover how DPM will adapt to Exchange server maintenance tasks.

As an Exchange administrator, it is important to keep an optimal Exchange environment that will serve the company or organization's need for a great e-mail experience. There are some maintenance tasks that are common to all.

The most common maintenance task for an Exchange administrator is the offline defragmentation and index purging. Before this is done, it is important that the DPM agent is disabled so no backup jobs are running during the Exchange server maintenance.

To disable a DPM agent, open the DPM console and click on **Management** followed by **Agents**. Right-click on the DPM agent you would like to disable and choose **Disable protection** from the drop-down menu.

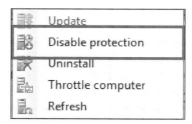

This will cause the backup jobs not to run, and when the maintenance task is done, simply right-click on the DPM agent again and choose **Enable protection** to get the scheduled backup jobs to run.

 If you have disabled a DPM agent, you will not be able to perform any recovery operations for that DPM agent.

For more information on how you can run ESEUTIL on the DPM server side, refer to the *Understanding how DPM can verify data integrity using ESEUTIL* recipe in this chapter.

Protecting a single Exchange mailbox database

This recipe will cover how to protect a single Exchange 2013 mailbox on a standalone server.

Getting ready

Before you start creating the **Protection Group** that holds the actual configuration for the backup schedule, you need to fulfill the following prerequisites:

▶ The Exchange server you would like to protect is a supported version of the DPM 2012 R2 protection

▶ A DPM agent is installed on all the servers that hold the data sources that you would like to protect

▶ The DPM agent reports **OK** in the DPM console's **Management** workspace

How to do it...

Go to **Protection** and click on **New** in the DPM console.

In the **Create New Protection Group Wizard Welcome** step, click on **Next >** to continue. In **Select protection group type**, choose **Servers** and click on **Next >** to continue. In the **Select group members** step, expand the **Exchange** and select **Mailbox Database** that you would like to protect with DPM. Click on **Next >** to continue.

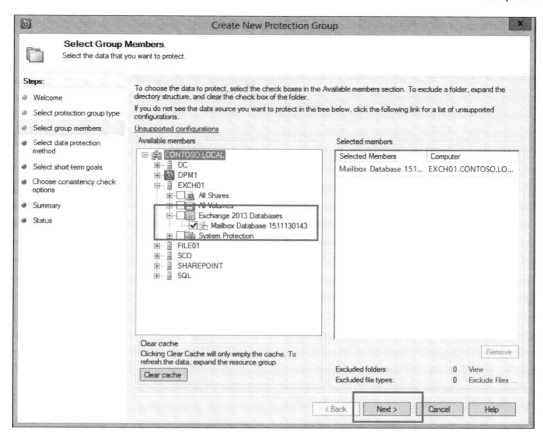

In **Select data protection method**, you decide the type of protection you would like to protect your Exchange data with. For the Exchange server workload, you can use **short-term protection** and **long-term protection** for your recovery goals.

Select the checkboxes next to the protection method you would like to use and click **Next >** to continue.

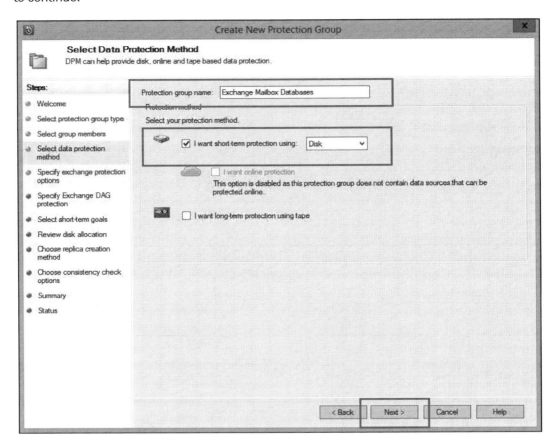

In **Specify exchange protection options**, you can choose to enable DPM to verify the data integrity using the ESEUTIL.EXE executable by selecting the checkbox for **Run Eseutil to check data integrity**.

> When you enable the DPM server to verify the backup consistency check, move the actual I/O impact from the Exchange servers to the DPM server.

If you have a standalone Exchange server, you choose the first option, which is **Run for both database and log files**. For a DAG configuration, you should choose the other option, which is **Run for log files only**.

For more detailed information on how to configure your DPM server to be enabled for data integrity verifications using ESEUTIL.EXE, refer to the *Understanding how DPM can verify data integrity using ESEUTIL* recipe in this chapter.

Click on **Next >** to continue to the next step.

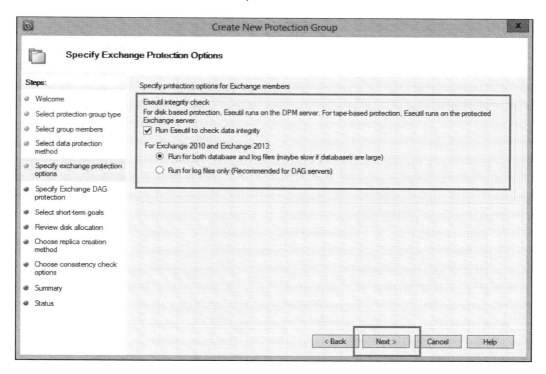

The next step is **Specify Exchange DAG protection**. For a standalone Exchange server, keep your databases in the left-hand side column called **Database copies selected for Full Backup**. This will make the federated log truncation execute.

 For more information on how you should design and protect your DAG-enabled Exchange server, refer to the *Understanding how DPM protects DAG configurations* recipe in this chapter.

Click on **Next >** to continue.

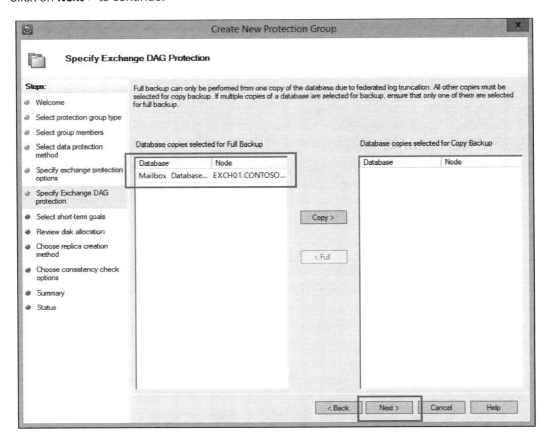

For the **Specify Exchange DAG protection** step, you choose which database should be selected for **Full Backup** or **Copy Backup**.

For a standalone Exchange server, you choose all your selected mailbox databases for **Full Backup**; only in a DAG scenario are you able to choose mailbox databases for **Copy Backup**. Click on **Next >** to continue.

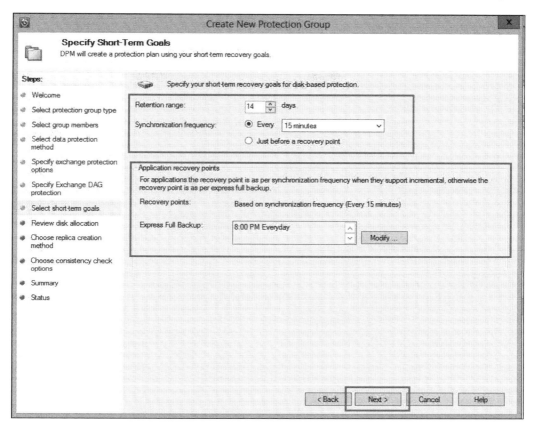

In **Specify short-term goals**, you will specify **Retention range**, which is the number of days you would like to keep the protected data in the DPM disk pool.

Next, you should configure **Synchronization frequency**, that is, how often the DPM agent should replicate the block level changes from the protected data source. You can synchronize every 15 minutes or **Just before a recovery point**.

In the **Application recovery points** section, you specify when to create recovery points for the protected data sources. Clicking on **Modify...** will open a window where you can choose the time of day and also specific weekdays for recovery point creation. Click on **OK** to get back to the **Select short-term goals** step.

When you are finished with your configuration, click on **Next >** to continue the **Review disk allocation** step.

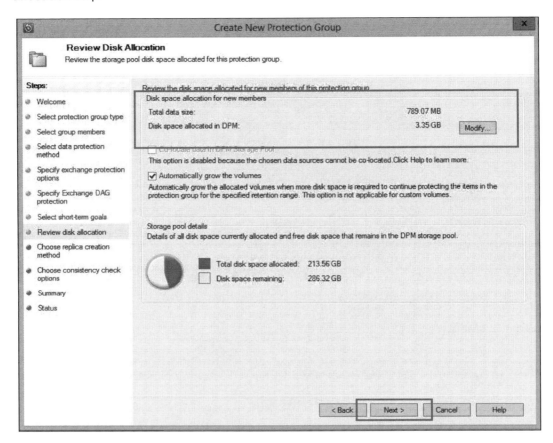

In the **Review disk allocation** step, you configure and review the disk space allocated for the protection group. Two specific volumes are created for all protected data sources that the DPM server is protecting, replica- and recovery-point volume. One of the auto-heal functions within DPM is **Automatically grow the volumes**. This feature will expand the volume when the threshold is reached; for more detailed information regarding the **Automatically grow the volumes** function, refer to the *Growing volumes automatically in the DPM disk pool* recipe in *Chapter 3, Post-installation Tasks*.

To continue, click on **Next >**.

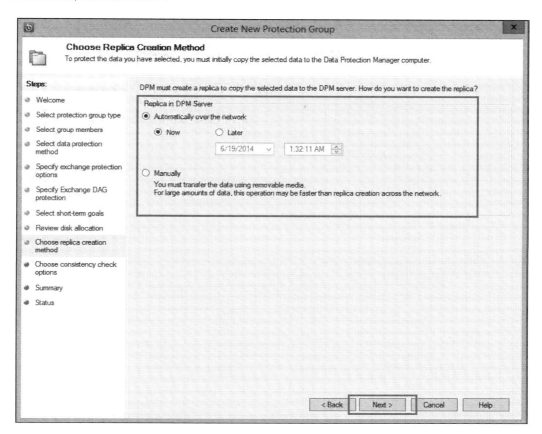

In **Choose replica creation method**, you can define how the DPM sever should create the replica of the protected data source. You can choose to create the replica **Now**, which means as the configuration of the protection group is finished, or you can schedule the replica creation **Later**. You can also create the replica manually; this is covered in the *Creating a replica manually* recipe in *Chapter 3, Post-installation Tasks*.

Click on **Next >** to continue.

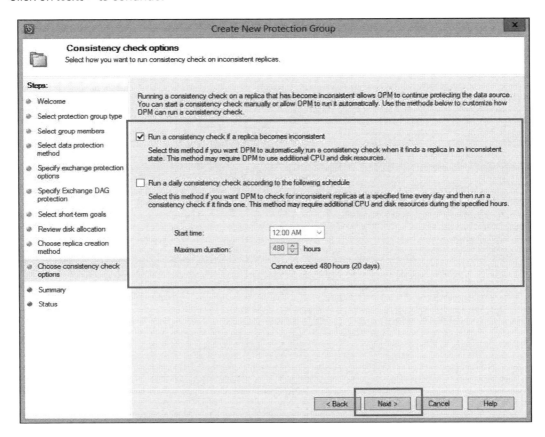

In **Consistency check options**, you specify whether the DPM should **Run a consistency check if a replica becomes inconsistent**; this is an auto-heal function within the DPM server technology. You can also specify to run a daily consistency check where you specify the start time and how many hours the task should run for.

To continue to the next step, click on **Next >**.

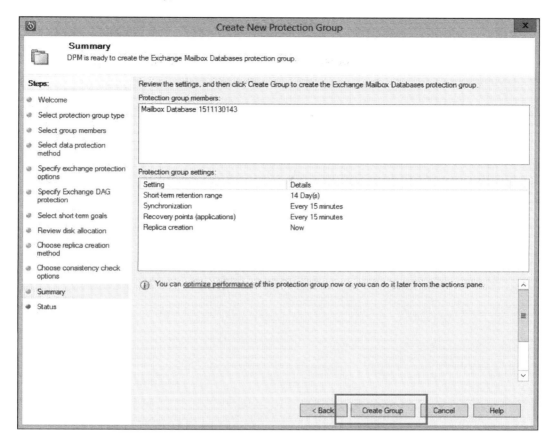

The **Summary** step is the last step in the protection group wizard. Here, you verify your configuration and click on **Create Group** to initialize the protection group, creating the replicas and applying the backup schedule with the configured options.

>
>
> You can also optimize the performance of a protection group by clicking on the optimize performance link; this is covered in the *Optimizing the Protection Group* recipe in *Chapter 3, Post-installation Tasks*.

The **Status** step will show you the progress of the protection group; this can also be verified in real time using **All jobs in progress filter** in the **Monitoring** task pane.

How it works...

Protection Group holds the actual configuration for your backup schedule, protected data sources, and specific configurations like **on-the-wire-compression**. The DPM server will call the DPM agents that are members of **Protection Group** to initialize the backup job; this is the **VSS Request** procedure that starts the VSS snapshot process on the protected server.

There's more...

If you try to perform parallel backups on multiple copies of the same Exchange Server database, then the backup procedure will fail.

For more information regarding how the DPM server operates, it is recommended that you read all the recipes in *Chapter 1, Pre-installation Tasks*.

Understanding how DPM protects DAG configurations

This section will cover how System Center Data Protection Manager 2012 R2 should be configured to protect an Exchange environment that is configured with DAG.

Getting ready

The most important part regarding your Exchange backup design is your restore scenario and how you should consider your disaster recovery scenarios. For item-level restore scenarios, which means restoring deleted items such as e-mails, you should take advantage of the **Deleted Item Retention** function. Within the Exchange server architecture, you have the option to restore hard deleted items using built-in tools within the Exchange server that could be accessed using **Exchange Management Shell** or **EMS**.

How to do it...

The protection for the DAG configuration is made in the **Specify Exchange DAG protection** step in the protection group wizard; for more information regarding the other steps, refer to the *Protect a single Exchange mailbox database* recipe in this chapter.

It is important to install a DPM agent on all DAG nodes so that you will be able to see both active and passive nodes.

When creating a new protection group using **Protection Group Wizard**, your DAG is listed under its DAG name in the **Select group members** step. When expanding your DAG name, your mailbox databases will be available for protection. If you further expand your mailbox databases, you will be able to see the DAG node members on which your database is located. If your mailbox database does not have any Exchange passive copies created, you will only see one node listed under the mailbox database name.

DPM is database role agnostic and can be configured to protect a server that hosts a collection of active or passive mailbox databases. This means that DPM does not care which database is active or passive and how the database is failing between nodes in your DAG configuration.

After including the mailbox databases on which there are nodes that you would like to include in your DPM protection, you need to configure the protection in the **Specify Exchange DAG protection** step. You can choose **Full Backup** or **Copy Backup**. For federated log truncation to be executed, the mailbox database must be chosen for **Full Backup**.

It is also possible to choose only one node per database to design a more suitable disaster recovery scenario from a DPM disk pool allocation perspective. Creating protection for all your mailbox databases that reside on every node in your DAG configuration will depend heavily on your DPM disk pool. It is always a decent idea to map the business continuity plan to your backup designs.

How it works...

Protection Group holds the actual configuration for your backup schedule, protected data sources, and specific configurations like **on-the-wire-compression**. The DPM server will call the DPM agents that are members of **Protection Group** to initialize the backup job; this is the **VSS Request** procedure that starts the VSS snapshot process on the protected server.

See also

▸ For more information regarding how the DPM server operates, it is recommended that you read all the recipes in *Chapter 1, Pre-installation Tasks*.

Understanding how DPM can verify data integrity using ESEUTIL

This recipe will cover how you enable DPM to verify the data integrity of your protected mailbox databases using `ESEUTIL.EXE`.

Getting ready

As mentioned in previous recipes, System Center Data Protection Manager 2012 R2 can verify the data integrity of the mailbox databases that it backs up by enabling the usage of `ESEUTIL.EXE` and `ESE.DLL`.

There are three different supported scenarios for this data integrity check via DPM:

- ▸ Copying `ESEUTIL.EXE` and `ESE.DLL` to the DPM server's BIN catalogue
- ▸ Installing Exchange Server Management Tool on the DPM server
- ▸ Using `FSUTIL` to create a hard link from the DPM server BIN catalogue

Either of these solutions will provide you with the same result, access to `ESEUTIL.EXE`, and other underlying technologies provided by the Exchange server technology so your DPM server can perform the process of data integrity verification.

 The `ESEUTIL.EXE` and `ESE.DLL` files are located in the BIN catalogue of the Exchange server.

How to do it...

To enable your DPM server to verify the data integrity of the backed up mailbox databases, simply select the **Run Eseutil to check data integrity** checkbox in the **Specify exchange protection options** step in **Protection Group Wizard**.

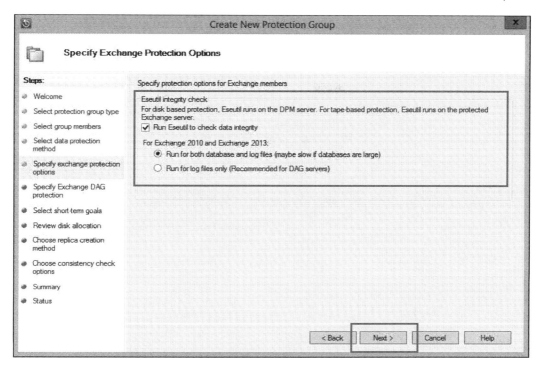

For a standalone Exchange server, it's recommended that you perform the data integrity check for both the databases and the log files. If you have not scaled your Exchange server environment and run all your companies' mailboxes in the same mailbox database, this verification can take some time. In the scenario that your Exchange server mailbox databases are large, it's recommended that you migrate some of the mailboxes to other mailbox databases to optimize the data integrity check.

For a DAG-configured Exchange environment, it's recommended that you just verify the data integrity on the log files instead of both the databases and the log files.

How it works...

DPM will cooperate with the Exchange server architecture that resides in ESEUTIL.EXE and ESE.DLL to verify the data integrity of the Exchange server workload databases. There are, however, two important facts. Data Protection Manger 2012 R2 will perform a Eseutil data integrity check on the backed up data if the DPM server has defined disk-based protection. If the DPM server has defined a tape-based protection, the Eseutil will run on the protected Exchange server.

See also

▸ For more information on how to create a hard link, refer to the information provided in Microsoft's TechNet article: `http://technet.microsoft.com/en-us/library/cc788097.aspx`.

 If you have set up a DPM-DPM-DR scenario, you must enable the data integrity check for the secondary DPM server, or the recovery point creation process will fail.

Restoring an Exchange mailbox database to its original location

This recipe will cover how to recover an Exchange mailbox to its original location.

Getting ready

Before you start **Recovery Wizard**, you should always verify that the DPM agent is reporting **OK** in the DPM console, or the local storage of the DPM server is enough.

How to do it...

In the DPM console, go to **Recovery** and choose the data source you would like to recover.

For File, Exchange, and SharePoint, you can use the search function.

Mark the data source and choose the date and time for the recovery. Right-click on the data source and choose **Recover...** to start **Recovery Wizard**.

In the **Review recovery selection** step, review the data source that is chosen for recovery and click on **Next >** to continue.

In the **Select recovery type** step, choose **Recover to original Exchange Server location** and click on **Next >**.

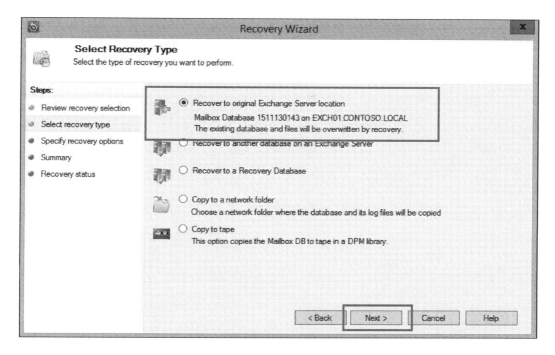

In the **Specify recovery options** step, configure the specific options for the recovery. At the top of **Recovery Wizard**, you will find the **Mount the databases after they are recovered** checkbox. If you want the databases to be mounted, you should select this checkbox.

If the recovery restores data over a poor WAN link, you can click on the **Modify...** link in the **Network bandwidth usage throttling** part to define how much bandwidth the restore job should consume.

If you have VSS hardware providers installed on the DPM sever and a LUN presented for the SAN storage of the protected data source, you can perform a SAN-based recovery by selecting the checkbox in the **SAN Recovery** part.

When the restore job has finished, you can send an e-mail to a specific addressed user or users, notifying them that the restore job has finished. This is enabled by selecting the checkbox in the **Notification** part. Click on **Next >** to continue.

> To be able to send e-mails, your DPM sever needs to have an SMTP server configured in the DPM options. Refer to the *Configuring e-mail notifications* recipe in *Chapter 3, Post-installation Tasks*.

In the **Summary** step, verify the recovery configuration and click on **Recover** to start the recovery.

In **Recovery Status**, you will be able to see the current state of the recovery. This could also be monitored in the **Monitoring** part of the DPM console.

> If you choose to restore the exchange mailbox database using the Latest technology, you can only restore it to its original location.

How it works...

When DPM initializes the recovery job, it will rely on the VSS architecture that is a part of the server operating system architecture.

There's more...

If the recovery job fails, you verify the alert that the DPM server will raise to inform you what has happened and guide you on how to create a possible scenario for the recovery to occur.

You cannot recover the database if the name of the Exchange Server database starts with a space. Make sure that the database name does not start with a space.

If you choose to search for a specific mailbox and restore it, you will have three possible restore scenarios:

- ► Recover the mailbox to an Exchange server database
- ► Copy to a network folder
- ► Copy to tape

The actual restore process of a single mailbox still involves the restore process of the entire mailbox database.

Restoring an Exchange mailbox database to an alternative location

This recipe will cover how to restore an Exchange mailbox database to an alternative location.

Getting ready

Before you start **Recovery Wizard**, you should always verify that the DPM agent is reporting **OK** in the DPM console, or the local storage of the DPM server is enough.

How to do it...

In the DPM console, go to **Recovery** and choose the data source you would like to recover.

 For File, Exchange, and SharePoint, you can use the search function.

Mark the data source and choose the date and time for the recovery. Right-click on the data source and choose **Recover...** to start **Recovery Wizard**.

In the **Review recovery selection** step, review the data source that is chosen for recovery and click on **Next >** to continue.

In the **Select recovery type** step, choose **Recover to another database on an Exchange Server** and click on **Next >**.

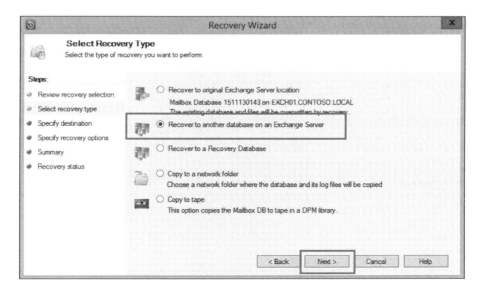

In the **Specify destination** step of **Recovery Wizard**, you need to choose an Exchange server that should be receiving the restorable data.

 For DPM to be able to list the other Exchange Server, it needs to be protected by the DPM server that is performing the recovery process.

Click on the **Browse...** button to choose your other Exchange Server and click on the **OK** button to return to the **Specify destination** step; you can also type in the FQDN for the Exchange server. Enter a name for the recovered mailbox database that should reside on the other Exchange server. When finished, click on **Next >** to continue.

In the **Specify recovery options** step, you configure the specific options for the recovery. At the top of **Recovery Wizard**, you will find the **Mount the databases after they are recovered** checkbox. If you want the databases to be mounted, you should select this checkbox.

If the recovery restores data over a poor WAN link, you can click on the **Modify...** link in the **Network bandwidth usage throttling** part to define how much bandwidth the restore job should consume.

If you have VSS hardware providers installed on the DPM sever and a LUN presented for the SAN storage of the protected data source, you can perform a SAN-based recovery by selecting the checkbox in the **SAN Recovery** part.

When the restore job has finished, you can send an e-mail to a specific addressed user or users, notifying them that the restore job has finished. This is enabled by selecting the checkbox in the **Notification** part. Click on **Next >** to continue.

 To be able to send e-mails, your DPM sever needs to have an SMTP server configured in the DPM options. Refer to the *Configuring e-mail notifications* recipe in *Chapter 3, Post-installation Tasks*.

In the **Summary** step, verify the recovery configuration and click on **Recover** to start the recovery.

In **Recovery status**, you will be able to see the current state of the recovery. This could also be monitored in the **Monitoring** part of the DPM console.

How it works...

When DPM initializes the recovery job, it will rely on the VSS architecture that is a part of the server operating system architecture.

There's more...

If the recovery job fails, verify the alert that the DPM server will raise to inform you what has happened and guide you on how to create a possible scenario for the recovery to occur.

Restoring an Exchange mailbox database to an Exchange Recovery Database

This recipe will cover how to restore an Exchange mailbox database to an Exchange Recovery Database.

Getting ready

In the scenario that you as a DPM administrator will provide a restore mailbox database for the Exchange administrators to extract specific Exchange objects from, you should restore your protected Exchange server data to **Recovery Database**.

Before you can restore your protected Exchange data to **Recovery Database**, you need to create one on the Exchange server that should receive the restored data. This is done using **Exchange Management Shell** or EMS. An example of how you can easily create **Recovery Database**, also called RDB, is to type in the following syntax:

```
New-MailboxDatabase –Recovery –Name RDB –Server EXCH01
```

The input followed by the `-Server` switch is your Exchange Server name; in this example, the Exchange server name is `EXCH01`.

Before you start **Recovery Wizard**, you should always verify that the DPM agent is reporting **OK** in the DPM console, or the local storage of the DPM server is enough.

How to do it...

In the DPM console, go to **Recovery** and choose the data source you would like to recover.

 For File, Exchange, and SharePoint, you can use the search function.

Mark the data source and choose the date and time for the recovery. Right-click on the data source and choose **Recover...** to start **Recovery Wizard**.

In the **Review recovery selection** step, review the data source that is chosen for recovery and click on **Next >** to continue.

In the **Select recovery type** step, choose **Recover to a Recovery Database** and click on **Next >**.

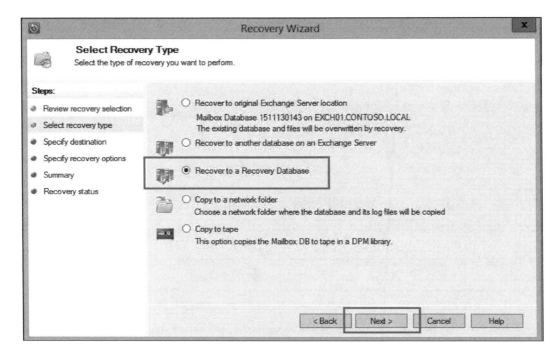

In the **Specify destination** step of **Recovery Wizard**, you need to choose an Exchange server that should be receiving the restorable data.

Click on the **Browse...** button to choose your other Exchange Server and click on the **OK** button to return to the **Specify destination** step; you can also type in the FQDN for the Exchange server. Next, you need to enter the name of **Recovery Database**, which you previously created. If the destination host uses remote storage, you must select the checkbox called **Destination host uses remote storage**. When all input has been completed, click on **Next >** to continue.

In the **Specify recovery options** step, you configure the specific options for the recovery. At the top of **Recovery Wizard**, you will find the **Mount the databases after they are recovered** checkbox. If you want the databases to be mounted, you should select this checkbox.

If the recovery restores data over a poor WAN link, you can click on the **Modify...** link in the **Network bandwidth usage throttling** part to define how much bandwidth the restore job should consume.

If you have VSS hardware providers installed on the DPM sever and a LUN presented for the SAN storage of the protected data source, you can perform a SAN-based recovery by selecting the checkbox in the **SAN Recovery** part.

When the restore job has finished, you can send an e-mail to a specific addressed user or users, notifying them that the restore job has finished. This is enabled by selecting the checkbox in the **Notification** part. Click on **Next >** to continue.

> To be able to send e-mails, your DPM sever needs to have an SMTP server configured in the DPM options. Refer to the *Configuring e-mail notifications* recipe in *Chapter 3, Post-installation Tasks*.

In the **Summary** step, verify the recovery configuration and click on **Recover** to start the recovery.

In **Recovery status**, you will be able to see the current state of the recovery. This can also be monitored in the **Monitoring** part of the DPM console.

How it works...

When DPM initializes the recovery job, it will rely on the VSS architecture that is a part of the server operating system architecture.

There's more...

When the recovery job has finished, you have performed just one half of the recovery process; next, you must open your **Exchange Management Console** on your Exchange server and perform `MailboxRestoreRequest`. The following example is a syntax to restore the alias `John Doe` mailbox:

```
New-MailboxRestoreRequest -SourceDatabase RDB -SourceStoreMailbox
'John Doe' -TargetMailbox jodo
```

If the recovery job fails, verify the alert that the DPM server will raise to inform you what has happened and guide you on how to create a possible scenario for the recovery to occur.

Restoring an Exchange mailbox database to a network folder

This recipe will cover how to restore an Exchange mailbox database to a network folder.

Getting ready

Before you start **Recovery Wizard**, you should always verify that the DPM agent is reporting **OK** in the DPM console, or the local storage of the DPM server is enough.

How to do it...

In the DPM console, go to **Recovery** and choose the data source you would like to recover.

 For File, Exchange, and SharePoint, you can use the search function.

Mark the data source and choose the date and time for the recovery. Right-click on the data source and choose **Recover...** to start **Recovery Wizard**.

In the **Review recovery selection** step, review the data source that is chosen for recovery and click on **Next >** to continue.

In the **Select recovery type** step, choose **Copy to a network folder** and click on **Next >**.

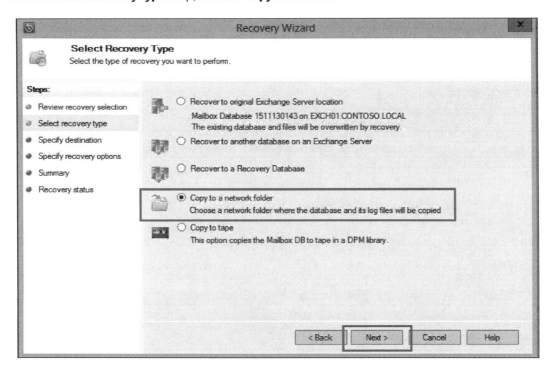

In the **Specify destination** step of **Recovery Wizard**, you need to choose where to restore the protected Exchange data.

Click on the **Browse...** button to choose a location and click on the **OK** button to return to the **Specify destination** step; you can also type in the FQDN for the server that should host the recovered files.

 For DPM to be able to restore protected Exchange server data to a network location, the listed server must be protected by the DPM server that is performing the recovery process.

In **Destination** path, you will see the path chosen to host the recovered data. Click on **Next >** to continue.

In the **Specify recovery options** step, you configure the specific options for the recovery. At the top of **Recovery Wizard**, you will find the **Bring the database to a clean shutdown...** checkbox; check only this option if the destination of the recovery job has the Exchange server application installed.

If the recovery restores data over a poor WAN link, you can click on the **Modify...** link in the **Network bandwidth usage throttling** part to define how much bandwidth the restore job should consume.

If you have VSS hardware providers installed on the DPM sever and a LUN presented for the SAN storage of the protected data source, you can perform a SAN-based recovery by selecting the checkbox in the **SAN Recovery** part.

When the restore job has finished, you can send an e-mail to a specific addressed user or users, notifying them that the restore job has finished. This is enabled by selecting the checkbox in the **Notification** part. Click on **Next >** to continue.

 To be able to send e-mails, your DPM sever needs to have an SMTP server configured in the DPM options. Refer to the *Configuring e-mail notifications* recipe in *Chapter 3, Post-installation Tasks*.

In the **Summary** step, verify the recovery configuration and click on **Recover** to start the recovery.

In **Recovery status**, you will be able to see the current state of the recovery. This can also be monitored in the **Monitoring** part of the DPM console.

How it works...

When DPM initializes the recovery job, it will rely on the VSS architecture that is a part of the server operating system architecture.

There's more...

If the recovery job fails, you should verify the alert that the DPM server will raise to inform you what has happened and guide you on how to create a possible scenario for the recovery to occur.

Copying the Exchange mailbox database to tape

This recipe will cover how to copy a protected Exchange mailbox database to tape. Many companies use this function for one reason: archiving.

Getting ready

Before you start **Recovery Wizard**, you should always verify that the DPM agent is reporting **OK** in the DPM console, or the local storage of the DPM server is enough. It is also critical that your tape library is operational and does not report any errors.

How to do it...

In the DPM console, go to **Recovery** and choose the data source you would like to recover.

 For File, Exchange, and SharePoint, you can use the search function.

Mark the data source and choose the date and time for the recovery. Right-click on the data source and choose **Recover...** to start **Recovery Wizard**.

In the **Review recovery selection** step, review the data source that is chosen for recovery and click on **Next >** to continue.

In the **Select recovery type** step, choose **Copy to tape** and click on **Next >**.

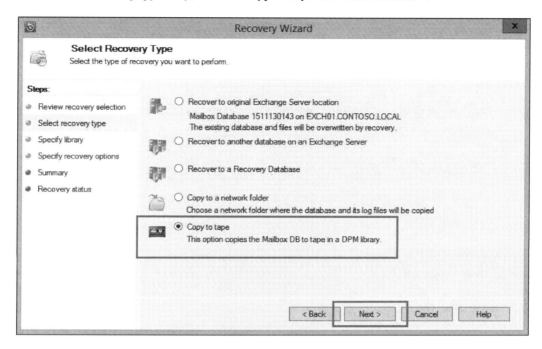

In the **Specify library** step of **Recovery Wizard**, you need to choose your **Primary library** for the copy process and, if needed, **Copy library** if you want multiple copies of the copied data.

Under **Tape options**, configure your **Tape label** and also the operation that you would like to perform on **Data on tape**. You are able to:

- ▶ Compress
- ▶ Encrypt
- ▶ Not compress or encrypt

When you have made your choices, click on **Next >** to continue.

In the **Specify recovery options** step, you configure the specific options for the recovery. When the restore job has finished, you can send an e-mail to a specific addressed user or users, notifying them that the restore job has finished. This is enabled by selecting the checkbox in the **Notification** part. Click on **Next >** to continue.

To be able to send e-mails, your DPM sever needs to have an SMTP server configured in the DPM options. Refer to the *Configuring e-mail notifications* recipe in *Chapter 3, Post-installation Tasks*.

In the **Summary** step, verify the recovery configuration and click on **Recover** to start the recovery.

In **Recovery status**, you will be able to see the current state of the recovery. This can also be monitored in the **Monitoring** part of the DPM console.

How it works...

When DPM initializes the recovery job, it will rely on the VSS architecture that is a part of the server operating system architecture. For a copy job to be successful, it is of major importance that the tape libraries are fully operational and do not report any errors.

There's more...

If the recovery job fails, you should verify the alert that the DPM server will raise to inform you what has happened and guide you on how to create a possible scenario for the recovery to occur.

9

Client Protection

In this chapter, we will cover the following recipes:

- ▶ Finding and understanding Company Protection Policy
- ▶ Understanding the prerequisites of client protection
- ▶ Creating a Protection Group for client protection
- ▶ Restoring client data via the DPM client
- ▶ Restoring client data from the DPM server
- ▶ Setting up the end user recovery feature
- ▶ Setting up the DPM self service recovery for SQL

Introduction

Protecting your client data has been a top priority for companies around the world for many years. The solutions have been varied and so has the outcome from the actual restore scenario, when something really needs to be "put back on track" for the end user to be able to continue his or her work.

System Center Data Protection Manager 2012 R2 provides one of the most sophisticated solutions regarding client protection; the biggest challenge is that no one really knows that this feature exists. As in every product, there will always be room for improvements, but what it all comes down to is how you, as an administrator, will design and manage the restore scenario for your end user's data.

The most common solution that many have both implemented and also struggled with is the folder redirection policy. The policy was a great thing when it was released in early Windows Server releases, but as most users tend to have a poor save strategy for their documents, the policy had some challenges regarding the matter of including the actual data that should be protected and most importantly, being able restore the data. The folder redirection policy focused on moving the contents of the `My Documents` folder to a specified share where third-party software backed up this NTFS share, providing a somewhat restore scenario.

With the client protection introduced in DPM 2007, many companies started to try out this feature. The development process regarding the client protection story was heavily improved by Microsoft, but not marketed in an optimal way.

Build **Backup as a Service** (**BaaS**) is a really simple thing when it comes down to delivering client protection. Via the Service Manager Portal, you can deliver the client backup service, get have an automated concept using either **System Center Orchestrator** (**SCO**) or **Service Management Automation** (**SMA**), and keep track of the clients using **Operations Manager**, also known as **OpsMgr** or **SCOM**.

The vision that Microsoft wants to deliver is to move the responsibility of backing up away from administrators, and leveraging the great possibilities of providing a self-service concept to the end users, building and providing services. DPM client protection can make this happen, and it is not very difficult to get started and design a company protection policy.

In this chapter, we will cover how to set up and explain the client protection feature for System Center Data Protection Manager 2012 R2.

This chapter will also provide you with information and setup steps for the End User Recovery and Self Service Recovery for SQL databases to enable simple services that the end user can actually rely on.

Finding and understanding Company Protection Policy

This recipe will cover the information you need to get started to design your client protection.

Getting ready

The client protection in DPM is really all about one thing: **Company Protection Policy**, also known as (**CPP**). This policy contains all the necessary information that DPM actually needs to start to provide protection that will, in the end, build an optimal restore scenario for the end user data.

How to do it...

The company protection policy contains five core components:

- ▸ Folder inclusion and exclusion
- ▸ Allowing users to specify protection group members
- ▸ File type exclusion
- ▸ Synchronization frequency
- ▸ Recovery point creation

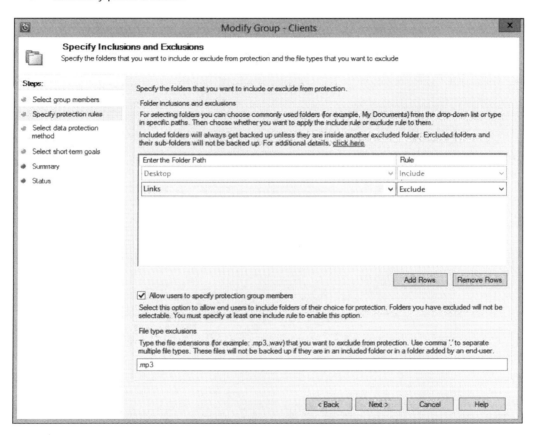

The folder inclusion and exclusion defines the folders that should be included in the company protection policy or the folders that should be excluded. The DPM administrator can choose between standard inclusion or exclusion options.

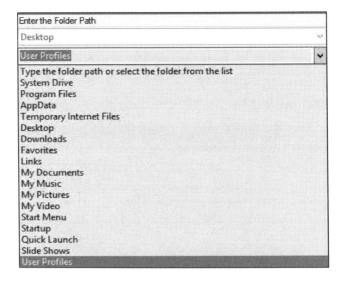

Providing a good Group Policy design with the combination of building an optimal restore scenario for client data, is something that is really beneficial for all the companies that build up this service.

You can also verify the company protection policy on the client side by right-clicking on the DPM client icon next to the watch, and choose **Restore** from the menu.

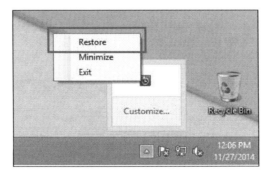

Now, click on the **Protected Items** tab, followed by the **Company Protection Policy** link.

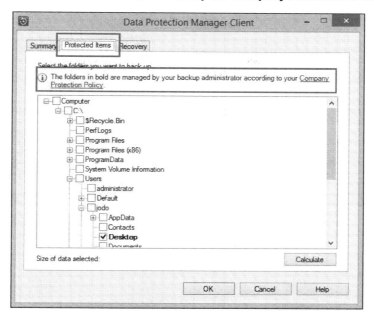

Company Protection Policy will summarize all the configuration and present it in an orderly manner.

How it works...

System Center Data Protection Manager 2012 R2 gives an easy, yet advanced client protection for companies of all sizes. When building a **Restore as a Service** (**RaaS**) service for a company or an organization, it is important to know the limits of the DPM software.

The DPM server should not be seen as a single server that can manage a massive scale of protection; Microsoft is more interested in providing an optimal and reliable service that maps nicely into the modern datacenter. Using the co-location feature on the DPM disk pool, you can protect 1000 clients per DPM server instance that builds up your BaaS, RaaS, or DRaaS for your protected data sources.

See also

 ▸ For more information regarding System Center Data Protection Manager 2012 R2, visit this blog: `http://robertanddpm.blogspot.com`.

Understanding the prerequisites of client protection

This section will cover the prerequisites that need to be in place at the client side, before you start to set up and configure the DPM client protection.

Before you start to set up your Company Protection Policy, you must verify that your client has all the prerequisite software, and also has a supported version of the Windows client operating system.

 Client inventory can be done via SCCM or Intune.

Supported Windows client operating systems are:

 ▸ Windows 8
 ▸ Windows 7
 ▸ Windows Vista

System Center Data Protection Manager 2012 R2 can protect clients in other domains if there is two-way transitive trust between the domains. This is something that you should avoid; it is better to place DPM servers in an untrusted domain and let them join that domain and then monitor and manage them via System Center Operations Manager 2012 R2.

You must have the .NET Framework 4.0 installed prior to the DPM agent installation for the DPM agent to be successfully installed.

The DPM client is the same as the DPM server agent, and it will track down the block level changes of files and folders that are included in **Company Protection Policy** and will replicate them from the client to the DPM server.

If the DPM client can't connect to the DPM server, the DPM client will temporarily store the block level changes on the client side, until the access to the DPM server is established again.

If your clients are connected to your company network via Direct Access, you also need to verify that ICMP is allowed between the DPM client and the DPM server. For the DPM client to be able to synchronize, it needs to be able to ping the DPM server, and vice versa.

The DPM client can communicate via:

▶ Direct Access
▶ PPTP
▶ SSTP
▶ L2TP

It is important that the client who accesses the company network via VPN or DA has at least 1 Mbps; if the computer is present in the company network, 256 Kbps is enough.

Creating a Protection Group for client protection

This recipe will cover some of the core fundamentals regarding client protection in DPM.

Getting ready

As mentioned in the introduction, client protection is a natural replacement for the folder redirection policy that will empower end users to perform both backups and restore the job under both restricted manners or as admins, depending on the scenario.

The client protection in DPM will provide you with a single administration point for up to 1000 clients per DPM server, using the co-location feature for the DPM disk pool configuration for the protection group. If you have multiple DPM servers, you just move your management to System Center Operations Manager 2012 R2 and start using the central console as your administrative point. Still, there should be just a single glass of pane for alerts and administration, which is something that you, as a DPM administrator, should always strive for.

How to do it...

When you have installed and attached the DPM server agent on your supported Windows operating system, you must create a **New Protection Group** or modify an existing one in the DPM console's **Protection** view.

First of all, in the **Welcome** step, you can select the checkbox next to **Do not show this Welcome page again** to skip this step the next time. Click on **Next >** to continue.

In the **Select protection group type** step, choose **Clients** and click on **Next >** to continue.

 When creating the protection group for clients, you can install the DPM agent afterwards. This is applicable only for clients.

In the **Select group members** step, you choose the clients from the **Computer name** column by either entering a FQDN for the client or by marking it in the list and clicking on the **Add >** button. The other option is to provide a text file to the DPM server that contains the FQDN for all the clients that you would like to add. It is important that all FQDN names are entered as a new line in the text file. Click on the **Add From File...** button to add multiple computers from a text file. Click on **Next >** to continue.

Next is the **Specify protection rules** step, where you define parts of **Company Protection Policy**. In **Folders inclusions and exclusions**, you define what should be included or excluded for the client protection; choose the appropriate options in the drop-down list according to your backup strategy and restore plan. If the protection group members can include catalogues, leave the checkbox next to the **Allow users to specify protection group members** option. As a DPM administrator, you can also exclude specific file types, such as `.mp3`, `.wav`, `.mov`, and so on.

 When you exclude a specific file type, be sure to have the correct syntax. To exclude all MP3 files, you should provide the MP3 file type as `.mp3` and not use a star.

Click on **Next >** to continue to the next step.

In the **Select data protection rules** step, define the name for the protection group and also choose whether you want to use only disk-based backup or combine it with tape. In this recipe, we will cover both options. Click on **Next >** to continue.

Next is **Select short-term goals**, where you define **Retention range**, which is the actual number of days for which the DPM server should store your protected data. Within the protection group configuration, you can define **Synchronization frequency** to identify the block-level changes on the client side and synchronize them to the DPM server. In **Client computer recovery points**, you list the number of recovery points that you want to create for the users' client data. To alter the number of recovery points and the time they occur for, click on the **Modify...** button. One difference when protecting clients as opposed to servers and applications is **Alerting options**. This option lists the number of days for which a client can be disconnected, before the DPM server triggers an alert that the affected client has not reported back. The numbers of days will start to count if the recovery point is not successfully created. Click on **Next >** to continue.

The next step is **Allocate storage**, where you define the storage configuration for the protection group. A specific client protection configuration has the possibility to define the size of the storage used from the DPM disk pool per protected client. In the **Disk space allocation for new members** field, you define **Data per computer**, which should be allocated in the DPM disk pool, and for disk optimization possibilities, you should also enable **Co-locate client computers in DPM Storage Pool**. This option will make it possible for you to protect a theoretical number of 1000 clients per DPM server, depending on the DPM server's possible resources. One important auto-heal function is **Automatically grow the volumes**; check this option and verify the storage summary in **Storage pool details**, and click on **Next >** to continue.

If you have chosen to use long-term protection, meaning tape, the next step is **Specify long-term goals**. Define your long-term goals and click on **Next >** to continue.

For more details regarding tape configuration, refer to *Chapter 13, Tape Management*.

Next is the **Select library and tape details** step; for more details, read *Chapter 13, Tape Management*. Create your configurations and click on **Next >** to continue.

Verify your configurations in the **Summary** step and click on the **Create Group** button to create the initial replica.

In the **Status** step, you can verify the progress.

How it works...

Protection Group contains **Company Protection Policy**, which holds the actual configuration.

The DPM client is dependent on the actual connection to the DPM server to be able to synchronize the file's block level changes. If the client is connected via an unstable connection, the DPM agent will still be able to create a recovery point for the selected data sources. However, the DPM client is also dependent on the connection to the DPM sever to be able to restore the data. This is something that is quite obvious but important to mention, as the backed up data resides on the DPM server and not on the client.

There's more...

Before the DPM server can start to receive data from the client to start to create the replica, the company protection policy must be delivered and adapted at the client side. The company protection policy will replicate within a few minutes and, in some cases, will take a bit longer, depending on the circumstances and challenges of the datacenter.

Restoring client data via the DPM client

This recipe will cover how you can restore your data from the DPM client, on the client side. When restoring data from the DPM agent on the client side, you must have a connection to the DPM server for verification.

Getting ready

The most important thing to bring up initially is who actually owns the backed up data. System Center Data Protection Manger 2012 R2 is sometimes used as a migration tool for end users. This is a very easy setup and is very helpful for the administrators in the company or organization. The actual owner of the protected data is the domain user. This opens up a great possibility; if a user receives a new laptop or desktop, he or she can easily restore My Documents folder from the DPM server to the new hardware. This process can easily be done and provided via a service offering in System Center Service Manager or via a simple PowerShell script that runs in the deployment phase of the new client.

How to do it...

To restore data from the DPM client, simply right-click on the DPM client icon next to the clock and choose **Restore**. This will open the **Data Protection Manager Client** window; click on the **Recovery** tab to continue.

To list all the recovery points available on the DPM server, click on the magnifying glass next to **Search for recovery points** on the field. After clicking on the magnifying glass, a list of recovery points will open; choose one and click on **Open...** to read the contents of the recovery point.

File Explorer will open a file explorer window that is addressed to the GUID ID of the recovery point. From here, you can simply drill down and open your data in the catalogue structure.

 If there are several users working on the same computer, you can only open the recovery points associated with your domain user.

When you have found the right file, simply right-click on it and choose **Copy**. Open the destination folder in file explorer, right-click on an empty space and choose **Paste**.

How it works...

The DPM client will connect to the DPM server to verify what recovery points are available, and then list them for the client to choose the most appropriate to restore from.

There's more...

It is crucial that the DPM client can connect to the DPM server for a restore to occur, as the actual protected data resides on the DPM server and not on the client. There are, of course, other methods to provide a restore scenario, but all of them are dependent either on storage, network, or both.

You could configure your Windows 8 clients to work with **File History**, but this will also be dependent on both network connectivity and/or storage that is either local or remote.

Looking at the third-party vendors in the market, there is no one who can claim that their product is not dependent on one of the two. Once again, it is proven that you as an administrator can never explicitly depend on a single software to sort and solve all your problems and challenges. What it all comes down to is knowing your services' data dependencies.

Restoring client data from the DPM server

This recipe will cover how to restore protected client data from the DPM server. Keep in mind that the DPM agent must have connectivity to the DPM server for a restore to the original location to occur.

Getting ready

Restoring data from the DPM server will always provide you with more options for the restore scenario. As mentioned in the *Restoring client data via the DPM client* recipe, you can perform a copy and paste operation from the recovery points that reside on the DPM server.

How to do it...

In the DPM console, go to the **Recovery** view and expand the client you want to associate with the restore process. Expand the node and drill down to the file you are looking for.

 You do not have a search feature for client-protected data.

Choose the correct date and time for the recovery point, right-click on the file or folder, and choose **Recover...** to continue. DPM will open **Recovery Wizard** and provide you with the first step, called **Review recovery selection**. Verify **Recovery items** and click on **Next >** to continue.

The next step is **Select recovery type**, where you will define if you want to restore the protected object to:

▶ The original location

▶ An alternate location

▶ Copy to tape

If you choose to restore to the original location, you only need to know that the DPM agent has a connection that is **OK** before you start the restore job.

 You can simply verify a DPM agent connectivity status by right-clicking on it and choosing **Refresh** in the **Agents... | Management** view in the DPM console.

In the **Specify Recovery Options** step, you configure the specific options for the recovery.

In the **Existing version recovery behavior** part, you define what DPM should do if the data source exists in the targeted location. **Create copy** will create a copy if the data source you are recovering already exists; **Skip** will skip to restore the data source if it already exists, and **Overwrite** will overwrite the data source if it already exists in the targeted location.

In the **Restore security** part, you define how the restored data source should apply to the security setting in the targeted location. The restored data can either keep its security settings that are present in the recovery point version, or apply the security settings of the targeted location.

If the recovery restores data over a poor WAN connection, you can click on the **Modify...** link in the **Network bandwidth usage throttling** part to define how much bandwidth the restore job should consume.

If you have VSS hardware providers installed on the DPM sever and a LUN presented for the SAN storage of the protected data source, you can perform a SAN-based recovery by selecting the checkbox in the **SAN Recovery** part.

When the restore job has finished, you can send an e-mail to a specific addressed user or users, notifying them that the restore job has finished. This is enabled by selecting the checkbox in the **Notification** part. Click on **Next>** to continue.

 To be able to send e-mails, your DPM server needs to have an SMTP server configured in the DPM options. Refer to the *Configuring e-mail notifications* recipe in *Chapter 3, Post-installation Tasks*.

In the **Summary** step, verify the recovery configuration and click on **Recover** to start the recovery.

In **Recovery Status**, you will be able to see the current state of the recovery. This can also be monitored in the **Monitoring** part of the DPM console.

How it works...

The DPM server will interact with the DPM agent on the client side to perform a restore operation. You, as a DPM administrator, have many more options than what are provided with the DPM client experience, but never forget that simplicity is of key importance for an end user.

There's more...

Building a RaaS, or Restore as a Service, is actually much more than just trying different software cooperate to deliver a service; it is understanding the optimal approach of the company or the organization.

Providing a Restore as a Service can be built from interaction between the different System Center family members, but most important is how they should deliver an optimal service for the customer and the actual end user.

Setting up the end user recovery feature

This recipe will cover how to configure the **End-user Recovery** (**EUR**), in your datacenter. There is some important information regarding how you can limit the risk of having end users overwriting or restoring production data by mistake; this is covered in the last section of this recipe.

Before you make any changes to the Active Directory schema, be sure to have a system state backup of all the domain controllers that hold any FSMO roles

Getting ready

End user recovery enables the possibility of end users being able to restore production data under a controlled manner, which means that you, as an administrator, can control what data they should be able to restore.

The EUR feature relies on the NTFS ACL in the operating system; if these are poorly configured, you will end up with a bad implementation of EUR.

There are some important tasks that you must fulfill before you add information to the Active Directory schema, which is part of your rollback plan if there are some unforeseen circumstances. Altering the schema configuration demands you to have:

- ▸ Communicated with the Active Directory administrators, regarding the schema update that needs to be done

- ▸ Made a backup of all the system states of domain controllers that hold any FSMO roles

- ▸ Provided a rollback plan that is accepted by your change management

As a DPM administrator, you cannot control which protected file server you enable for end user recovery. All servers that have the file server role enabled and protected via DPM will be enabled for end user recovery.

How to do it...

The initial task to enable End-User recovery is to configure the Active Directory of your domain that the DPM server is a member of. This can be done via the DPM console by entering the **Management** view and clicking on the **Options** button followed by the **End-user Recovery** tab.

Click on the **Configure Active Directory** button to enter your credentials that have the sufficient rights to add information to the Active Directory schema; then, click on **OK**.

System Center Data Protection Manager 2012 R2 will prompt you with an informational window, stating that you will configure your Active Directory to support end user recovery; click on **Yes** to continue.

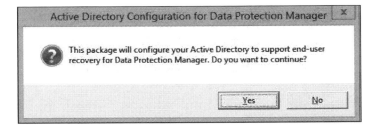

DPM will open the **Active Directory Configuration for Data Protection Manager** window, which will inform you that it will take a few moments for the Active Directory to be configured. Click on **OK** to continue.

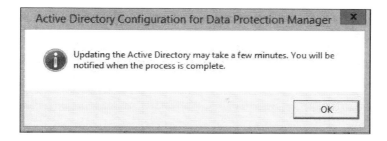

After you have clicked on the **OK** button, the DPM server will initialize the update of the Active Directory schema.

Before you make any changes to the Active Directory schema, you must have a backup of the system state of the domain controllers that hold the FSMO roles. Also, you must inform the Active Directory administrators and provide a roll-back plan.

If you have not provided an FQDN for the domain, or for some reason, the DPM server could not connect to the domain, you receive an error stating that there was a problem, and DPM has not started to configure or alter your Active Directory yet.

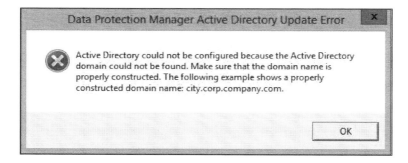

If you face this error, you can still enable End-User Recovery by running the executable that creates the configuration. Copy the `DPMADSchemaExtentions.exe` executable to the domain controller that owns the schema FSMO role. Right-click on the file and choose **Run as administrator**.

 The file is located on the DPM server at `%Program Files%\Microsoft System Center 2012 R2\DPM\DPM\End User Recovery\`.

Once again, **Active Directory Configuration for Data Protection Manager** will be presented; click on **Yes** to continue.

The first window that appears is **Enter Data Protection Manager Computer Name**. It is important to enter the DPM server NetBIOS name; if your DPM server FQDN is **DPM.contoso.local**, you should enter DPM in the text field and click on **OK** to continue.

Next is **Enter Data Protection Manager Server Domain**; if your DPM server is joined to the **contoso.local** domain, you should enter contoso.local in the text field and click on **OK** to continue.

The next step is **Enter Protected Computer Domain Name**; enter the name of the file server that you want to enable the end user recovery for. If the file server is a member of the same domain as the DPM server, then just leave the text field blank and click on **OK** to continue.

The last step is the **Active Directory Configuration for Data Protection Manager** window, which will inform you that the update of the Active Directory schema might take a few minutes. Click on the **OK** button to continue.

When the configuration is done, you will see the **Active Directory Configuration for Data Protection Manager** window inform you that the update was successful.

 There is a known bug is the initial R2 release with the script to update the Active Directory schema used by the executable. Apply the latest update rollup from Microsoft, and the script is updated.

You can now go back to your DPM server and select the checkbox in the DPM server options under the **End-user Recovery** tab next to **Enable end-user recovery** and click on **OK**.

You will be prompted with an informational window that will inform you that end user recovery settings will take effect when the protection groups have been successfully synchronized.

How it works...

The End-user Recovery function relies on the shadow copy client, in combination with the schema extensions that you provided to your domain controllers during the preparations for the EUR feature. The key component of the EUR is, of course, the VSS architecture within the operating system that must be working in an optimal state. The health state can, and should, be monitored by System Center Operations Manager in order to provide the most health state satiation for your production environment.

There's more...

You can limit the possibility for end users to restore and overwrite production data that resides on the file server by altering some registry values. When the end users want to restore some data, they will do that by right-clicking on the catalogue and choosing **Restore previous versions**.

The end user can choose what recovery point in time they want to restore from, and have three options:

- **Open**
- **Copy**
- **Restore**

As a DPM administrator, you must provide an easy approach for the end users that also protects them from their own mistakes. By disabling the **Restore** button, you can make the experience more bulletproof, as the end user can only open a recovery point or copy it to an alternative location.

 Remember, if you provide a poor NTFS configuration to your shares, you will have a poor control of who can restore files. You must provide good NTFS and ACL rights for your shares before enabling End-user Recovery.

To do this, type either of the following commands into the Command Prompt, and then press *Enter*:

- `REG ADD HKLM\Software\Microsoft\Windows\CurrentVersion\Explorer /v NoPreviousVersionsRestore /t REG_DWORD /d 1`
- `REG ADD HKCU\Software\Microsoft\Windows\CurrentVersion\Explorer /v NoPreviousVersionsRestore /t REG_DWORD /d 1`

You can add the DWORD registry entry as part of a user's logon script. It's recommend that you add the DWORD entry to the `HKEY_LOCAL_MACHINE` subkey. This is for two reasons:

- The `HKEY_LOCAL_MACHINE` subkey is not overwritten by policy updates
- The `HKEY_CURRENT_USER` subkey can be written to by logon scripts that use nonadministrator permissions

As a DPM administrator, you should also always consider building a RaaS service via System Center Service Manager and the integration of System Center Orchestrator or Service Management Automation.

Setting up the DPM self service recovery for SQL

This recipe will cover how to configure and enable the end users to be able to restore SQL databases to an alternate location, using **DPM Self Service Recovery**.

Getting ready

The ability to restore your own databases as a SQL administrator is always an important task; this also applies to the fact that the restore scenarios are always performed via the same procedure by using a supported and easy-to-manage solution from System Center Data Protection Manager.

The user who is enabled to restore databases via the self-service feature should never be able to restore the databases to their original location, as this task is something that should be performed under controlled circumstances by the DPM administrator with the cooperation of the SQL database administrators.

 You can't use the self-service recovery feature on a client side if you have the DPM agent installed.

How to do it...

The initial step is for the DPM administrator to configure some DPM roles in **Self-Service Configuration Tool for SQL Server** that could be accessed from the **Protection** task area in the DPM console.

Click on the button at the top of the DPM console called **Self service recovery**, and the **DPM Self Service Recovery Configuration Tool for SQL Server** will open.

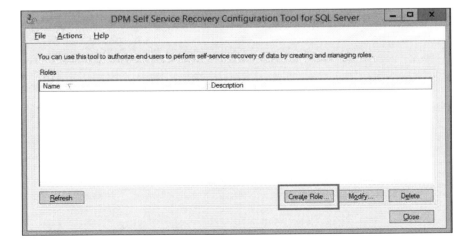

Click on the **Create Role...** button to get started.

The **Create New Role** wizard will open, which consists of five steps:

1. **Getting started**
2. **Specify security groups**
3. **Specify recovery items**
4. **Specify recovery targets**
5. **Summary**

In the **Getting started** step, click on **Next >** to continue.

Next is the **Specify security groups** step, where you should enter a **Role name** followed by a **Description**, and then **Add** a security group. Enter a name for the role that is easy to understand; the name could be part of the naming convention that is used for a specific service that you offer to your end users within your datacenter.

Type in a **Description** and add a security group by clicking on the **Add** button. Provide the information in the `domain\user` format; remember that multiple groups can be part of the same DPM role. Click on **Next >** to continue.

 When you click on the **Next >** button to continue, the DPM server will verify that the security group that you have entered is present in the Active Directory. If the DPM server can't find the security group, DPM will give you an alert.

In the **Specify recovery items** step, you must enter **SQL Server Instance or Availability Group** followed by **Database Name**. Click on **Add** and enter the **SQL Server Instance or Availability Group** name followed by **Database Name**; click on **Next >** to continue.

The last configurable step is **Specify recovery targets**; if you just click on **Next >** to continue, you will skip to configure the recovery target. If you don't configure the recovery target, the end users will still be able to restore the SQL databases as flat files to any location where they have permissions to write. In an environment where you are striving to create an orderly restore, you must define recovery targets; select the checkbox next to **Allow users to recover the databases to another instance of SQL server**. It is also very important to guide the restore process as much as possible; therefore, enter **SQL Server Instance** followed by **Recovered Files Path**, which is the file path where DPM should place the restored files.

 You can have multiple recovery targets.

Click on **Next >** to continue to the **Summary** step.

Verify your configuration and click on **Finish** to finalize the configuration. You will get a message saying **The DPM role configuration has been successfully saved**.

You now have the ability, via **DPM Self Service Portal**, to connect you to the DPM server and create **Restore job**, but first, you must install it on the client operating system.

Insert the DPM media and on the splash screen under **Install**, click on the **DPM Self Service Recovery** link.

 The Self Service Recovery depends on .NET and you need to have this operating feature installed for the installation process to continue.

Follow the installation guide and when it has successfully finished, you will have a new icon on your desktop called **Microsoft System Center 2012 R2 DPM Self Service Recovery Tool**. Start the application and connect to the DPM server that you previously configured the DPM role on.

Click on the **New Recovery Job...** button to initialize **Recovery Wizard**. Select the checkbox next to **Do not show this Welcome page again if you don't want to show the Welcome** step the next time. Click on **Next >** to continue.

Recovery Wizard consists initially of seven steps:

1. **Welcome**
2. **Specify database details**
3. **Specify recovery point**
4. **Select recovery type**
5. **Specify database state**
6. **Specify recovery options**
7. **Summary**

In **Specify database details**, you will be prompted with the available databases that the security group that your account is a member of has permissions to restore.

 You can always change a DPM role via the DPM console for any additional configurations required.

Choose **SQL Server Instance Name or Availability Group,** followed by **Database Name**, and click on **Next >** to continue.

In the **Specify recovery point** step, you choose the recovery point of the SQL database that you need to restore and click on **Next >** to continue when you have chosen the date, time, and the media that you should perform the recovery job from.

The next step is **Select recovery type**, where you can either choose **Recover to any instance of SQL Server** or **Copy to a network folder**. If you choose to recover to the SQL server, you will have an additional step in the wizard called **Specify alternate recovery location**. Click on **Next >** to continue.

 It's a design recommendation that you should let the SQL database administrators restore their databases to a restore SQL server.

In the configuration you made for the DPM role associated with the SQL database, you defined the instance and location of the restore jobs. This is the first thing that **Recovery Wizard** will resolve for you.

 You can have multiple recovery targets configured for one DPM role.

Choose your recovery location and click on **Next >** to continue.

Next is **Specify database state**, where you can either choose **Leave database operational**, which is the default option, or you can choose **Leave database non-operational** but able to restore additional transaction logs. Choose your option and click on **Next >** to continue.

In the **Specify recovery options** step, you can enter an e-mail address for notifications when the recovery job has finished. Click on **Next >** to continue to the **Summary** step, where you verify the summary before you click on the **Recover** button.

How it works...

The DPM self-service portal connects itself to a specific DPM server that the end user defines. From the connection, security group membership for the user domain account and configuration provided in the DPM roles, **Recovery Wizard** will provide you with the possible restore scenarios within a controlled restore job.

 All synchronization jobs on the destination server will be canceled during the recovery.

There's more...

You can monitor the recovery job via the DPM console or via the self-service recovery portal on the client.

10
Workgroup Protection and CBA

In this chapter, you will learn the following recipes:

- ▸ Understanding workgroup protection
- ▸ Understanding CBA protection
- ▸ Setting up workgroup protection
- ▸ Setting up certificate-based authentication

Introduction

In a datacenter, you will sometimes end up with non-domain attached servers that you need to provide a supported restore scenario for. System Center Data Protection Manager 2012 R2 will provide you with two different scenarios to leverage:

- ▸ Workgroup protection
- ▸ Certificate-based authentication

Workgroup protection is a simpler approach. This is suitable for scenarios where you need a quick and simple approach regarding simple non-clustered environments with a low security demand for a workgroup attached server.

Certificate-based authentication will be more suitable in the scenario where you need to provide a restore service for a nontrusted domain with higher security demands.

In this chapter, we will cover how to protect workgroup servers either via NTLM authentication or via certificate-based authentication, which is also known as CBA.

Understanding workgroup protection

This recipe will cover the information you need to understand both the prerequisites and also help you understand what could be expected from the workgroup protection approach for System Center Data Protection Manager 2012 R2.

Getting ready

Before you start to provide a restore scenario for your workgroup servers, you must understand the supported scenarios where you can use the workgroup protection.

Compared to the normal protection provided by DPM for domain joined servers, you will, for example, not able to protect clustered servers.

The workgroup server could also be a member of another domain that you don't trust. CBA is not a prerequisite for workgroup protection.

The following list can be protected via workgroup protection:

► Files
► System States
► SQL Server
► Hyper-V
► Primary DPM server via a secondary DPM server (DPM-DPM-DR)

You don't need to open any additional firewall ports to get started with the workgroup protection. The *Firewall configuration* recipe in *Chapter 1, Pre-installation Tasks* will provide you with the information you need to get communication configured between your DPM server and workgroup servers.

How to do it...

To be able to provide a restore scenario for your workgroup servers, you need to have the DPM agent installed on the targeted server that hosts the workload that you need to protect. System Center Data Protection Manager 2012 R2 also needs an authentication mechanism as the server is not domain-joined. This authentication mechanism resides in a local account and the configured setup via the DPM Cmdlets.

The DPM agent installation cannot be pushed from the DPM server; it must be installed manually due to it not being able to authenticate. For information regarding how to install a DPM agent manually, refer to the *Installing the DPM agent manually* recipe in *Chapter 3, Post-installation Tasks*.

If your company has IPSEC enabled, System Center Data Protection Manager 2012 R2 will adapt to that communication and will still be able to provide a restore scenario for the classified services within your modern datacenter.

When the DPM agent has been installed, you must configure it to use the NTLM authentication between the workgroup server and the DPM server and also define the DPM agent as **NonDomainServer**.

 The DPM agent uses NTLM CHAP v2 for workgroup protection.

When the DPM agent has been configured, you must attach the DPM agent to the DPM server either via the console or via the DPM management shell.

How it works...

The DPM server will use the local DPM account that is defined during the configuration phase and also provided by the DPM administrator during the attachment configuration to establish relations and trust between the DPM server and the protected data sources.

There's more...

The local service account created during the configuration phase of the DPM agent needs to update its password as well as the configuration on the DPM server side. This is accomplished via the updatepassword switch for the SetDpmServer Cmdlet.

Understanding CBA protection

This recipe will cover the information you need to understand both the prerequisites as well as what can be expected from certificate-based authentication for System Center Data Protection Manager 2012 R2.

A service provider must always be able to provide a restore scenario for data sources that reside in a domain that he or she does not trust. Looking at a normal company, the IT department should be seen as service providers and not IT professionals. Their job is to deliver optimal services to the company or organization in the most efficient way.

The following workloads can be protected using CBA:

- Files
- SQL Server
- Hyper-V
- Secondary DPM server

When protecting data sources that are clustered, you can protect them using certificate-based authentication. There are some limitations that are important in order to gain knowledge before setting up the protection. Currently, Microsoft does not support the protection of the Hyper-V environment using CSV volumes or DAG-configured Exchange servers.

How to do it...

The certificate-based authentication consists of four configuration steps:

1. Install a certificate.
2. Install the DPM agent.
3. Recognize the DPM server.
4. Attach the DPM agent.

You must also consider the following:

► Each computer you want to protect should have at least.NET Framework 3.5 with SP1 installed.

► The certificate you use for authentication must comply with the following:

  □ X.509 v3 certificate
  □ **Enhanced Key Usage** (**EKU**) should have client authentication and server authentication
  □ The key length should be at least 1024 bits
  □ The key type should be exchange
  □ The subject name of the certificate and the root certificate should not be empty
  □ The revocation servers of the associated Certificate Authorities should be online and accessible by both the protected server and DPM server
  □ The certificate should have an associated private key
  □ DPM shouldn't support certificates with CNG Keys
  □ DPM shouldn't support self-signed certificates

► Each computer you want to protect (including virtual machines) must have its own certificate.

How it works...

The authentication mechanism and trust is established via the usage of certificates and specific bin files that are created during the configuration of the DPM agent. The DPM server bin file must be copied from the DPM server to the BIN catalogue on the server that you want to protect. The bin file that is an output of the configuration steps for the DPM agent must be copied from the protected server to the DPM server's `windows/system32` catalogue.

See also

▸ For more information regarding System Center, refer to this blog: `http://robertandthecloud.blogspot.se/`

Setting up workgroup protection

This recipe will cover the steps you need to perform to configure workgroup protection for non-domain joined servers within your datacenter.

Getting ready

Read and understand the *Understanding workgroup protection* recipe in this chapter.

How to do it...

From an elevated Command Prompt, open the `bin` catalogue that resides in the installed DPM agent catalogue. The default path is `%systemdrive%\Program Files\Microsoft Data Protection Manager\DPM\bin`.

To configure the DPM agent, use the `setdpmserver.exe` executable with the `-isnondomain` switch.

 The local account is not a member of the local administrator group; it is a low privilege account.

Open an elevated Command Prompt and type as shown in the following screenshot:

```
setdpmserver -dpmservername DPMSERVERNAME -isnondomainserver -username
USERNAME
```

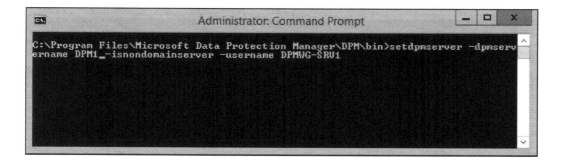

You will be prompted to provide a password for the local account. Enter the password and verify it in the next input question.

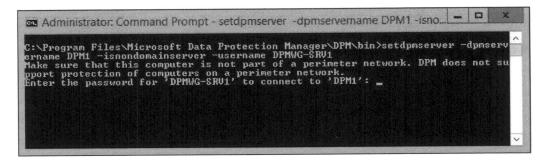

The `setdpmserver` executable will prompt you with the result. If you receive `Configuration completed successfully!!!`, then you know that all went well with the DPM agent configuration.

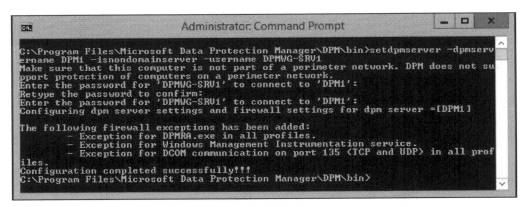

Now that you are finished on the client side, the next step is to attach the DPM agent to the DPM server. Open the DPM console, go to **Management**, and click on **Install** in the top-left corner of the DPM console. In **Protection Agent Installation Wizard**, click on **Attach agents** followed by **Computer in a workgroup or untrusted domain**. Click on **Next >** to continue.

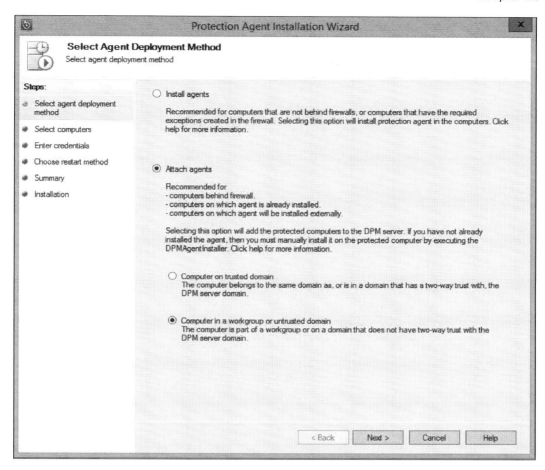

In the **Select computers** step, enter **Computer name**, **Username**, and **Password** and click on **Add >** to add the computer to the **Selected computers** list.

 You can only enter one server at a time.

Click on **Next >** to continue.

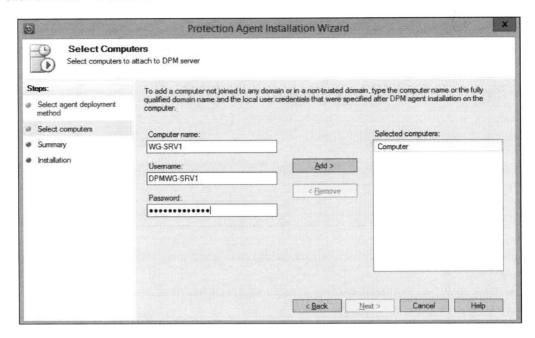

The next step is the **Summary** step, where you verify the configuration and click on **Attach** to attach the DPM server agent to the DPM server.

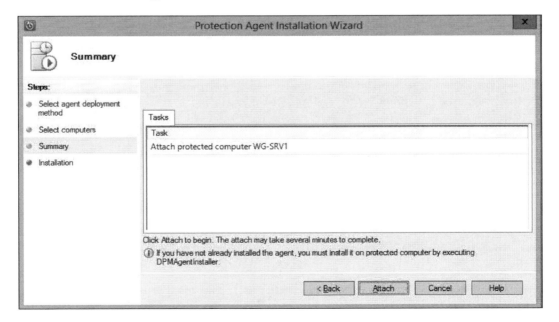

In the **Installation** step, you can follow the progress of the installation.

How it works...

Using the `-isnondomainserver` switch on the `setdpmserver` executable will create a local account on the workgroup server that you wish to protect using System Center Data Protection Manager 2012 R2. This account is provided both in the agent configuration as well as on the DPM server side; the DPM server authenticates to the DPM agent using the local credentials of the dedicated service account.

 Be sure to have a decent naming convention for the accounts that you use for workgroup protection.

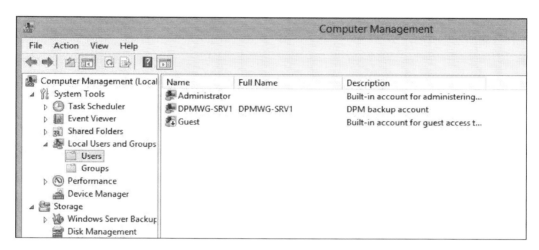

There's more...

When you want to create a Protection Group or include the workgroup server into an existing Protection Group, you will find the workgroup server under the Workgroup node.

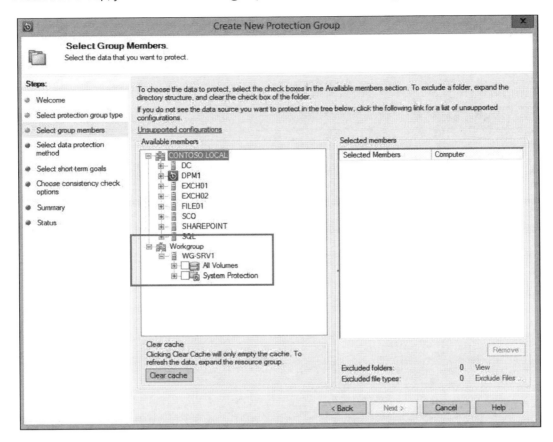

See also

▶ For more information regarding System Center, visit this blog: `http://robertandthecloud.blogspot.se/`

Setting up certificate-based authentication

This recipe will cover how to set up the certificate-based authentication protection, which is also known as CBA.

Getting ready

To be able to configure certificate-based authentication protection for your workloads in your modern datacenter, you need to have a **Certificate Authority** (**CA**) role installed with a **Clear Revocation List** (**CRL**) that both servers can access. This recipe will not cover the installation and setup of a CA; read this article for guidance: `http://technet.microsoft.com/en-us/library/cc731183.aspx`.

How to do it...

The protection process to get started with certificate-based authentication is divided in five steps:

1. Create a DPM certificate template
2. Configure a certificate on the DPM server
3. Install the DPM agent
4. Configure a certificate on the protected server
5. Attach the DPM agent to the DPM server

First, you must configure a certificate template that you can reuse when creating certificates for certificate-based authentication protection. It is important that the template has both client authentication and server authentication.

A recommended approach is to set up a template for web enrollment that is dedicated to the CBA feature in System Center Data Protection Manager 2012 R2. Open an MMC on your CA server and add the **Certificate Templates** snap-in. Find and right-click on the **RAS and IAS Server** template and select **Duplicate Template**.

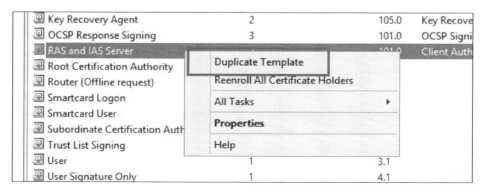

In the **Properties of New Template** window, leave the default settings for Capability settings.

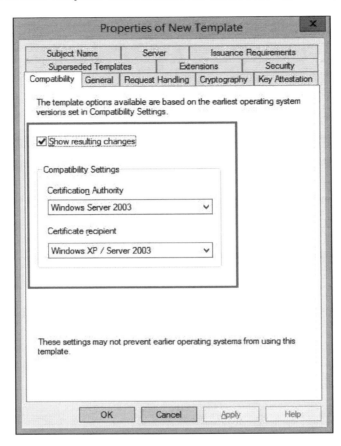

Go to the **General** tab and change **Template display name** to something more suitable.
Change **Validity period** to a timeframe that meets your organizations demands. Last,
select the checkbox next to **Publish certificate in Active Directory**.

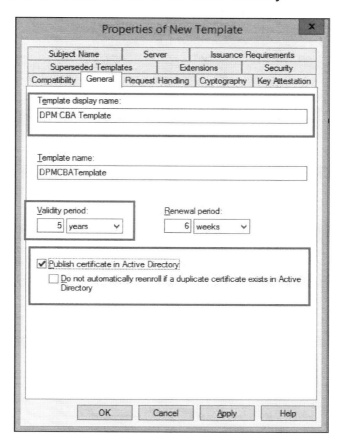

In the **Request Handling** tab, select the **Allow private key to be exported** checkbox.

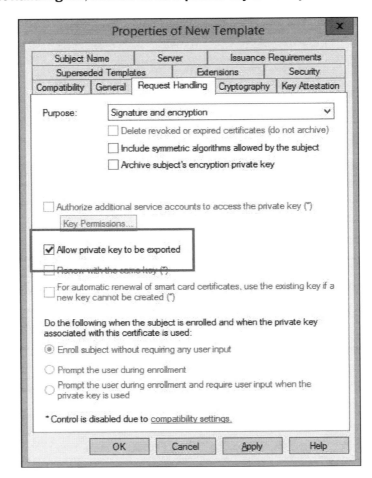

Click on **OK** to close **Properties of New Template**. Now, you must make the template available for use by opening the **Certificate Authority** snap-in in Microsoft Management Console.

Right-click on **Certificate Template** and choose **New** followed by **Certificate Template to Issue**.

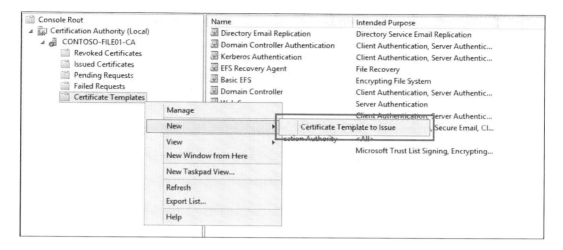

In **Enable Certificate Templates** window, select the previously created template and click on **OK**.

The template will now be available when you obtain a certificate.

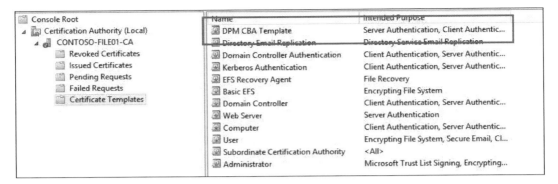

With that configured, you must now enroll the certificate. To do this, open the MMC console with the **Certificate Template** snap-in one more time. Double-click on your template and verify that **Build from this Active Directory information** is selected and **Common Name** is selected in **Subject name format** followed by **DNS name** on the **Subject Name** tab of the template.

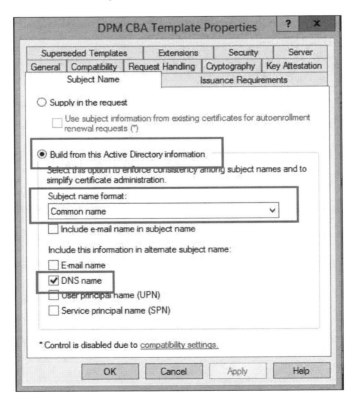

In the **Security** tab, verify that **Authenticated Users** have been assigned Enroll permission.

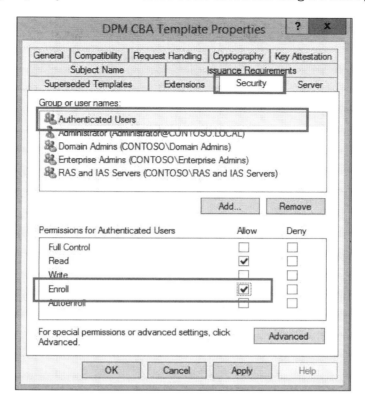

The next step is to request a certificate based on the template you previously created.

On the DPM server, open an MMC and add the **Certificates** snap-in with the focus of management of Computer account and Local computer. Expand **Personal** and right-click on **Certificate**; choose **All Tasks** followed by **Request New Certificate...**.

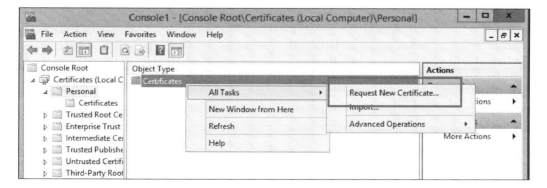

The **Certificate Enrollment** window will show you the before you begin information; click on **Next** to continue. In **Select Certificate Enrollment Policy**, mark **Active Directory Enrollment Policy** and click on **Next**.

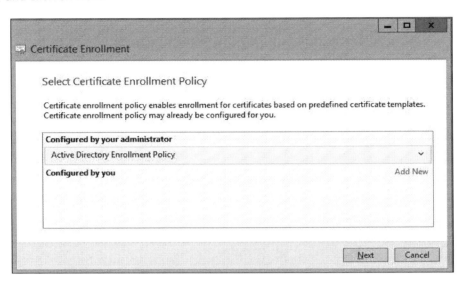

In the **Request Certificates** step, you check the template you created previously and click on **Details** followed by **Properties**.

In the properties of the template under the **General** tab, you should provide a **Friendly name** for the certificate, to make it easier to identify.

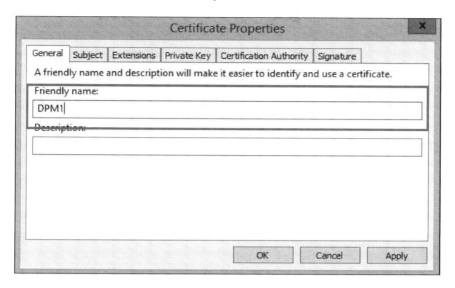

The enrollment process will begin, and it will provide you with the finished result within a short amount of time.

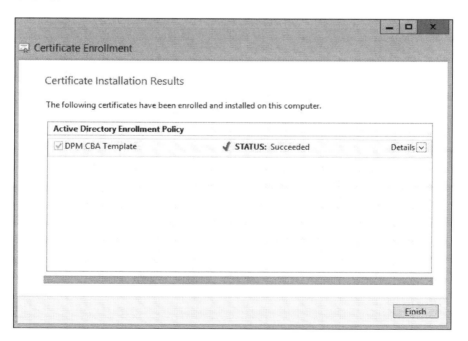

Click on **Finish** to quit the certificate enrollment. The certificate must reside in the `Local Computer\Personal\Certificates` store.

The next step is to configure the DPM server, so it will use the CBA option for communication. As the communication uses both certificates and specific generated BIN files, you need to have the thumbprint of the certificate in Local Computer.

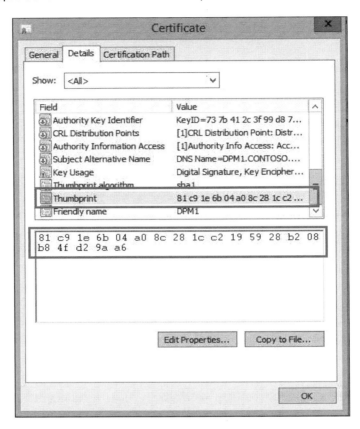

Mark the thumbprint and copy it, paste it to Notepad, and remove the spaces. This information is critical when configuring DPM in the next step.

Open the **DPM Management Shell** tool and use the `Set-DPMCredentials` PowerShell Cmdlet. The following syntax should be used when configuring the DPM server for certificate-based authentication:

```
Set-DPMCredentials -DPMServerName DPM1.contoso.local -Type Certificate -
Action Configure -OutputFilePath C:\ -Thumbprint YOURTHUMBPRINT
```

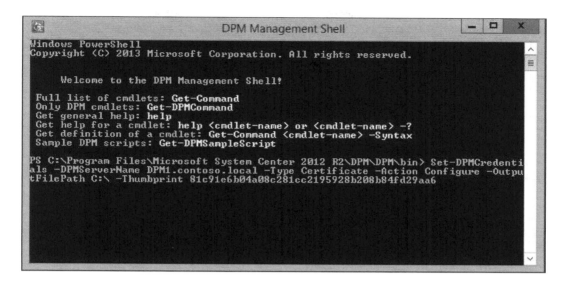

The BIN file that is created is located at C:\; copy the file into the BIN catalogue of the server that you want to protect using CBA as well as the BIN catalogue of the DPM server itself.

 When you paste the edited thumbprint from your Notepad, you may end up with an extra "?" in front of the actual thumbprint; remove this for your configuration to work.

You have now configured your DPM server for CBA using the BIN file and the certificate. If your BIN file is lost, you can regenerate it again using the -Action Regenerate switch in the Set-DPMCredentials setup.

 The CBA feature uses both TCP and UDP port 6076 for its wrapper service.

The next step is to install the DPM agent; read the *Installing the DPM agent via the DPM console* in *Chapter 3, Post-installation Tasks*. After the DPM agent has been installed, you must create a certificate for the untrusted server and configure the DPM agent.

Open your web browser on the server you want to protect and enter the URL for the CA. Choose **Request a certificate**.

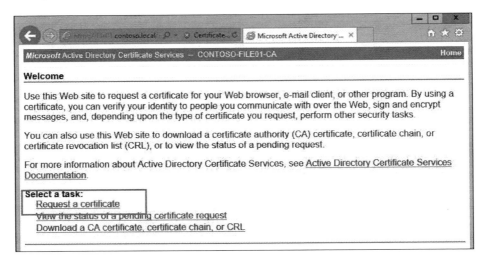

Next, choose to click on **advanced certificate request**.

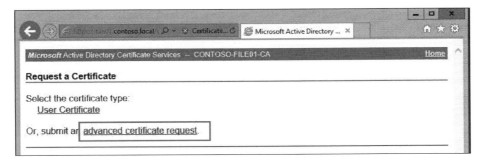

Click on **Create and submit a request to this CA**.

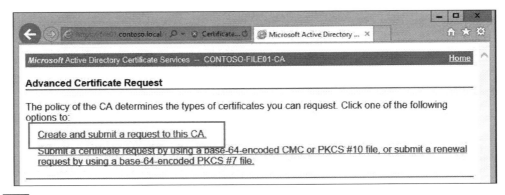

Using v3 certificate templates is not supported for web enrollment. To make your certificate template visible in the web enrollment browser, you need to change the certificate template under the Subject Name tab from Build this from Active Directory information to Supply in the request.

In **Advanced Certificate Request**, you choose your template from the drop-down list and provide a Name in **Identifying Information For Offline Template**.

Under **Key Options**, verify that the size is larger than 2048 and in the bottom, provide Friendly Name.

 Add the URL for the CA in the trusted sites for it to be able to run all the necessary scripts.

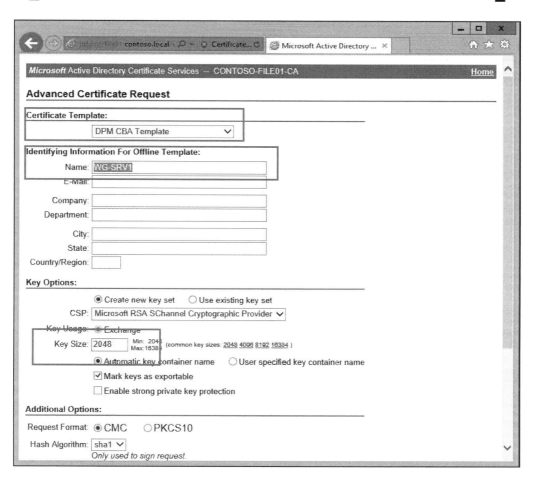

Click on the **Submit** button at the bottom of the page and the request for the certificate starts. When the request has finished, you will end up with the Certificate Issued page; click on **Install** this certificate.

The certificate will be installed under the current user personal certificate store. It needs to be exported. Right-click on the certificate and choose **All Tasks** followed by **Export...**; **Certificate Export Wizard** opens. Click on **Next** to continue. In the **Export Private Key** step, choose **Yes, export the private key**, and then click on **Next** to continue.

Choose the default options in **Export File Format** and click on **Next** to continue.

In the **Security** step, select the checkbox next to **Password** and enter a password; click on **Next** to continue.

In the **File to Export** step, provide a location and a name for the certificate; click on **Next** to continue.

Verify the configuration and click on **Finish** to export your certificate; remember the location and the name of the certificate. Now, you must import the certificate to the local computer store, right-click on **Personal**, and choose **All Tasks** followed by **Import...** to start the guide. Follow the steps and you will have the certificate imported.

Now, it's time to configure the DPM agent on the untrusted or workgroup server. Copy the thumbprint of the certificate we just imported and paste it into Notepad; remove all the spaces and keep it for later usage.

Open an elevated Command Prompt on your computer and run the `setdpmserver` executable with the following syntax:

```
SetDpmServer -DPMCredential CertificateConfiguration_
YOURDPMSERVERBINFILE.bin -OutputFilePath C:\ -Thumbprint
CERTIFICATETHUMBPRINT
```

It is now time to attach the DPM agent to the DPM server. Before you do this, you must copy the BIN file created on the workgroup or untrusted server to the DPM server's `Windows/system32` catalogue. When this is taken care of, you are ready to attach the DPM agent to the DPM server via **DPM Management Shell**.

The attachment process cannot be done via the DPM console GUI; it must be performed via PowerShell. Open **DPM Management Shell** and use the `Attach-ProductionServerWithCertificate.ps1` script.

How it works...

Certificate-based authentication uses both certificates and the bin files generated by the DPM server and the protected computer to verify the access.

See also

▸ For more information regarding how to create great restore scenarios, visit this blog: `http://robertanddpm.blogspot.com`

11
Azure Integration

In this chapter, we will cover the following recipes:

- ▶ Understanding the prerequisites for the Microsoft Azure backup service
- ▶ Configuring your DPM server for online protection
- ▶ Registering your DPM server
- ▶ Configuring the protection groups to enable online protection
- ▶ Manually creating online recovery points
- ▶ Recovering production data from Azure
- ▶ Troubleshooting Microsoft Azure Backup Agent

Introduction

With the System Center 2012 SP1 release, Microsoft presented a new feature that provided online protection that could easily integrate with the System Center Data Protection Manager server software. As Microsoft released the 2012 R2 version of System Center Data Protection Manager, great effort to optimize the online protection feature was made.

In the Microsoft Azure Management Portal, Microsoft created a service called backup vault that can easily be connected to both DPM servers as well as the WSB feature for Windows 2012 Server. Using certificates and explicit passphrases, Microsoft can assure not just a great feature to reduce the tape management for companies, but also a high degree of security. This chapter's recipes will walk you through the complete configuration of your System Center Data Protection Manager 2012 R2 server. We will cover how System Center Data Protection Manager 2012 R2 integrates with Microsoft Azure and provides an online protection for your datacenter.

The steps to get started are:

1. Sign up for Azure services
2. Install a Microsoft Azure Backup agent
3. Register your DPM server with the Azure service
4. Start protecting your production data

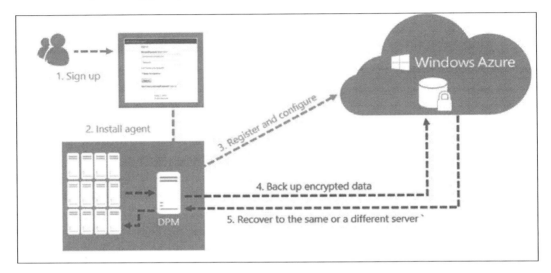

Understanding the prerequisites for the Microsoft Azure backup service

The online protection will provide you with a great opportunity to place your production data in Azure, which means that you can securely provide and fully optimize an offsite replication for the company production data that represents the datacenter's hosted services.

There are some considerations that you must keep in mind:

▶ The online protection is only available for primary DPM servers

▶ The retention time for your production data in Azure is 99 years

▶ You can protect Hyper-V, SQL, Client, SharePoint, Exchange, and File resources with the online protection

- You must have a DPM disk pool attached to the DPM server

- The restore process consists of two separate steps

- Microsoft Azure Backup Agent will use the Windows Identity Foundation 3.5 and Microsoft .NET Framework 4 features

The certificate used for the backup vault in Azure must fulfill the following prerequisites:

- To upload the certificate to the vault, you must export it as a `.cer` format file that contains the public key

- The certificate should be an X.509 v3 certificate

- The key length should be at least 2048 bits

- The certificate must have a valid Client Authentication EKU

- The certificate should be currently valid with a validity period that does not exceed 3 years

- The certificate should reside in the Personal certificate store of your local computer

- The private key should be included during the installation of the certificate

- You can create a self-signed certificate using the makecert tool or use any valid SSL certificate issued by a **Certification Authority** (**CA**) trusted by Microsoft, whose root certificates are distributed via the Microsoft Root Certificate Program

Configuring your DPM server for online protection

This recipe will cover how you should configure your DPM servers to enable online protection. We will use the Microsoft Azure Portal to create the Backup Vault, we will create certificates for secure authentication, and finally, we will download and install the Microsoft Azure Backup Agent.

Getting ready

Before you can register your DPM server, you need to have **Backup Vault** up and running in Azure. First, you must register an account for Azure services; you can register an account at this URL: `http://azure.microsoft.com`.

How to do it...

Go to your DPM console and click on **Management** followed by the **Manage subscription** button in the top-left section of the console.

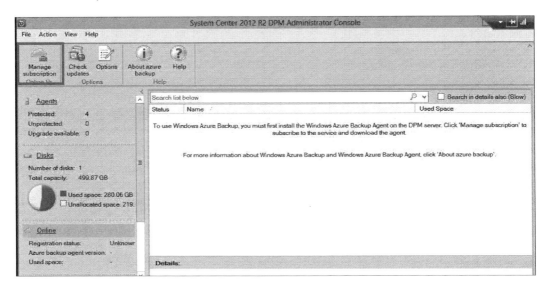

Your DPM server will open the Microsoft Azure web page; provide your credentials to log in.

First, you must register **Recovery Services**. To do this, click on **Recovery Services** on the left-hand side of the Azure portal.

Next, create your **Backup Vault** by clicking on the **CREATE A NEW VAULT** link in the middle of the portal.

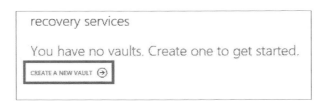

A new interactive screen opens, and you should click on **BACKUP VAULT**.

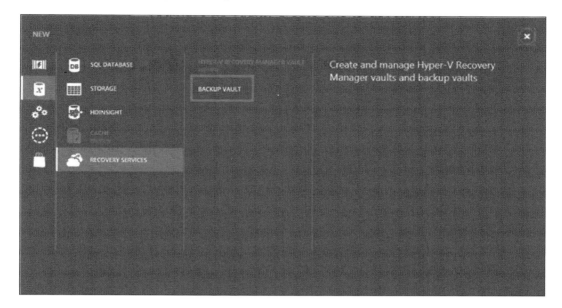

Click on **QUICK CREATE**.

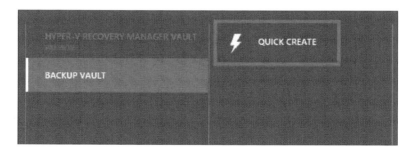

Enter a **NAME** for the backup vault and choose the **REGION** for which Microsoft Azure datacenter should host your service. To finish your configuration, click on **CREATE VAULT**.

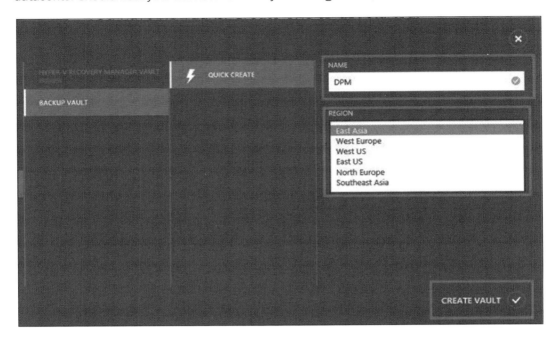

In the Azure portal, you will now notice the backup vault being created. When Azure is finished, the **STATUS** value will change from **Creating** to **Active**.

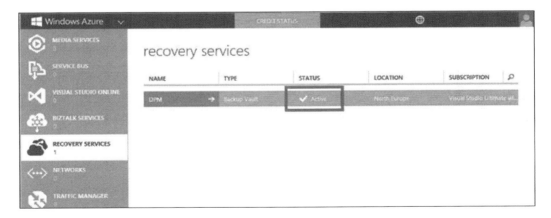

Now, it's time to create a certificate that must be used between your DPM server and your backup vault in Microsoft Azure. You should use the `MakeCert.exe` executable that is available as part of the Windows SDK, which you can download from this URL: `http://msdn.microsoft.com/en-US/windows/desktop/bg162891`.

Open an elevated Command Prompt window and use the following syntax for your certificate configuration:

```
makecert.exe -r -pe -n CN=CertificateName -ss my -sr localmachine -eku
1.3.6.1.5.5.7.3.2 -len 2048 -e 01/01/2016 CertificateName.cer
```

Change the `CertificateName` to any name you prefer.

Keep in mind that the certificate must:

- ▸ Have a key length of 2048 bits
- ▸ Have a valid validity period that does not exceed 3 years

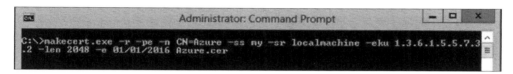

The certificate will be placed under the same catalogue as the `MakeCert.exe` executable. Next, you must upload the certificate to your Microsoft Azure backup vault. Go to your **Microsoft Azure Management Portal** web page to provide the certificate to the Microsoft Azure Backup Vault. Click on **Manage Certificate** in the center of the Microsoft Azure Portal.

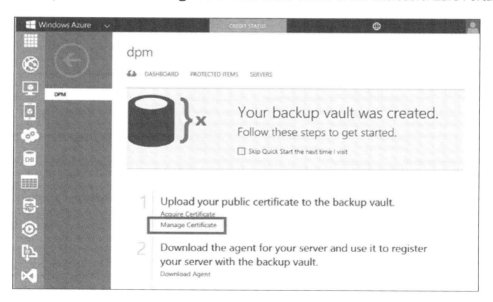

Browse the certificate you just created and click on the checkmark to continue.

The certificate will now be uploaded to **Microsoft Azure Backup Vault**. When your certificate has successfully been uploaded to your **Microsoft Azure Backup Vault**, you must install **Microsoft Azure Backup Agent**. Click on the **Download Agent** link to continue.

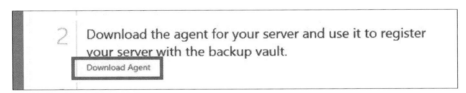

Next, you must choose which version of the Microsoft Azure Backup Agent you want to download and install. Choose the Microsoft Azure Backup Agent for **Data Protection Manager** and click on the checkmark to continue.

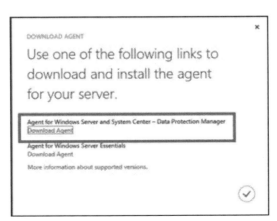

The Microsoft Azure Backup Agent will be downloaded after you have chosen your download options. Click on **Run** to continue.

You will be prompted with **Supplemental Notice**. Choose **I accept the terms of the Supplemental Notice**. Then, click on **OK** to start the installation of the Microsoft Azure Backup Agent.

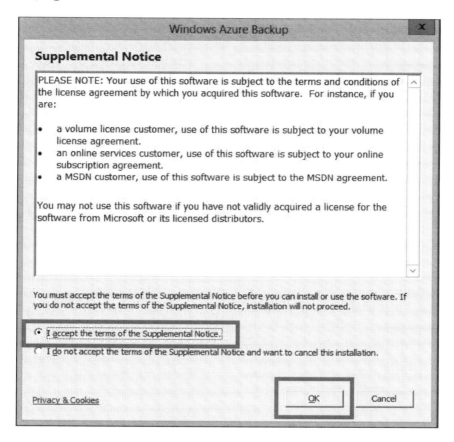

The Microsoft Azure Backup Agent consists of three steps:

1. **Prerequisites Check**
2. **Installation Settings**
3. **Installation**

You will be prompted with **Prerequisites Check**, that verifies that you have the **Windows Identity Foundation** feature installed on the DPM server and **Microsoft .NET Framework 4**. If these features are not installed, they will be installed by the prerequisites checker. Click on **Next** to continue.

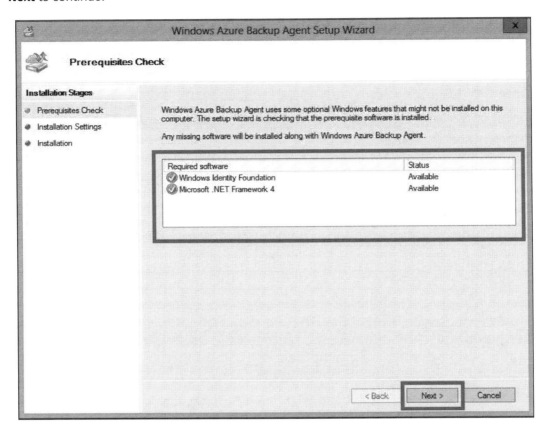

Under the installation settings, you can configure the installation path for the Microsoft Azure Backup Agent and **Cache Location**. Microsoft Azure Backup Agent must have a cache location to keep track of the files the DPM server backs up. The Microsoft Azure Backup Agent must have at least 2.5 GB of local free space for the cache location, but 15 GB is recommended.

Click on **Install** to continue the installation of the Microsoft Azure Backup Agent.

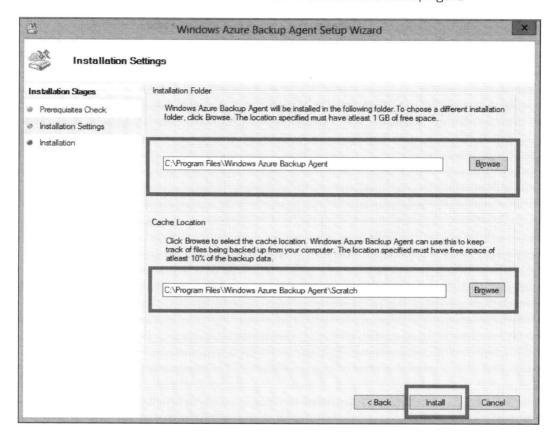

After the installation has finished, it will present a summary. The next step is the registration of your DPM server.

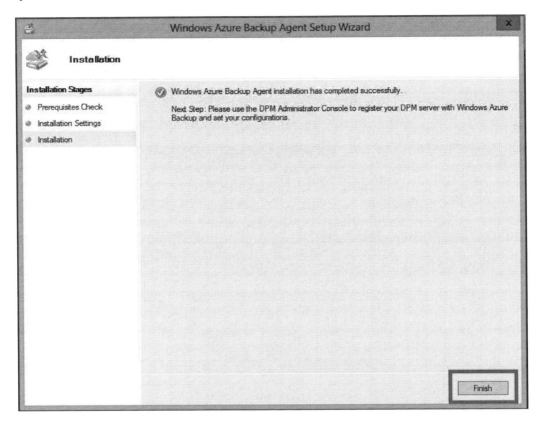

Registering your DPM server

In the previous recipe, we performed the required configurations that make it possible to start using the online protection provided by Microsoft Azure. This recipe will cover how to register your DPM server with the Recovery Services within Microsoft Azure.

How to do it...

Open the DPM console, and on the left-hand side, choose **Management**, then choose **Online** followed by **Register** in the top-left part of the console.

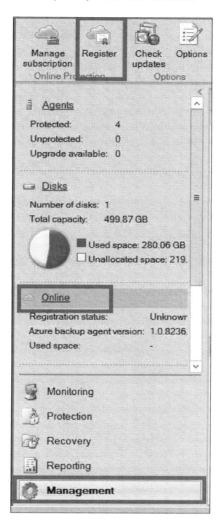

Click on **Browse** to point out your certificate.

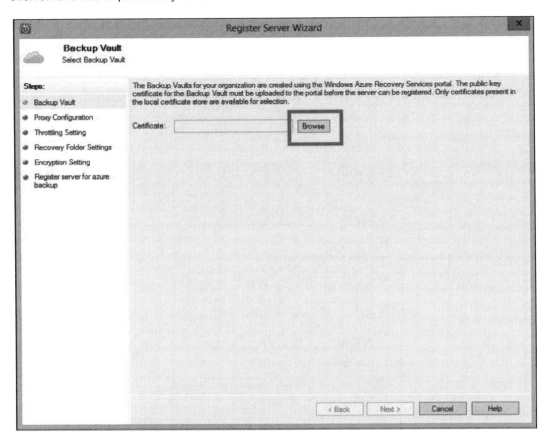

Choose the certificate you just created by marking it, and click on **OK**.

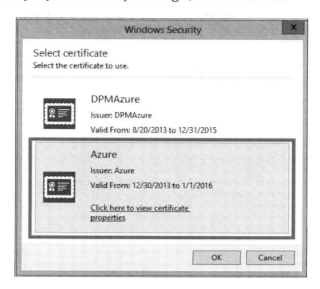

Now, choose your backup vault and click on **Next >**.

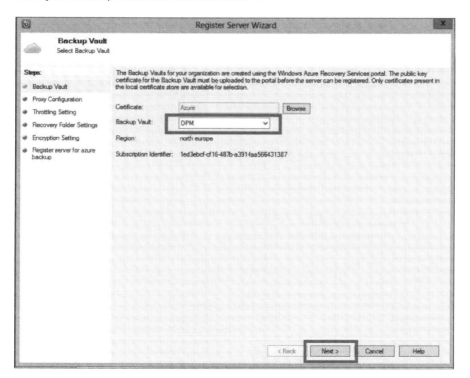

In the next step, you have the option to configure **Proxy Configuration**. Enter the address, port, and (if needed) the username and password used by your DPM server so the Microsoft Azure Backup Agent can communicate with your Azure service. When you are finished, click on **Next >** to continue.

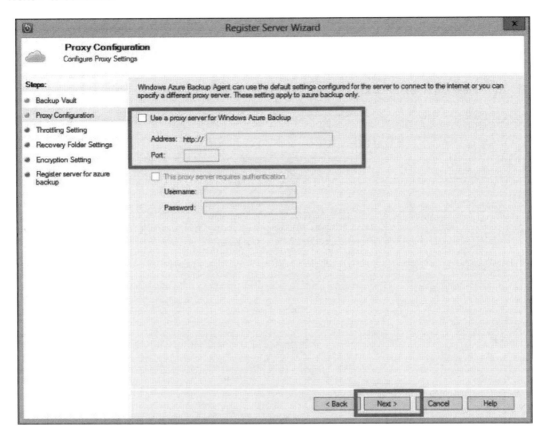

In the next step, you will configure **Throttle Setting** for your Microsoft Azure Backup Agent. If you have the scenario of a limited network bandwidth, you have the possibility to define your business hours and the amount of bandwidth the Microsoft Azure Backup Agent should consume. When you have finished your configuration, click on **Next >** to continue.

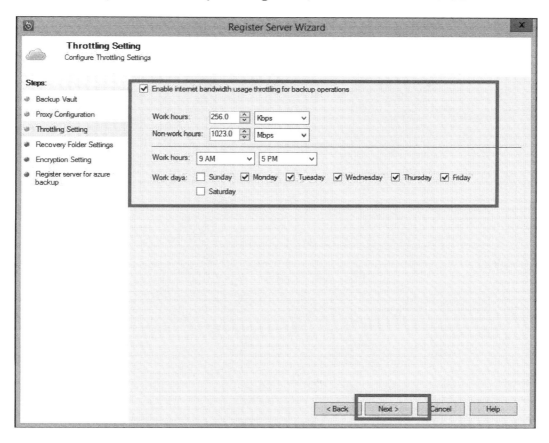

Recovery Folder Settings will help you define where you want to temporarily place the restored data from Azure before you let DPM move the data from the recovery folder to the production servers via the DPM agent. A recommendation is to use a separate disk for this purpose; click on **Browse** to point out your catalogue and click on **Next >** to continue to the next step.

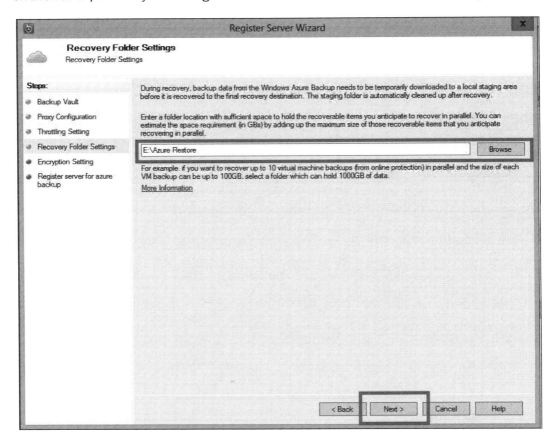

In the **Encryption Setting** step, it is important to remember one thing: copy the passphrase to the clipboard. Click on **Generate passphrase** followed by **Copy to clipboard**. You will receive a message that your passphrase has been copied to the clipboard. It is now a very good idea to open Notepad and paste the passphrase from the clipboard, save the file, and print the file and lock it away. Click on **Register** to register your DPM server with your Backup Vault.

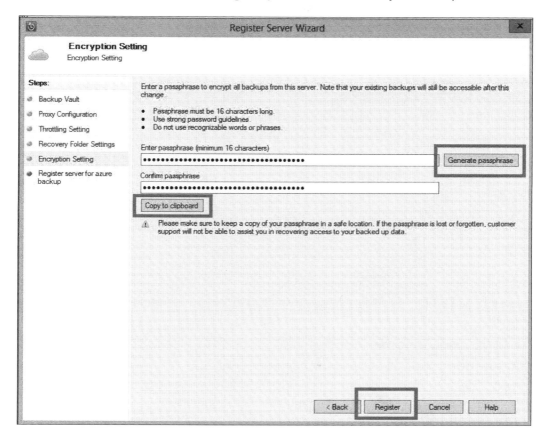

You will receive a message that your DPM server is successfully configured to use your backup vault in Azure. Click on **Close** to continue to the next step; enable the online protection.

Configuring the protection groups to enable online protection

After you have registered your DPM server with your Azure Backup Vault, you are ready to configure your protected production data. This recipe will cover how to start protecting the workloads present in your datacenter and enable them for online protection.

Getting ready

What's worth mentioning again is that you can place the following workloads in your backup vault:

- ▶ SQL
- ▶ Hyper-V
- ▶ SharePoint
- ▶ Client
- ▶ Exchange
- ▶ File

You can either create a new Protection Group or modify an already configured Protection Group for online protection. In this example, I already have a Protection Group and will show you how to add the online protection for my DPMDB that is a SQL database that is supported for online protection.

How to do it...

The modify wizard for a Protection Group contains a few steps that are specific to online protection. The first one is the **Select data protection method** step.

To enable the online protection for your protected production data, just select the checkbox for **I want online protection** followed by **Next >**.

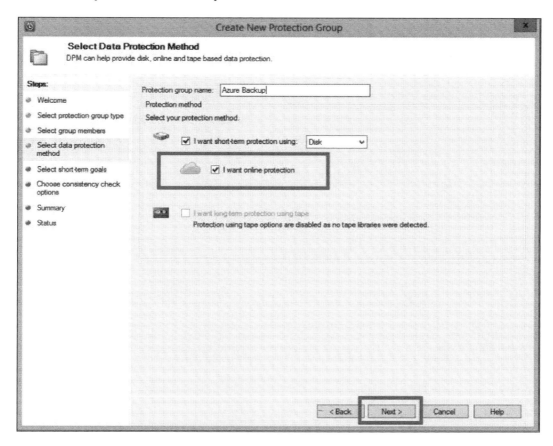

The second step is **Specify online protection data**. In this step, you will choose which workloads you would like to enable for online protection. Select the checkbox for your production data and click on **Next >**.

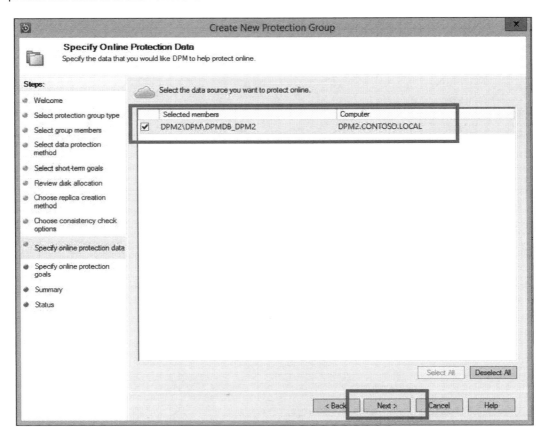

The next step is **Specify online protection goals**. Here, you can define your online protection goals using a daily or weekly synchronization frequency. As mentioned previously, you have the possibility to store data for 99 years and also to synchronize your DPM server data twice per day.

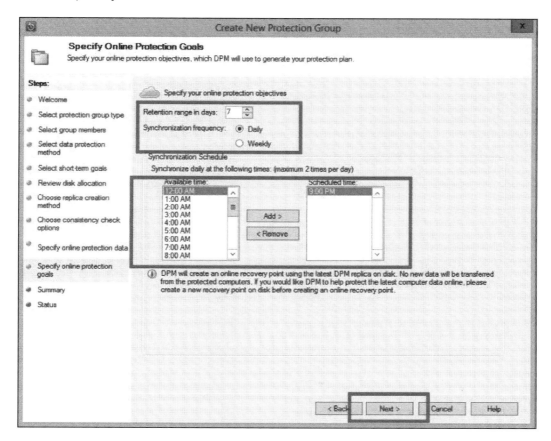

For the weekly synchronization frequency, you can choose specific weekdays and decide whether the synchronization should occur weekly or biweekly. You can have your DPM server synchronize your protected data up to every 4 weeks.

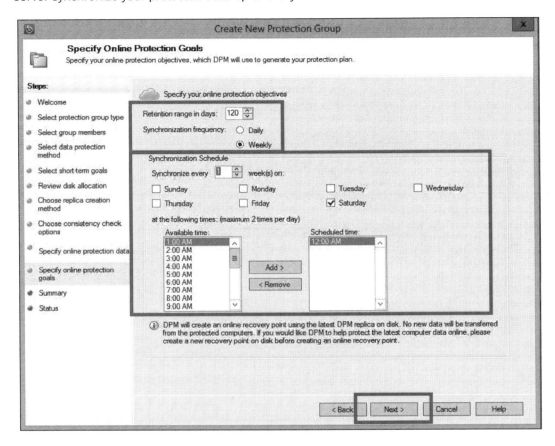

After you have run through these steps, you will notice that your production data is set to **Enabled** for **Online Protection** in the DPM console.

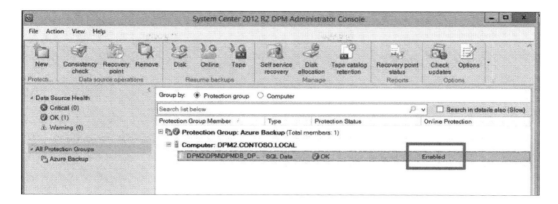

Now, you have provided online protection and archiving. To enable the online protection with the retention of 99 years, you must add the UR5 for DPM 2012 R2. More information can be found at this URL: `http://blogs.technet.com/b/dpm/archive/2015/02/11/update-rollup-5-for-system-center-2012-r2-data-protection-manager-is-now-available.aspx`.

Manually creating online recovery points

This recipe will cover how to manually create a recovery point for archiving purposes and automatically replicate it to your associated Recovery Service in Azure. This requires that you complete all configuration that is presented in the previous recipes of this chapter.

Getting ready

In some scenarios, you want to manually create recovery points for your production data. The prerequisites are that you have the online protection enabled for the data source(s) present in your Protection Group.

How to do it...

To create a recovery point manually for your protected production data, right-click on the data source and choose **Create recovery point...**.

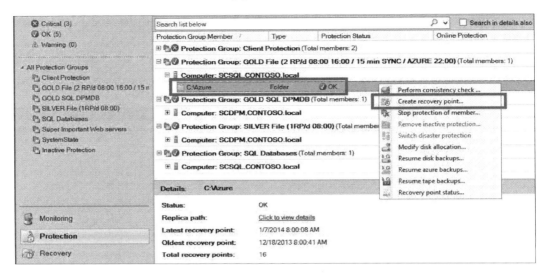

You will now be prompted with the **Create recovery point** wizard. Choose **Online protection** from the drop-down menu, followed by clicking on the **OK** button.

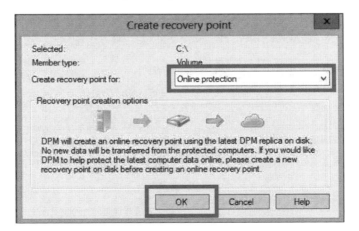

Now, your DPM server will create a backup and store it in Azure; you can follow the progress in the **Create Recovery Point** task window.

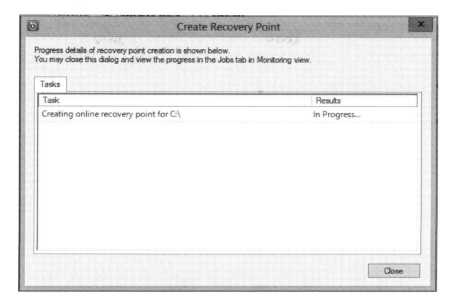

The progress can also be monitored in the DPM console monitoring display.

 Always keep in mind that bandwidth is very important. It's always important to verify your network performance from on-premises to Azure via your **Internet Service Provider** (**ISP**). You can use the tool available at `http://azurespeedtest.azurewebsites.net` to verify your network latency depending on your closest Azure datacenter.

Recovering production data from Azure

The main purpose of creating a backup of production data is to be able to restore it. This recipe will provide the information needed to restore production data from Microsoft Azure to your production environment.

Getting ready

As mentioned in the introduction of this chapter, the restore process from Azure is a two-step process for DPM. During the registration phase, we pointed out something called **Recovery Folder Setting**; now this folder comes into play during the restore process. As mentioned, the focus of DPM is to be an easy restore function in a modern datacenter; this also applies to the Azure restore operations.

How to do it...

To restore your production data from Azure, you must go to **Recovery** within the DPM console.

On the left-hand side of the console, you will find your protected data sources both active and inactive. Start by expanding the tree so that your data source will be visible; in my case, this is the C drive of my SQL server.

Next, you must choose the right date followed by choosing the right time from the drop-down list.

Finally, to start the restore, right-click on the data source and choose **Recover**.

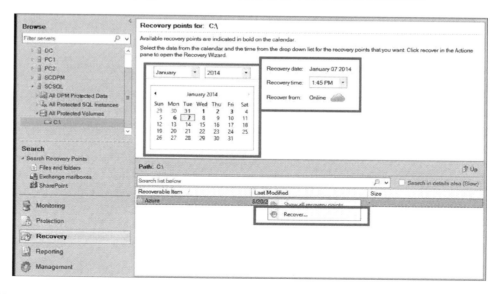

Recovery Wizard will open and present the actual restore process. Click on **Next >** to continue.

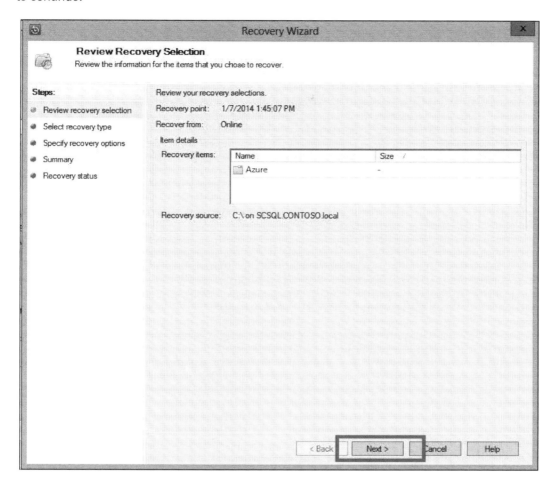

Now you need to choose the recovery type for the restore operation. You can choose to restore the data to its original location or an alternate location; in this example, I will choose to restore my data to its original location. Mark the radio button and click on **Next >** to continue.

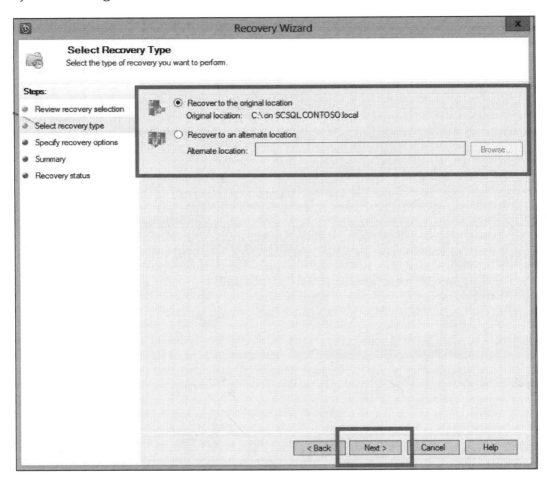

Last, you must choose **Specify recovery options**, which will manage your **Existing version recovery behavior**, **Restore security** settings, and so on. Click on **Next >** to get to **Summary**.

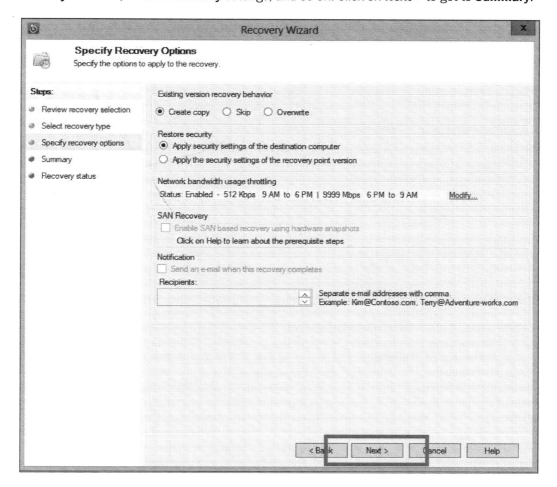

In the **Summary** step, you need to verify your suggested restore operation. If it fits your needs, click on the **Recover** button to start the recovery process.

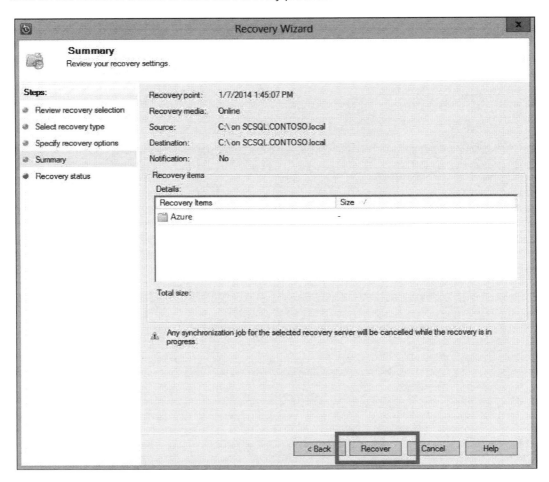

During the restore process, you can either monitor the work progress in the **Recovery status** window or in the DPM console under **Monitoring** and apply the **All jobs in progress** filter.

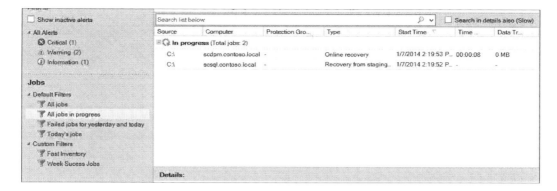

When the restore operation is finished, DPM will raise an alert regarding the status of the restore job indicating the status of the restore. In this case, the restore was successful, so the DPM server raised an informational alert.

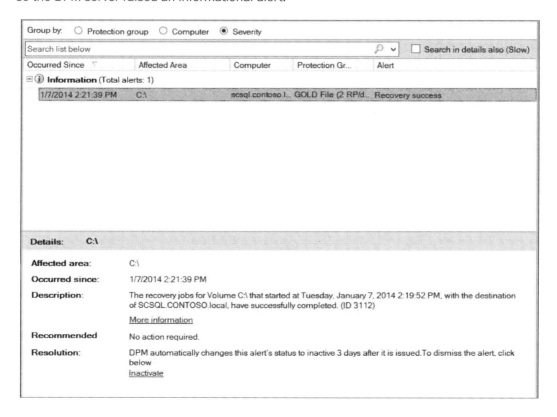

Keep in mind that Azure is applicable for all kinds of company sizes. An example is for the company to be able to perform a daily or weekly backup of the DPMDB; this is a great example of how a DR scenario for DPM could look like.

Troubleshooting Microsoft Azure Backup Agent

There are several steps in the process of getting the Microsoft Azure Backup Agent operational; this recipe will cover troubleshooting for the following scenarios:

- ▶ Installation
- ▶ Network connectivity

How to do it...

For a successful installation of Microsoft Azure Backup Agent, these prerequisites must be met:

- ▶ The account that is being used to install Microsoft Azure Backup Agent is a member of the local Administrators group on the server or has been granted the similar permissions
- ▶ Microsoft Azure Backup Agent is supported to be installed on Windows Server 2008 R2 SP1 operating systems and higher
- ▶ Always use the latest version that you can download from the Microsoft Azure Management Portal

If the prerequisites are met and you are facing challenges with the network connectivity, you should start your troubleshooting by verifying the following:

- ▶ Check whether you can connect to the Internet from your DPM server
- ▶ Verify your firewall rules so that they allow communication from the DPM server on port 443
- ▶ If your company has a proxy server, you should verify the configuration
- ▶ Use the **Network Monitoring** tool to start troubleshooting more advanced network connectivity issues

12
Disaster Recovery

In this chapter, we will cover the following recipes:

- ▶ Understanding the primary/secondary DPM server scenario
- ▶ Enabling a DPM server to be a secondary DPM server
- ▶ Enabling the chaining of DPM servers
- ▶ Understanding the replication process from the primary to secondary DPM server
- ▶ Switching from the primary to secondary DPM server
- ▶ Restoring data from a secondary DPM server
- ▶ Restoring a DPM server

Introduction

Disaster recovery has been a natural component of the business continuity plan for many years. The most important fact to realize is that disaster recovery can be presented in many shapes and can also be transformed over a period of time within companies and organizations.

System Center Data Protection Manager 2012 R2 can be designed and implemented by applying the disaster recovery concepts. Use a primary DPM server that manages your on-premises workloads, which builds up services and replicates the services' data dependencies to a secondary site. There, leveraging the concept of executing a failover if the primary protection fails is one part of the many disaster recovery scenarios that System Center Data Protection Manager 2012 R2 can provide to your business continuity plan.

The most important fact regarding planning disaster recovery scenarios is that there is no best practice that you can apply. Building and planning disaster recovery concepts requires hard work, but a successful disaster recovery concept is worth it, big time. The secret of delivering a successful disaster recovery plan is pre-studies, planning, processes, having a good understanding of dialogues, and knowing the software limitations.

In this chapter, we will cover how to set up disaster recovery by using primary and secondary DPM servers, also known as DPM-DPM-DR designs.

Understanding the primary/secondary DPM server scenario

This recipe will cover the information needed for you to understand the concepts of a primary and secondary DPM server scenario, also known as DPM-DPM-DR.

Building a disaster recovery design using the DPM-DPM-DR approach needs some initial consideration. The very first thing to check or decide is whether all protected data sources on the primary DPM server should be replicated to the secondary DPM server and whether they will be enabled for disaster recovery.

The most important part here is to understand that there are no best practices—nothing that you can simply download and just apply. Determining what protected workloads should be enabled for a disaster recovery scenario must come from the pre-study and classification process of the services' data dependencies. You must perform a classification that will define the retention time or the level of synchronization or recovery point creation but is also enabled for disaster recovery.

Enabling a DPM server to become a secondary DPM server is a simple process and will be covered in the *Enabling a DPM server to be a secondary DPM server* recipe in this chapter.

The secondary DPM server will replicate the primary DPM server recovery points for protected data sources. The secondary DPM server can protect more than one primary DPM server. This is important to remember when implementing the disaster recovery scenario. A DPM server could also be enabled for chaining, which means that it is both a primary and a secondary DPM server.

There are several different scenarios where a classic DPM-DPM-DR scenario could fit, but the most common one for the chaining feature is its ability to act as a primary DPM server within datacenter A and also replicate the protected data to datacenter B, which is located in another part of the country or the world.

 Using the Backup Vault in Azure also could be considered a light version of implementing disaster recovery.

The most efficient way to create a truly optimal disaster recovery scenario based on the DPM-DPM-DR scenario, is to leverage the power of Hyper-V and to build virtual DPM servers that will map into the **Disaster Recovery as a Service** (**DRaaS**) instance and when more resources are needed, an automated installation process will initialize.

Enabling a DPM server to be a secondary DPM server

This recipe will cover how to enable the DPM-DPM-DR scenario, which means enabling the secondary DPM server feature, so that you can build a disaster recovery site for your organization or company.

Getting ready

In the scenario that your datacenter needs additional protection from a disaster recovery scenario, you can provide protection in numerous ways. One way is to provide a secondary DPM site where your production data can be located in the scenario of a disaster of your primary datacenter.

There are two different approaches that a secondary DPM sever could be used for:

- ▸ Chaining
- ▸ Cycling

The chaining approach is the traditional primary secondary DPM server approach, where the primary DPM server is the dedicated primary protection for all datacenters and locations.

Enabling the secondary protection is a two-step process that consists of the following steps:

- ▸ Connecting the secondary DPM server with the primary DPM server
- ▸ Choosing what protected data sources on the primary DPM server should be replicated to the secondary DPM server

How to do it...

1. To enable a DPM server to become a secondary DPM server, it must be connected to the primary DPM server. On the DPM server that should become a secondary DPM server in the protection process, go to **Management** view and click on **Agents**. In the top-left corner of the console, click on the **Install** button to start **Protection Agent Installation Wizard**.

2. In **Select Agent Deployment Method**, click on **Install agents**, followed by the **Next >** button.

3. The next step is **Select Computers**. DPM will list all the computers that are members of the same domain that the DPM server is a member of. Add the primary DPM server that holds the data that you want to enable for disaster recovery protection. Click on **Next >** to continue.

 A secondary DPM server can protect multiple primary DPM servers.

4. **Enter Credentials** is the next step, and now you must enter an account that has administrative rights to the server that you would like to install the DPM agent to. If you have selected a node within a cluster, DPM will then prompt you with the possibility to install DPM agents to the other cluster members that are discovered via the cluster service. When you have entered the credentials, click on **Next >** to continue.

5. In the **Choose Restart Method** step, you can choose whether the DPM server should be restarted or not after the connection from the secondary DPM server has been made to the primary DPM server. There is no need for you to restart your primary DPM server when you are attaching the secondary DPM server; this is just an optional step of the wizard. Choose the option that you see fit and click on **Next >** to continue.

6. In the **Summary** step, you can verify the information and click on **Install** to initialize the installation and configuration process of the DPM agent.

7. When you have attached the secondary DPM server to the primary one, you are ready to enable the disaster recovery protection for the selected workloads that the primary DPM server is protecting or all of the primary protected workloads. To enable a workload for a disaster recovery protection, you must create **Protection Group** on the secondary DPM server and include the primary protected workloads.

8. On the secondary DPM server, go to **Protection** and in the top-left corner of the console, click on **New** to create a new **Protection Group** via **Create New Protection Group Wizard**.

9. In the **Welcome** step, click on **Next >** to continue to **Select protection group type**; choose **Server** and click on **Next >**.

10. The next step is **Select group members**, where you will see all the servers that have an attached DPM agent. Expand your primary DPM server; your primary protected data sources will be listed under the **Protected Servers** node.

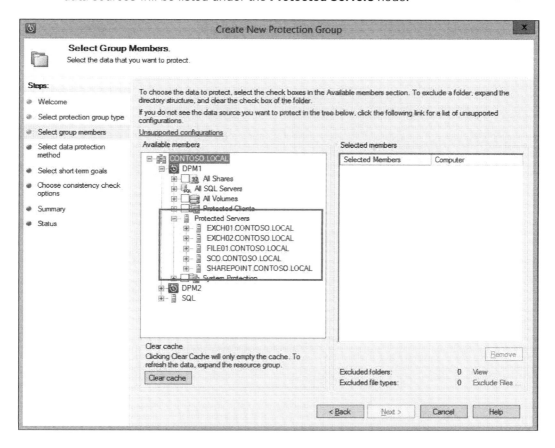

11. Choose the primary protected data sources that you want to enable for secondary protection and click on **Next >** to continue. You will be prompted with a friendly reminder to protect the primary DPM server database, if this is unprotected.

12. Next is the **Select data protection method** step, where you choose to use either the disk and tape or just the disk. Remember to provide an optimal naming convention for your **Protection group name**. Choose the option that meets your needs and click on **Next >** to continue. In this recipe, we will cover the disk and tape options.

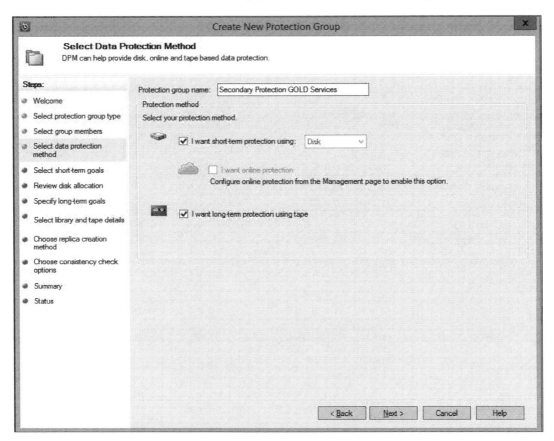

 The Azure service Backup Vault is currently just available on a primary DPM server.

13. In the **Select short-term goals** step, you define:

- Retention days
- Synchronization frequency

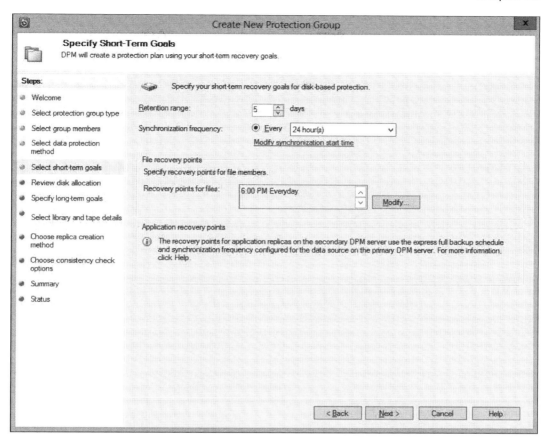

14. Enter the number of days that you would like to store the primary protected data on your secondary DPM server and also adjust the synchronization frequency to meet your business continuity plan. Regarding the secondary DPM server protection for Applications: they are protected without you having to decide the actual time for synchronization. When it comes to files, you can change the actual time for the replication; this is done by clicking on the **Modify...** button. Adjust the time schedule to fit your needs and click on **OK** to get back to the former wizard step. Click on **Next > ** to continue.

 You can optimize a protection group via the staggering function and also the on-the-wire-compression feature. Click on the link named Modify synchronization start time in the wizard.

15. The next step is the **Review disk allocation** step. System Center Data Protection Manager will suggest the disk space needed for you to protect your primary protected data sources. If you wish to change the disk allocation, click on the **Modify...** button. In the **Review disk allocation** step, you can also enable the Co-location feature by selecting the checkbox next to **Co-locate data in DPM Storage Pool**.

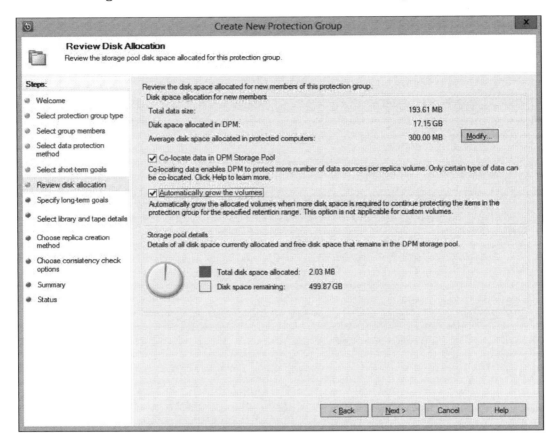

16. One of System Center Data Protection Manager's auto-heal functions is the auto-grow feature. To enable this feature, simply select the checkbox next to the **Automatically grow the volumes** checkbox. Click on **Next >** to continue to the next step.

 The Co-location feature is only available for the SQL, Hyper-V, and Client protection.3

17. The next step is **Select long-term goals**. Define your long-term goals and click on **Next >** to continue.

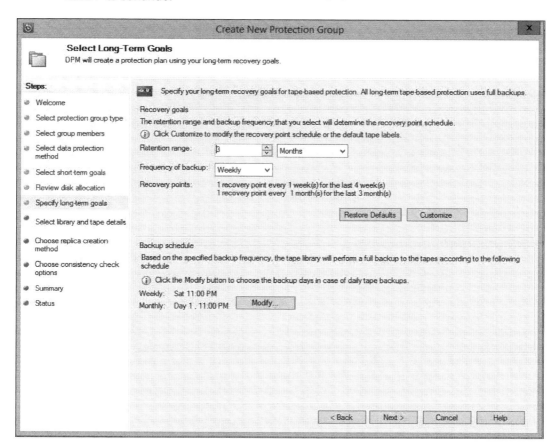

For more detailed instructions regarding long-term goal configurations, read the *Configuring tape optimization for DPM* recipe in *Chapter 13, Tape Management*.

18. The next step is **Select library and tape details**, where you configure the last tape configurations for the protection group.

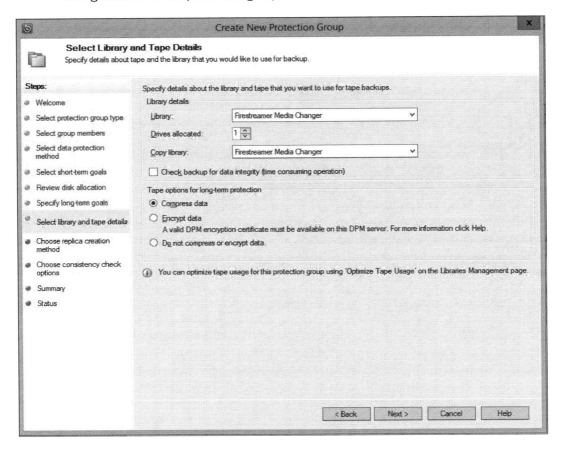

Choose the appropriate tape configuration and click on **Next >** to continue.

19. The next step is **Choose Replica Creation Method** and here is where you decide how or when the actual replica should be created on your secondary DPM server.

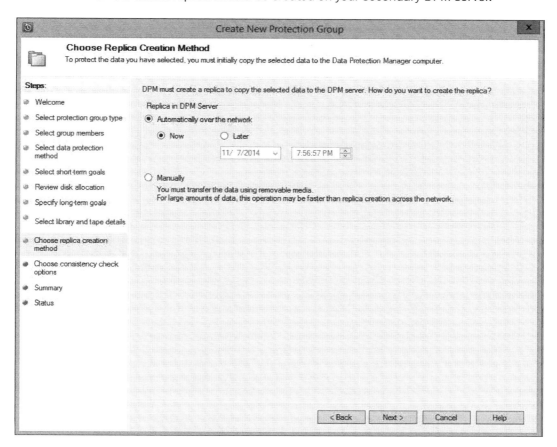

You are now able to create the Now replica, which means that after **Protection Group Wizard** is finished, the replica creation will start. You can also choose to schedule the replica creation process or create it manually. Click on **Next >** to continue to the next step.

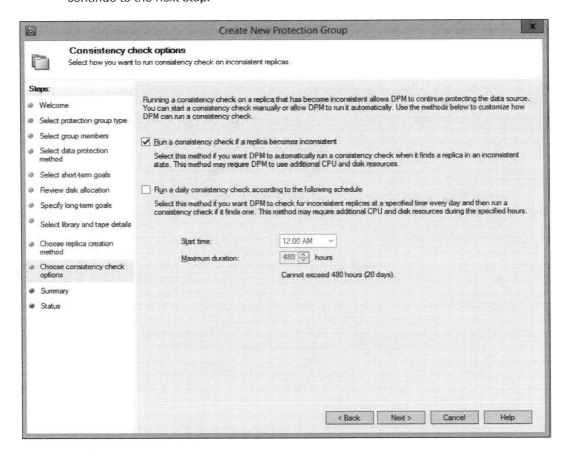

20. The next step is **Choose consistency check options**, where you are able to enable a second auto-heal function for DPM. By default, the checkbox next to **Run a consistency check if a replica becomes inconsistent** is the second auto-heal function. You can also schedule a consistency check to start on a daily bases. When you have finished your configuration, click on **Next >** to continue.

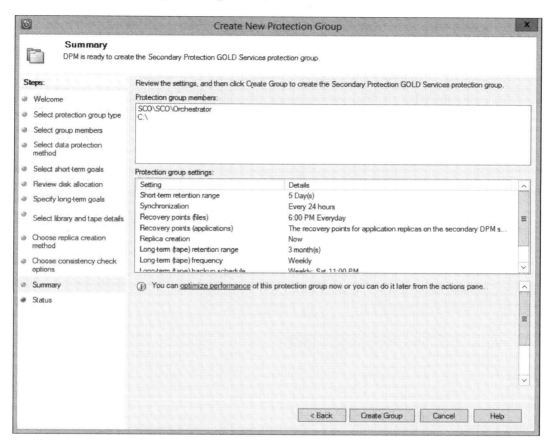

21. In the **Summary** step, you verify your configuration and click on the **Create Group** button to create your Protection Group.

How it works...

The installation process is more or less just an attach procedure, and just using the attach option instead of the install option will also work just fine.

The secondary DPM server will query the primary DPM server-specific VSS writer called DPM writer, which will create the replication process from the primary DPM server to the secondary.

There's more...

As System Center Data Protection Manager uses the DCOM objects to initialize the DPMRA services to provide a VSS request from the DPM agent, it is critical that the secondary DPM server is also a member of the selected groups and configurations on the server that hosts the protected data source as the primary DPM server.

Enabling the chaining of DPM servers

This recipe will cover what chaining of DPM servers is and also how to set it up.

Having multiple datacenters is, in many cases, necessary for your business to be able to provide a true disaster recovery scenario or solution.

How to do it...

Enabling chaining between DPM servers is done via installing or attaching the primary DPM server to the secondary DPM server. In the scenario that you have two DPM servers that are either located in two physical locations or are protecting one half of the datacenter each, you need to enable a disaster recovery solution that makes it possible for one DPM server to be both primary for its protected data sources and also a secondary DPM server for the other DPM servers protected data sources:

1. On each DPM server that should become a secondary DPM server in the protection process, go to the **Management** view and click on **Agents**. In the top-left corner of the console, click on the **Install** button to start **Protection Agent Installation Wizard**.

2. In **Select Agent Deployment Method**, click **Install agents** followed by the **Next >** button.

3. The next step is **Select Computers**. DPM will list all the computers that are members in the same domain that the DPM server is a member of. Add the primary DPM server that holds the data that you want to enable for disaster recovery protection. Click on **Next >** to continue.

A secondary DPM server can protect multiple primary DPM servers.

4. **Enter Credentials** is the next step and you must now enter an account that has administrative rights of the server that you would like to install the DPM agent to. When you have entered the credentials, click on **Next >** to continue.

5. In the **Choose Restart Method** step, you can choose whether the DPM server should be restarted or not after the connection from the secondary DPM server has been made to the primary DPM server. There is no need for you to restart your primary DPM server when you are attaching the secondary DPM server to the primary; this is just an optional step of the wizard. Choose the option that you see fit and click on **Next >** to continue.

6. In the **Summary** step, you can verify the information and click on **Install** to initialize the installation and configuration process of the DPM agent.

How it works...

The installation process is more or less just an attach procedure and just using attach instead of install will also work just fine.

The secondary DPM server will query the primary DPM server-specific VSS writer. This VSS writer is called DPM writer, and it will create the replication process from the primary DPM server to the secondary.

There's more...

The most important part regarding enabling features in a product is to actually map them to the corresponding business need. It's a very poor and frankly, a very bad idea to enable a lot many features if there is no actual need.

Understanding the replication process from the primary to secondary DPM server

This recipe will cover the information needed to understand how the replication process will vary for different workloads between a primary and a secondary DPM server.

With the intention to build a disaster recovery solution for your company, it is crucial that you have knowledge of how the DPM server software will operate when replicating the protected data sources data from a primary DPM server to a secondary DPM server.

The primary DPM server will have its backup schedule, which will map the actual definition of the restore plan that is presented in the business continuity plan for the company. When enabling a secondary DPM server protection, either via chaining or standard DPM-DPM-DR protection, the DCOM object managing the DPMRA service will be updated with the secondary DPM server computer account. This makes it possible for the secondary DPM server to make a secondary copy of the protected data.

 The secondary DPM server will replicate the primary protected data sources that lie on the primary DPM Server. The secondary DPM server will create its copy from the data that resides on the primary DPM server.

When setting up a protection group on your secondary DPM server that includes primary protected data sources from the primary DPM server, enable the DPM-DPM-DR scenario.

The secondary DPM server will start its replication of the primary DPM servers' protected data sources every midnight. Using the staggering function for protection group optimization is a good way to push the replication starting point forward in time.

You must always keep in mind that the product that you use to build up your disaster recovery solution will never be better than the actual design that you have decided. Mix the different solutions or products provided in the System Center suite and Microsoft Azure.

Switching from the primary to secondary DPM server

This recipe will cover how to switch a secondary DPM server to a primary DPM server for a protected data source.

Building a disaster recovery solution also includes controlled failover tests between resources that are part of the plan. This is also applicable to the DPM-DPM-DR scenario that you build up by using primary and secondary DPM servers.

The most common problem, when building a disaster recovery scenario, is that companies and organizations miss the fact that they must verify that their disaster recovery strategy really works on a regular basis. In DPM, this can be verified really easily, either via the DPM server console taking ownership of a protected workload, or via PowerShell creating an automated scenario that will adapt to the business continuity plan that is set and regulated within the company.

How to do it

On the secondary DPM server, you open the DPM console and navigate to the **Protection** view of the console. Right-click on the data source for which you want to change the DPM server protection, and choose **Switch disaster protection** from the drop-down list.

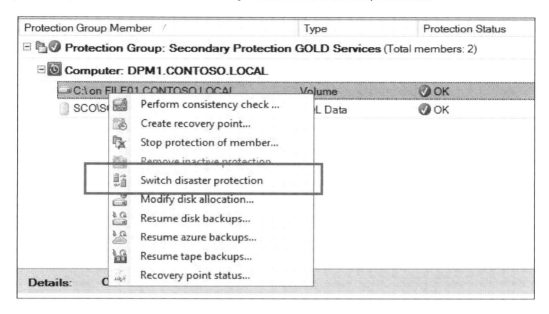

You will be prompted with a warning box, making you aware of the fact that you are about to switch protection from the primary DPM server to the secondary DPM server.

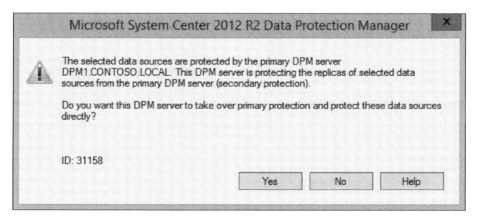

Click on **Yes** to start the switch protection job. The **Switch Disaster Protection** window will open and keep you informed of the progress of the job; you can also monitor the job in the Monitoring view of the DPM console using the **All jobs in progress** filter.

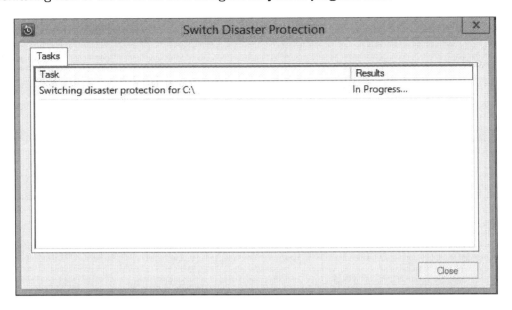

After the job has completed, you will see a significant change in the secondary DPM server console. The switched protected data sources will be listed in the DPM console with the **Protection-Switched** attribute.

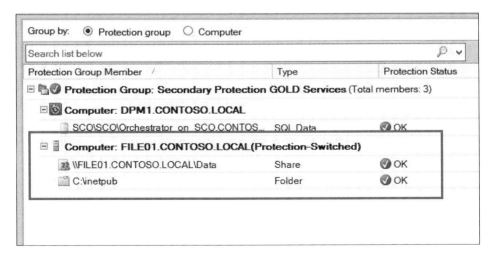

The reasons for which you want to switch your protection from a primary DPM server to a secondary DPM are two most common scenarios:

▸ Your primary DPM server has crashed

▸ You want to restore data to its original location from a date or point in time that only resides in a recovery point on the secondary DPM server

To switch back the protection, right-click the data source and choose **Switch disaster protection** and a similar warning box will appear; the context now has changed.

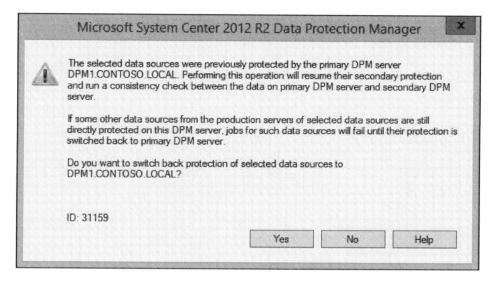

Click on **Yes** to switch back to what was previously the primary DPM server to continue to use it as the primary choice of protection.

How it works...

When you switch the protection for a protected workload or data source from a primary DPM server to a secondary DPM server, the secondary DPM server will communicate to the protected data source DCOM object that it should initialize the actual process of making it the primary DPM server for the protected data sources.

The secondary DPM server must have network access to the primary protected data source to be able to verify access to the DCOM object.

In the former primary DPM server, an alert will be raised with the message that the former primary DPM server is no longer the primary protection for the data sources that reside in or build up the workload.

There's more...

The process of switching the protection from a primary DPM server to a secondary DPM server can only be performed on a data source level; you cannot switch an entire protection group. If there's a need to switch all protected data sources on a secondary DPM server, you can use either automation via SMA, System Center Orchestrator, or strict PowerShell.

Restoring data from a secondary DPM server

This recipe will cover how to restore data from a secondary DPM server and what limitations there are.

Getting ready

The concept of having a primary and secondary DPM server is based either on the standard DPM-DPM-DR scenario or on chaining. The result has the protected data sources that are hosted by the workload application on a secondary off-site location.

How to do it...

In the secondary DPM server console, go to the **Recovery** view and choose the data source, the point in time for the restore, and right-click on the object and choose **Recover...** to start **Recovery Wizard**.

The Recovery Wizard consists of five steps:

1. **Review Recovery Selection**
2. **Select Recovery Type**
3. **Specify Recovery Options**
4. **Summary**
5. **Recovery Status**

In **Review Recovery Selection**, DPM will present to you the data source that you have chosen to restore. Verify the information and click on **Next >** to continue.

The **Select Recovery Type** step provides you with the options available for the restore job. You can choose to restore the secondary protected data sources to:

- ► **Recover replica to primary DPM server**
- ► **Original location**
- ► **Alternate location**
- ► **Copy to tape**

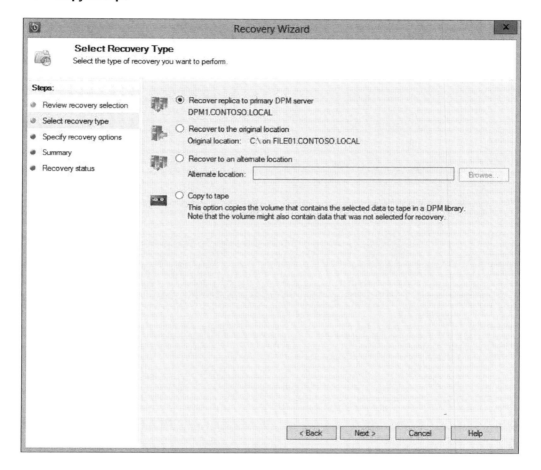

Choose the option that will apply to your restore job and click on **Next >** to continue.

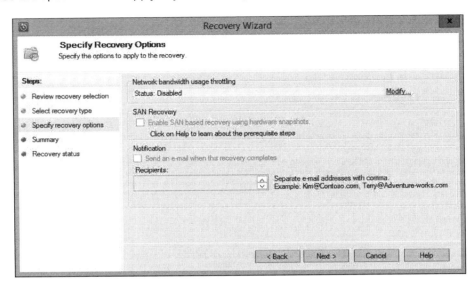

Specify the recovery options in the **Specify Recovery Options** step and click on **Next >** to continue.

In the **Summary** step, verify the restore job configuration and click on **Recover** to start the recovery job.

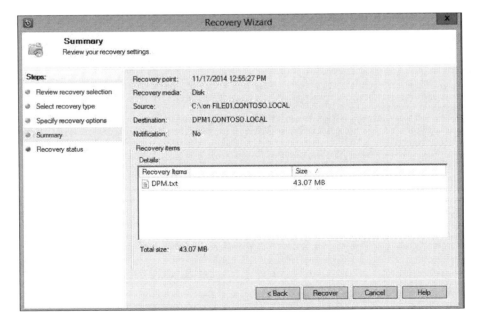

You can keep track of the progress via the **All jobs in progress** filter located in the **Monitoring** view of the DPM console.

How it works...

When you perform a switch operation on a protected data source that resides on a primary DPM server, the secondary DPM server reaches out to the DCOM object managing the DPMRA services on the server hosting the DPM agent and providing it with the information that the previously secondary DPM server is now the new primary DPM server.

There's more...

For more information regarding how to use the switch operation, refer to the *Switching from primary to secondary DPM server* recipe in this chapter.

If you want to restore the secondary protected data source to its original location, you must first switch the protection. If you forget to perform the switch operation, you will get this error message as a friendly reminder:

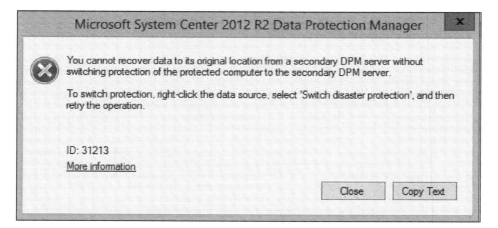

Restoring a DPM server

This recipe will cover how to restore a DPM server.

The most important component of a DPM server is the DPMDB database. It is very important that you have a clear and working strategy for how you provide reliable protection for it.

Getting ready

There are two critical facts that you must consider when restoring a DPM server:

- ▸ The DPM disk pool is in a healthy state
- ▸ You must have a good backup of the DPMDB

How to do it...

There are two scenarios:

- ▸ Restoring the DPMDB from a secondary DPM server
- ▸ Using the DPMSYNC executable

The first approach is quite straightforward. From the secondary DPM server, you simply choose to restore the primary DPM server DPMDB to its original location. When the job is done, you run the DPMSYNC executable with the -SYNC switch before you open the DPM console.

The second approach is to restore a dumped version of the DPMDB by using the DPMSYNC executable with the -RestoreDb switch. Remember to also run the DPMSYNC executable with the -SYNC switch before you open the DPM console.

How it works...

The best way to provide good protection for a DPMDB is to use a secondary DPM server that will provide protection for the primary DPM server database.

 The switch to create the local SQL dump via the DPMSYNC executable has been removed, as this operation should or could be made via the SQL Server Management Studio.

There's more...

For more information regarding System Center, visit this blog: http://robertanddpm.blogspot.com/.

13
Tape Management

In this chapter, we will cover the following recipes:

- ▸ Understanding the basics of tape backups
- ▸ Installing tape libraries and stand-alone tape drives
- ▸ Understanding the concept of VTL
- ▸ Understanding how DPM manages tapes
- ▸ Configuring tape optimization for DPM
- ▸ Understanding tape reports in DPM
- ▸ Configuring the short erase feature
- ▸ Understanding tape management tasks

Introduction

Tapes have been the definite archive media for many years and will probably continue to be used for this purpose for many years to come. What seems to be the most natural transition for backup and restore operators is to migrate the archive feature to other solutions, such as **Backup Vault** in Azure. For more information regarding the Backup Vault Azure recovery service, refer to *Chapter 11, Azure integration*.

In this chapter, we will cover tape management in System Center Data Protection Manager 2012 R2 and provide you with the information to get started with archiving your data to tape media. It will teach you the basics of tape management and some more advanced concepts of configuring, tape optimization, and last but not least, report handling.

Understanding the basics of tape backups

This recipe will cover the basics of tape usage for backups. If you are new to backup and restore solutions, this recipe will provide you with the core concepts presented in the easiest manner.

All organizations or companies have important production data that is either online or accessible, which needs to be protected and archived. System Center Data Protection Manager 2012 R2 will provide you with the features needed to let you have a rich experience providing archiving and backing up your product data to the tape. The most important part regarding tape backups is to determine the production data that should be archived in some manner. The organization must have a classification done prior to the actual implementation; the production data that is critical or has major impact on the company's business continuity plans should be archived. A rule of thumb, never archive production data if there is no need. It will only incur more cost on the organization in the long run compared to having an actual strategy of what data needs to be, or should be archived.

System Center Data Protection Manager 2012 R2 protects its data by making the data source an explicit member of **Protection Group**. A protection group can be seen as backup jobs' configuration regarding time, specific options that are related to the type of workload, and how to archive data on a tape using **long-term protection**.

If you have a standalone tape drive, tape library, or a virtual tape library, you will be provided with two additional steps in **Protection Group Wizard** when modifying or creating a new protection group. These are:

1. Specify long-term goals
2. Select library and tape details

In **Specify long-term goals**, you define your **Recovery goals** and **Backup schedule**. DPM will provide you with a default value for the recovery goals' configuration, that is, a **Retention range** for three months and a weekly backup. If the default recovery goal configuration does not meet your requirements, you can simply click on the **Customize** button and enter the number of recovery goals that you want and also create a customized label. There is a slight chance that the recovery goals can occur at the same time; this can be managed by choosing an appropriate option in the **Option** part of the **Customize Recovery Goal** window. A recovery goal can have a backup frequency that can be **Yearly**, **Monthly**, **Weekly**, or **Daily** with the maximum **Retention range** limit up to 99 years. It is also possible to have a copy library option that will provide an offsite backup to another location.

The last part that you can choose to configure if you are not satisfied with the default options is the **Backup Schedule** by clicking on the **Modify...** button in the **Specify long-term goals** step of **Protection Group Wizard**.

You can have up to three different recovery goals based on the grandfather-father-son relationship.

In the **Select library and tape details** step, you have the possibly of configuring a dedicated tape library if you have many present in your DPM server. The number of **Drivers allocated** and **Copy Library** can be configured per **Protection Group**. If you are about to protect or archive confidential data, you have the chance to provide the DPM server with a dedicated certificate that will encrypt the written data. It is critical that you do not lose the certificate as it is the key component of your restore capabilities. You can also compress the data that is written to the tape, but it is impossible to both compress and encrypt the data written on to the tape. There is a built-in data integrity to check the DPM server technology that will verify the data written to the tape; keep in mind that this is a time-consuming process, but is critical if you need to ensure the data consistency.

System Center Data Protection Manager 2012 R2's main focus is to deliver a rich and stable restore function for your modern datacenter or private cloud. Microsoft is accomplishing this by not using incremental technology when writing data to a tape; instead, the DPM server will allocate two tapes per **Protection Group** and write a full backup to the tape. This will result in a longer backup time, but you will gain speed when performing a restore as you are not using the incremental restore chain of tapes.

Installing tape libraries and stand-alone tape drives

This recipe will cover the installation process of a standalone tape drive, tape library, or **Virtual Tape Library** (**VTL**), as well as how to make it available for the DPM server.

Getting ready

System Center Data Protection Manager 2012 R2 is compatible with the majority of tape libraries and standalone tape drives present on the market. The reason is that DPM has a standard SCSI communication that all hardware vendors use.

 To verify that the tape library is compatible, run the DPM compatibility tool `DPMLibraryTest.exe`. Download the tool from this URL: `https://onedrive.live.com/?cid=885774776d4f197a&sc=documents&id=885774776D4F197A%21128`.

How to do it...

After you have installed the hardware, you boot up your DPM server and open **Device Manager**. If you have installed a tape library, you should see both the media changer and the provided tape drives. Keep in mind that some hardware vendors are rebranding other vendors' hardware, and sometimes, this makes it a bit more challenging to find the suitable driver for the media changer and/or tape drives.

> With the UR3 for DPM 2012 R2, the synthetic fiber channel support is working, and this will make it possible to provide a physical tape library to a virtual DPM server that is using Hyper-V as its hypervisor.

How it works...

After the hardware shows up without any failure in **Device Manager**, you can open your DPM console. Go to **Management and Libraries** and click on the **Rescan** button in the top-left section of the console. In the window that pops up, click on **Yes** to continue and when the rescan operation is finished, it will prompt you with another window. Click on the **OK** button to close the dialogue. Your tape library, standalone tape drive, or VTL should now be visible in the DPM console.

> For some vendors' needs, you should also refresh the console before the tape library, standalone tape drive, or VTL is visible in the DPM console.

There's more...

Microsoft has not provided a hardware-compliant list or HCL for DPM. The approach is more that if the vendors are using Microsoft-certified drivers, you will know that it will work and is compatible with the DPM software.

Another trick to verify that the hardware is supported with the usage of DPM is to verify that the driver could be found in the Microsoft catalogue services that you can access via this URL: `https://catalog.update.microsoft.com/v7/site/Home.aspx`.

In the scenario where you have multiple secondary DPM servers that have enabled the DPM-DPM-DR scenario for your organizations' protected data sources, you can share a tape library between DPM servers. The first and most important part is that the tape library must use a fiber channel; it is not optimal to use SCSI and it will not work using an iSCSI target:

▶   Use only the fiber channel as the primary communication media.

▸ The physical tape library must be presented to all DPM servers that use it.

▸ For the server that should be **Library Server**, the media changer or tape library and the tape drives should be enabled in the device manager.

▸ For the servers that should be **Library Clients**, the media changer or tape library must be disabled in the device manager of the servers. The tape drives must be enabled in the device manager.

▸ Configure **SQL Named Pipes Protocol** on all SQL servers.

▸ Use a service account for the TLS feature.

For detailed instructions, follow the instructions provided by this blog post: `http://robertanddpm.blogspot.se/2013/11/tape-library-sharing.html`.

Understanding the concept of VTL

This recipe will cover the concept of a virtual tape library, also known as VTL, and how DPM can leverage it.

For many companies, there is no interest in writing the production data to an actual tape. The reason is that they only need the grandfather-father-son relation or granularity and that is only possible by defining long-term recovery goals. This can be accomplished using a VTL, which could be a hardware box or software that you install on the DPM server.

A VTL solution is installed and configured the same way as a physical tape library and from a DPM perspective, should be managed the same way regarding its long-term recovery goals.

A virtual tape library simulates a media changer and a number of tape drives. Instead of using tapes, the VTL software or solution writes the backed-up data to individual files that represent a tape. Different vendors use different file setups and extensions.

The advantage of using VTL is to gain the granularity of tape to the speed of a disk-based backup or restore. This also enables you to customize your storage for the VTL software or solution. You can either choose to have a lot of storage but lack the speed or the opposite. Always keep in mind that you should map your restore scenarios, as defined in your business continuity plan.

There's more...

There are two vendors that you should consider to choose if you are implementing a VTL solution:

▸ Cristalink's VTL Firestreamer
▸ VTL from EMC DATA DOMAIN

See also

▶ http://www.cristalink.com/fs/.

▶ http://www.emc.com/data-protection/data-domain/data-domain-virtual-tape-library.htm.

Understanding how DPM manages tapes

This recipe will cover the information that you need to understand how DPM manages tapes.

System Center Data Protection Manager 2012 R2 is a focused restore product. This reflects from a tape management perspective and how DPM writes protected data to tapes.

The DPM server could write data directly to the tape by using an incremental technology, but this is not a recommended approach as the vision of DPM is to use the backup-to-disk technology as its primary choice.

DPM will write a full backup to the tape and never create long incremental tape chains that could be seen as a risk in the restore process. DPMs are, of course, able to span and divide the protected data sources between tapes, but this is not the same technique as incremental tape backup.

System Center Data Protection Manager 2012 R2 will present accurate information regarding your tape status. Information regarding when your tape is offsite ready, which means that you can remove it from the tape library, or whether it's free or has other statuses will be presented to you in a real time experience and will also be provided to System Center Operations Manager if you monitor your DPM servers.

All information regarding the status of your tapes will be found in the **Monitoring and Management** parts of the DPM console.

Within the DPM console, you can find the current tape status by clicking on **Management and Libraries**; you can also find information regarding different tape alerts in the **Management** part of the DPM console. There, you will see the tape libraries present, as well as all the tape drives.

A tape will be marked as offsite ready when three of the following conditions are met:

▶ The tape is full

▶ The expired dataset

▶ The Write Period Ratio is crossed

Configuring tape optimization for DPM

This recipe will cover how to optimize tape usage for DPM.

Getting ready

When Microsoft released the 2007 version of System Center Data Protection Manager, a new feature called **co-location** was introduced. The purpose of co-location was to create a tape optimization scenario where the DPM administrators could store data more efficiently on allocated tapes. The co-location feature was also introduced in the disk allocation methodology regarding Hyper-V, SQL, and client protected data sources that were placed in the DPM disk pool.

In the release of System Center Data Protection Manager 2012 R2, there is more GUI-based configuration for the co-location feature for tape optimization that will be described in this recipe.

How to do it...

To enable long-term co-location for your protected workloads, there are some key points that you should be aware of. The first thing you need to configure is to create new sets of tape optimization by using the GUI and then associate protection groups to the set.

Go to **Management** in the DPM console and click on **Libraries**. In the DPM console, you will now be able to click on the **Optimize usage** button in the top-left section of the DPM console. The **Tape Optimization Setup** window will pop up; click on the **Create** button to create your **Tape Optimization Set**. When you click on **Create**, a new window will appear, which will present you the **Protection Group** options that could be chosen for tape optimization. Select the checkboxes next to the name of the Protection Groups field that you would like to collocate, and click on **OK**.

 Only Protection Groups that have long-term protection configured will be presented as possible choices for co-location.

How it works...

By enabling this feature, your DPM server will write multiple protected data sources that are members of the same optimization set on the same tape. The DPM administrator has some further configurations that could be made, which are described in the next part of this recipe.

There's more...

As a DPM administrator, you can control three important options:

- ▸ The co-location of protection groups with different retention time
- ▸ The Write period
- ▸ The Expiry tolerance

If your Protection Groups that have long-term retention goals configured have different retention time for the tape protection, you can still co-locate them on the same tape. By clicking on **Modify** in the **Tape Optimization Setup** window, you are able to uncheck the checkbox next to **Don't allow backups of different retention periods co-locate on the same tape** in the **Select tape co-location details** section.

In the modify view of **Optimization Set**, you can also configure advanced configurations for the tape co-location options by clicking on the **Advanced** button in the **Select tape co-location** details section. Here, you will be able to configure **Write period**, that is, the number of days, weeks, months, or years for which the tape will be available for writing. When the period expires, the tape will be marked Offsite Ready. The second part is **Expiry tolerance**, which defines the maximum time a recovery point can lie expired on an active tape. This could also be set to any number of days, weeks, months, or years depending on your configuration.

Understanding tape reports in DPM

This recipe will explain the two reports in DPM that will provide you with the information that you will need to keep track of your tapes' rotation schedules, and so on.

As the DPM administrator who is responsible for the company's restore plans, it's critical that you have a good understanding of when a tape is marked Offsite Ready and when you are able to reuse these tapes.

In the DPM console, you click on **Reporting** to enter the reporting area of the console. You have two different tape reports that are very useful:

- ▸ Tape Management
- ▸ Tape Utilization

The **Tape Management** report provides you information regarding how to manage tape rotation and lists all the libraries that are below the free tape threshold. It's important to know that data is collected per library and is aggregated for all libraries.

The **Tape Utilization** report will give you the data needed to determine the trends that will assist you in capacity planning.

All DPM reports are generated and provided via SQL Server Reporting Services, which is one of the prerequisites for DPM installation.

If you don't want to access the DPM console to generate your reports, you can easily subscribe to them and have them sent to you in PDF, HTML, or Excel format.

As all the data is stored in the DPM database, you can also create your own reports using **Report Builder**.

Configuring the short erase feature

This recipe will cover how to configure your DPM server to enable short erase.

Getting ready

Erasing tapes is always a time-consuming process, and this is a very common scenario regardless of the product, as the tape will be formatted. A faster way is to perform a short erase.

How to do it...

Enter the DWORD `UseShortErase` in the registry on the DPM server and reboot the server:

`HKEY_LOCAL_MACHINE\SOFTWARE\Microsoft\Microsoft Data Protection Manager\Agent`

Provide the value of 00000000 in a DWORD.

How it works...

Short erase means that the data written to tapes will be overwritten with a NULL value that makes it appear empty

There's more...

For a tape to be erased, it must not contain any recovery points that are within the retention time.

Understanding tape management tasks

This recipe will cover standard tape management tasks for a DPM server environment.

As a DPM administrator, you are responsible for tape management tasks that could result in very negative scenarios if neglected.

Within the DPM console, you can perform all the tape management tasks that are associated with your responsibility.

The following list presents all the tape management tasks in DPM that you should perform:

- ▶ Add or remove tapes
- ▶ Inventory tapes
- ▶ Mark a tape as free
- ▶ Identify an unknown tape
- ▶ Re-catalog an imported tape
- ▶ View tape contents
- ▶ Mark a tape as a cleaning tape
- ▶ Erase a tape

For a detailed explanation, refer to this TechNet article:

`http://technet.microsoft.com/en-us/library/jj628066.aspx.`

14
Monitoring and Automation

In this chapter, we will cover the following recipes:

- ▶ Understanding how the System Center family should be your base for service delivery
- ▶ Understanding System Center Operations Manager 2012 R2
- ▶ Understanding System Center Orchestrator 2012 R2
- ▶ Understanding the DPM PowerShell Cmdlet
- ▶ Installing System Center Operations Manager
- ▶ Installing System Center Orchestrator
- ▶ Installing the DPM Central Console
- ▶ Understanding how to configure System Center Orchestrator for DPM automation

Introduction

When it comes to delivering an actual service, close cooperation between different products is important, as they are the pillars the service is built up from. A modern datacenter is a frequently used term by Microsoft, but what is more important is the three pillars that define the modern datacenter:

- ▶ Highly automated
- ▶ Highly resilient
- ▶ Able to deliver well-structured services

Being able to provide a highly automated concept for your Baas, RaaS, or DRaaS service is critical. What is most important is that there are no guidelines for how this should or could be automated. The best advice you can get is to start small and then expand the automation experience.

For a modern datacenter to adapt and adjust the resources it can provide to the services, it must be resilient. If a number of servers are just in standby, the datacenter should be able to scale its resources in order to meet the current demands for the level of resources needed to be allocated.

Building a modern datacenter more or less starts out by defining what should be the service offerings. Once again, Microsoft provides both whitepapers and best practices, but these should be seen as professional advice for how you could build, design, and implement a cloud solution and not just how you should implement a cloud solution.

By building a proactive monitoring of both the fabric and the tenants using the cloud, you gain not just the possibility to reduce the business impact, but also gain the possibility to verify that your resource distribution within the modern datacenter and cloud are working in an optimal way.

When it comes down to what building services is all about, it can only be said with this sentence: *all good designs come from knowing your services' data dependencies*. In this chapter, we will cover how to get started with the monitoring and automation of your System Center Data Protection Manager 2012 R2 environment that builds up your BaaS, RaaS, and DRaaS services in your modern datacenter.

Understanding how the System Center family should be your base for service delivery

This section will present a good starting point for you, regarding how you can use the System Center family to build your on-premises services for your modern datacenter.

Before you can start to install a server software, you need to define what services should be available within your modern datacenter. It is not about installing products and using as much PowerShell as possible, it is all about building and designing services that are reliable and useful to both your end users and deciding what brings great value to the company or organization.

Start simple; think of perhaps three services that you should provide as service offerings to your organization. Keep it simple and do not add complexity, as this will only lead to complex administration and make it difficult to troubleshoot.

The System Center family is more than just a bunch of different products; it's a toolbox for you to use when designing the workflow of the process or service.

The integration between different System Center family members could be done via:

- ▶ Software
- ▶ Management Packs
- ▶ Connectors
- ▶ PowerShell
- ▶ Other

The first four members in this list are Microsoft's way of integrating System Center products or solutions. However, the last point is to emphasize that there is so much more than what meets the eye, and here is where your own creativity comes in. You should initially work with the standard ways provided by Microsoft but still have rich experience when integrating different solutions or products, as long as you keep two important facts in mind:

- ▶ Never add complexity
- ▶ Always keep your solutions within a supported scenario

System Center Data Protection Manager 2012 R2 can cooperate with:

- ▶ **System Center Operations Manager** (**SCOM**)
- ▶ **System Center Orchestrator** (**SCO**)
- ▶ **System Center Configuration Manager** (**SCCM**)
- ▶ **System Center Virtual Machine Manager** (**SCVMM**)
- ▶ **System Center Service Manager** (**SCSM**)
- ▶ **Service Management Automation** (**SMA**)
- ▶ **Windows Azure Pack** (**WAP**)

The last two in the list, SMA and WAP, are not branded System Center components but are very important when you deliver services within a modern datacenter or any cloud. Windows Azure Pack is at an early stage of development but is extremely useful. WAP or Windows Azure Pack should be considered a portal that has the function of self-service for cloud, for example, IaaS to provision virtual machines, databases, and more. The SMA or Service Management Automation is a product that cooperates with System Center Orchestrator, but neither is dependent on the other.

When building, a backup as a service or BaaS, for example, you could build it up by using the schema presented in this figure:

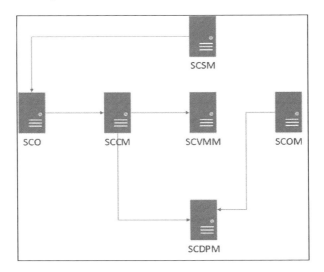

End users would open the web browser and go to the Service Manager portal website. From there, they order the client backup that is part of the BaaS service offering. System Center Orchestrator or Service Management Automation will start and install a DPM agent to the client. When that is done, System Center Orchestrator or Service Management Automation will verify that there is a need for a new DPM server instance for the BaaS service. If this is true, System Center Virtual Machine Manager will start a deployment of a new DPM server instance to the BaaS service. When the load for the BaaS service is within resource tolerance, System Center Configuration Manager will start the configuration of the DPM agent and System Center Orchestrator, or Service Management Automation will make the DPM agent a member of the specified protection group.

For more information regarding integration and to see the possibilities of System Center, follow this blog: `http://robertanddpm.blogspot.com`.

Understanding System Center Operations Manager 2012 R2

This section will give you a very short introduction to what System Center Operations Manager is all about on a very high level.

System Center Operations Manager is a Microsoft solution to build a monitoring experience that you could rely on if it is designed the right way. The biggest difference between Operations Manager and other third-party software that claims the market is that Operations Manager will provide you with deeper knowledge and richer monitoring—an alert experience.

Providing a proactive monitoring experience that is based on a product comes from building a design that is applicable to the organization and operators for the modern datacenter. A thorough pre-study regarding what is really important to know before you get started with the actual implementation of Operations Manager is of key importance, if you want to achieve a decent proactive monitoring experience.

Planning is the most important part of building a proactive monitoring experience. Before you begin to install the software, you need to have a clear plan or roadmap regarding what features and functions should be installed depending on your pre-study, which will define:

- Service classifications
- Network topologies and components
- Windows Server technologies
- Alert management
- ITIL processes
- Services data dependencies
- Management scenarios

These are just a few points that should be defined and documented, before you start to install and build a proactive monitoring experience for your company or organization.

System Center Operations Manager is the hub or central point in your datacenter, which monitors the current states of the different services and also provides a realistic remedy solution with the integration of System Center Orchestrator or Service Management Automation.

Providing a "one look, one solution" approach via distributed applications is something that works well for a service desk or owners of a service within the company datacenter. A distributed application is built from the components that are defined in the monitoring packs you imported and distributed in System Center Operations Manager.

From the start, System Center Operations Manager 2012 R2 is more or less an empty box that you add intelligence and logic to via different management packs. The monitoring logic that is stored in the management packs is then distributed to the SCOM agents via an internal mechanism.

For a high-end implementation of Operations Manager, it is important that the service accounts and security group be defined in the Active Directory.

The following list presents the service accounts and security group that must be defined:

- **OMAA**: OM Server action account
- **OMDAS**: OM Config and Data Access service account
- **OMWRITE**: OM Reporting Write account

> ▸ **OMREAD**: OM Reporting Read account
> ▸ **SQLSVC**: Service Account for SQL Server
> ▸ **SCOMAdmins**: OM administrator security group

You must also provide a security group in the Active Directory called SCOMAdmins and make the OMAA and the OMDAS members of that security group.

Building a decent monitoring solution does not start with the installation of software. The initial part is to understand the demands and wishes of the organization that will be administrating and operating the proactive monitoring solution.

Understanding System Center Orchestrator 2012 R2

This section gives you a basic introduction to what System Center Orchestrator 2012 R2 is, and why it is an important component in the BaaS, RaaS, or DRaaS service that you are providing in your datacenter.

An everyday situation for many companies is the repetitive tasks that consultants or employees perform; the majority of these tasks could easily be automated. This is where System Center Orchestrator comes in. System Center Orchestrator, formerly known as Opalis, is a graphical automation engine that companies or organizations can use to easily automate these repetitive tasks.

System Center Orchestrator provides a graphical programming experience for automated workflows that will eliminate these simple repetitive tasks. Your automation is built in what Microsoft calls runbooks. A **runbook** is built up from linking different activities from different integration packs together, so that they represent a workflow or process.

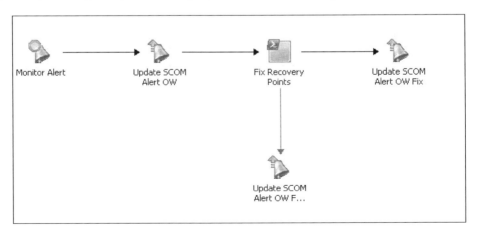

Building an automation workflow comes from the possibilities of using multiple activities from different integration packs, as the preceding figure exemplifies. You can mix different activities from different integration packs, to fit your automation concept.

 Microsoft provides you a rich automation possibility when using System Center Orchestrator, but for more complex automation workflows, it is recommended that you work with **Service Management Automation**, also known as **SMA**.

To be able to connect System Center Orchestrator to different solutions, you must define a prerequisite configuration setting for the activity. This is done after you have imported the integration packs, and this is done under the **Options** menu in **System Center 2012 R2 Orchestrator Runbook Designer**.

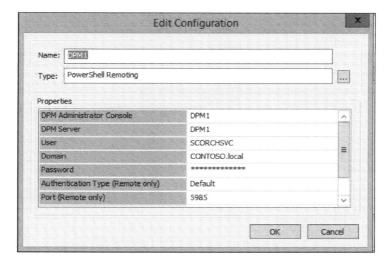

Every activity is linked together and System Center Orchestrator can pass the information from one activity to another via the data bus. One important part regarding error management within a runbook is the fact that System Center Orchestrator 2012 R2 does not care whether the activities within the runbook finish successfully or not. System Center Orchestrator 2012 R2 only cares about the fact that it could start or run its runbook.

For more information regarding how to install and setup System Center Orchestrator, refer to the *Installing System Center Orchestrator* recipe in this chapter.

Understanding the DPM PowerShell Cmdlet

As mentioned in this chapter, automation is a key concept for a modern datacenter. PowerShell is the most natural choice to work with either System Center Orchestrator 2012 R2 or Service Management Automation.

PowerShell is flexible and gives you the ability to build up your solution for a workflow or process any way that you want. PowerShell also brings another important fact to the table; if you are using PowerShell, you can be sure that the script that you build up will be supported by Microsoft, as you are working with predefined Cmdlets from Microsoft.

DPM PowerShell Cmdlets can be accessed after you have imported the modules, or you can simply open **DPM Management Shell**.

With the 2012 R2 release, the number of PowerShell Cmdlets matches the actual number of possible commands presented in the DPM console. This actually means that all you can do in the DPM console can also be done via System Center Data Protection Manager 2012 R2 PowerShell Cmdlets.

This link contains the complete Cmdlet reference for System Center Data Protection Manager 2012 R2: `http://download.microsoft.com/download/A/0/B/A0BB6495-3010-43A8-B06C-6B0F0E8F92D9/SC2012R2_DPM_Cmdlets.pdf`.

The guide contains all the DPM PowerShell Cmdlets for the 2012 R2 release, and is a great tool to use when you are developing your automation workflows or PowerShell scripts.

The first example is used to add disks to the DPM disk pool and the second example is to add a SQL database to a protection group. Let's start with the first example:

`$Disk = Get-DPMDisk -DPMServerName dpm1`

The first line will list all the disks that the `dpm1` server has listed in its **Disk Management** specification and store the output in the variable `$Disk`:

`Add-DPMDisk $Disk[3]`

The last line adds the fourth disk to the DPM disk pool.

 The first disk is listed as number zero in the array of disks presented in the $Disk variable.

The next example will add a SQL database to a protection group.

```
$ps = Get-ProductionServer -DPMServerName DPM
```

This first line will list all the servers that have a DPM agent installed and attached to it and store it in the $ps variable.

```
$SQL = Get-Datasource -ProductionServer $ps[0] -inquire
```

The second line will inquire or ask a specific production server to list all the data sources available for protection and add that information to the variable $SQL.

```
$newpg = New-ProtectionGroup -DPMServerName DPM1 -Name SQLDB
```

The third line of PowerShell will create a new protection group called SQLDB on the DPM server named DPM1 and store that in the $newpg variable.

```
Add-ChildDataSource -ProtectionGroup $newpg -ChildDataSource $SQL[0]
```

The fourth line will add specific databases as protected data sources from the $SQL variable we created earlier to the new protection group that we created in the third line.

```
Set-DataSourceDiskAllocation -Datasource $SQL[0] -ProtectionGroup $newpg
```

The fifth line will create a disk allocation for the first database listed in the $SQL variable for the newly created protection group that we created and stored in the $newpg variable.

```
Set-ReplicaCreationMethod -ProtectionGroup $newpg -Now
```

The sixth line will provide information on how you should create your replica for the protected data source. In this case, we will create the replica now, hence the Now switch.

```
Set-PolicyObjective -ProtectionGroup $newpg -RetentionRangeDays 2
```

The seventh line will set the number of days for the retention range.

```
Set-ProtectionGroup $newpg
```

The eighth line will create the actual protection group and start to create the replica for the selected SQL database.

For more advanced scripts, you can take a look at this blog post:

```
http://robertanddpm.blogspot.se/2013/10/powershell-script-for-adding-
specific.html
```

Installing System Center Operations Manager

This recipe will cover the installation of System Center Operations Manager 2012 R2. Note that this guide meets the minimum requirements to set up System Center Operations Manager with the purpose of monitoring and managing a BaaS, RaaS, or DRaaS service, based on System Center, Azure, and Windows Server.

This recipe will cover a very basic installation of System Center Operations Manager, so that you can have as a decent starting point.

Getting ready

The most important part before you start to install a System Center product is to have a plan for its purpose. When this plan and strategy are done, you can sit down and provide the prerequisites before you start the installation.

For System Center Operations Manager 2012 R2, the prerequisites for the management servers are:

- .NET Framework 4 or .NET Framework 4.5
- Windows Remote Management must be enabled for the management server

For the Operations Manager console role, you must have:

- .NET Framework 4.0 installed

Operations Manager needs to have SQL Server 2012 SP2 to store its operational and data warehouse database.

System Center Operations Manager is built for different roles:

- Management Server
- Operations Console
- Web Console
- Reporting Server

The reporting server role should be installed on the backend SQL that is hosting the operational and data warehouse databases. If this is not installed, System Center Operations Manager 2012 R2 will not be able to generate reports for you, via the operational console.

For a high-end implementation of Operations Manager, it is important that the service accounts and security group are defined in the active directory.

The following list presents the service accounts and security group that must be defined:

- **OMAA**: The OM Server action account
- **OMDAS**: The OM Config and Data Access service account
- **OMWRITE**: The OM Reporting Write account
- **OMREAD**: The OM Reporting Read account
- **SQLSVC**: The Service Account for SQL Server
- **SCOMAdmins**: The OM administrator security group

You must also provide a security group in the active directory called SCOMAdmins and make the OMAA and the OMDAS members of that security group. Also, make the SCOMAdmins group a member of the local administrator group on every server that is hosting any roles of the Operations Manager installation.

How to do it...

The installation process for System Center Operations Manager 2012 R2 is divided into two steps:

1. The installation of the backend SQL server
2. The installation of selected Operations Manager roles

Insert the SQL server media and run `setup.exe` as an administrator; the **SQL Server Installation Center** will then start. Click on **Installation** followed by **New SQL Server stand-alone installation or add features to an existing installation**.

Setup Support Rules will run; click on **OK** when it is finished.

Next is the **Product Key** step; enter your product key and click on **Next >** to continue.

In **License Terms**, select the checkbox next to **I accept the license terms** and click on **Next >** to continue.

The next step is **Product Updates**, select the **Include SQL Server product updates** checkbox and click on **Next >** to continue.

In the **Install Setup Files** step, the SQL server installation will provide the installation bits for the installation process. Click on **Install** to continue.

The next step is **Setup Support Rules**, which will alert you if there are any prerequisites that are not fulfilled. Click on **Next >** to continue.

In the **Setup Role** step, choose **SQL Server Feature Installation** and click on **Next >** to continue.

In the **Feature Selection** step, choose from the following features:

- ▶ **Database Engine Services**
- ▶ **Full-Text and Semantic Extractions for Search**
- ▶ **Reporting Services—Native**
- ▶ **Management Tools Basic and Complete**

Click on **Next >** to continue. The **Installation Rules** step will verify your selections and in the details view, you can verify the issues, if any; click on **Next >** to continue.

Next is the **Instance Configuration** step; always use a named instance in SQL for its purpose. Choose the **Instance root directory** and click on **Next >** to continue.

Verify the **Disk Space Requirements** step and click on **Next >** to continue.

In the **Server Configuration** step, you start by adding the SQL service account credentials and be sure to change **Startup Type** for **SQL Server Agent** to **Automatic**. Click on the **Collation** tab and verify that you have the Latin1_General_100_CI_AS collation.

Operations Manager has formerly been installed using SQL_Latin1_General_CP1_CI_AS, but due to issues regarding searches and so on, Microsoft has not updated TechNet with this information. The Operational Data warehouse database will be installed by using the old collation, regardless of whether you choose the new collation.

Click on **Next >** to continue.

Next is the **Database Engine Configuration** step; add your SA account for the SQL instance or add the SCOMAdmin group. Click on **Next >** to continue.

Choose the **Install and configure** option in the **Reporting Services Configuration** step. Click on **Next >** to continue.

Click on **Next >** to continue and in the **Ready to Install** step, click on **Install** to start the installation.

You can follow the installation process in the **Installation Progress** step. When the installation of the SQL server instance is finished, you will see the **Complete** step, providing you a summary of the installation.

The next step is to install the first management server in the management group for your Operations Manager environment. On all servers that should be members of the management group, make sure that the global security group SCOMAdmins is a member of the local administrator group.

Insert the SCOM media and in the splash screen, click on **Install**.

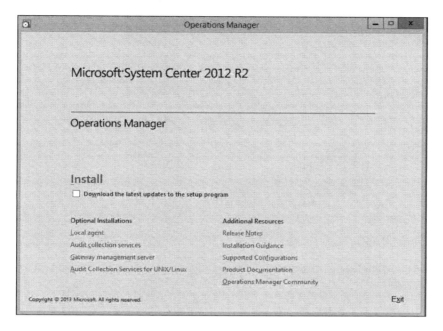

In **Select features to install**, choose to install:

▸ Management server

▸ Operations console

It is not recommended that you place the SQL installation and OpsMgr installation in the same server. This will not only make it unsupported to monitor nontrusted domains using the SCOM gateway server, but most importantly, it is also hard to scale out the solution. Start with a minimum of:

▸ One SQL server

▸ Two Management servers

Click on **Next >** to continue.

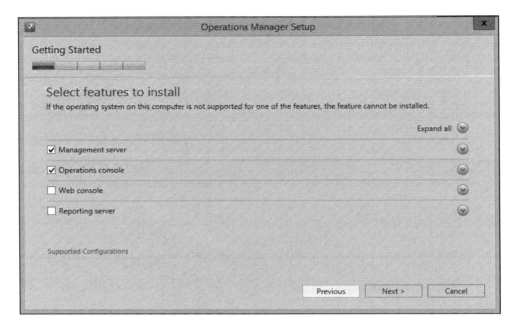

In the **Select Installation Location** step, you can choose the default location and click on **Next >** to continue.

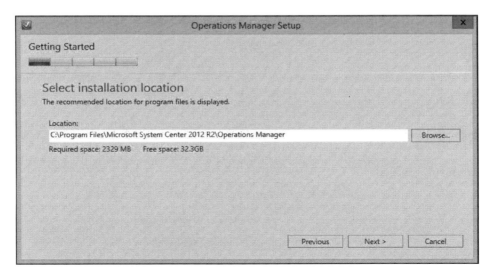

A prerequisite check will run and provide you with feedback, if anything needs to be handled. Solve these issues and then click on **Next >** to continue.

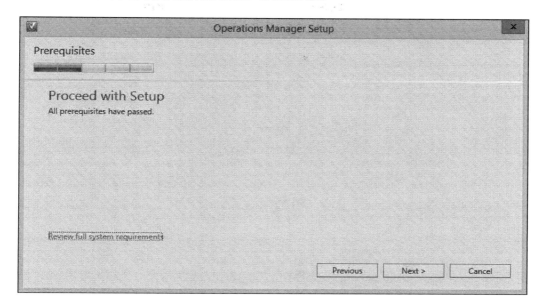

The next step is **Specify an installation option**. Choose **Create the first Management server in a new management group** and provide a name for the management group.

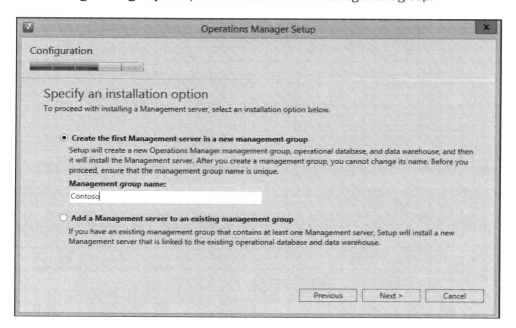

Keep in mind that you can't change the management group name afterwards, so think twice before you choose your name. Click on **Next >** to continue.

The next step is the licensing step. Select the checkbox next to **I have read, understood, and agree with the license terms**. Click on **Next >** to continue.

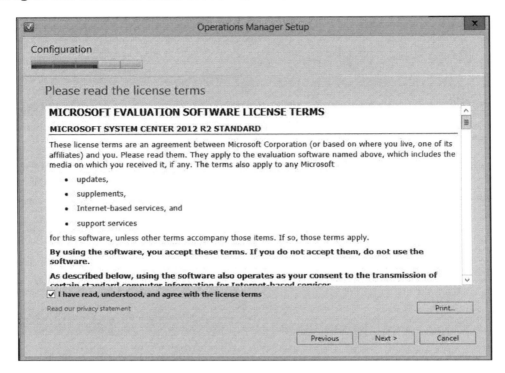

Next is the **Configure the operational database** step, where you provide the SQL server configurations. Change the size of the database from 1000 MB to 5000 MB. Click on **Next >** to continue.

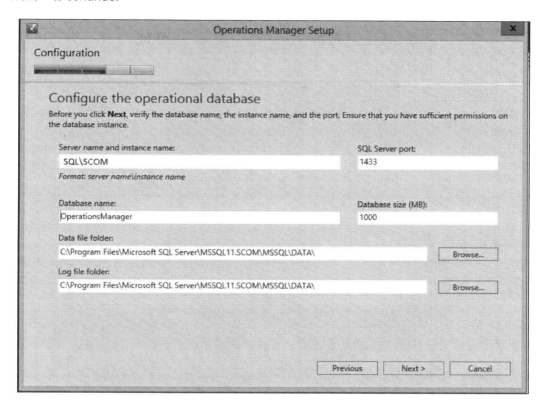

Provide the SQL configurations for the Operations Manager data warehouse database. Choose **Create a new data warehouse database** and change the size from 1000 MB to 10000 MB; click on **Next >** to continue.

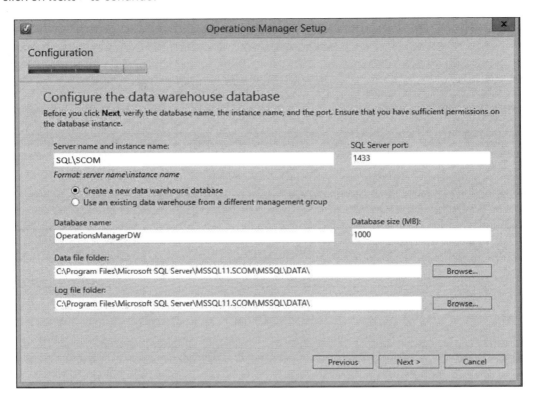

Next is the **Configure Operations Manager accounts** step. Provide the credentials and click on **Next >** to continue.

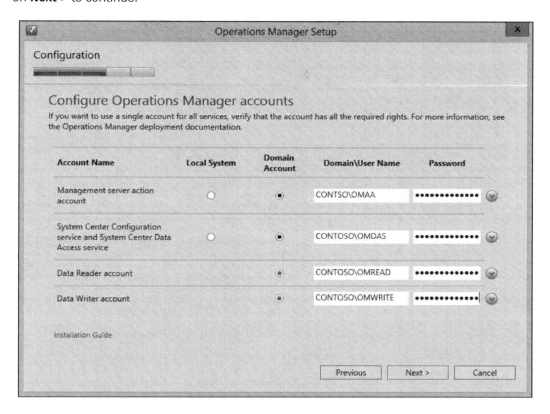

If you want to help Microsoft improve Operations Manager, you can choose to do this in the **Help improve Operations Manager** step. Choose your configuration and click on **Next >** to continue.

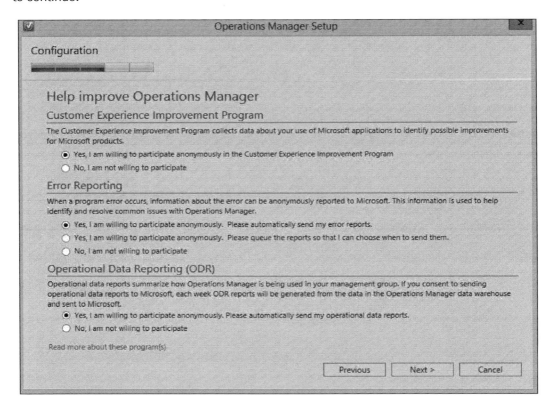

Always be in control of your updates; never automate this. In the **Microsoft Update** step, choose **Off** and click on **Next >** to continue.

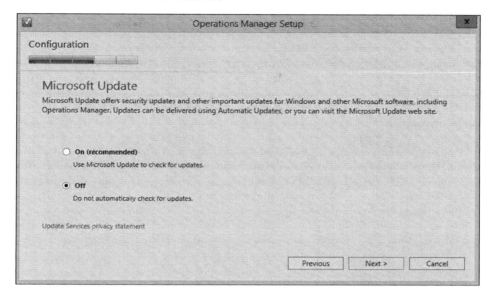

In the **Installation Summary** step, verify your configuration and click on **Install** to start the installation.

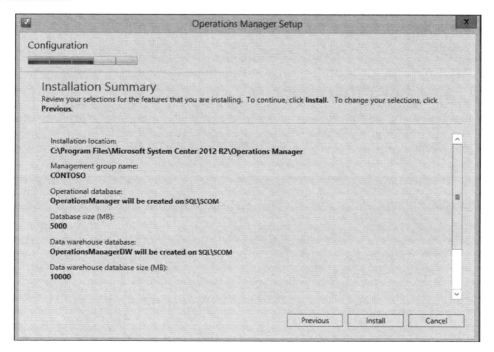

When the installation has finished, you will see the end result in the **Setup is complete** step.

How it works...

System Center Operations Manager is the Microsoft System Center component that provides a proactive monitoring experience by leveraging the monitoring logic, provided by management packs. For more information regarding datacenter management based on private and public cloud strategies, visit `http://robertandthecloud.blogspot.in/`.

There's more...

For a more high-end approach, you must have correctly scaled the Operations Manager environment, so you know that the actual health state of the management group is healthy and can function in the way that your organization needs.

Remember to register the SPN of your SQL server and management servers, or you will have an alert for Operations Manager.

Also, provide the license key using PowerShell via the Operations Manager Shell by using the following syntax:

```
Set-SCOMLicense -ProductId XXXXX-XXXXX-XXXXX-XXXXX-XXXXX
```

Installing System Center Orchestrator

This recipe will cover the basic installation of System Center Orchestrator.

Getting ready

System Center Orchestrator is a System Center family member that provides you with the capability to create automation via a GUI. The installation is quite straightforward, but always keep in mind that if you provide a poor SQL installation, you will end up with a poor experience of the solutions that use these SQL server instances.

System Center Orchestrator must have some service accounts and a security group in Active Directory defined:

- ► **SCORCHSVC**: The service account for Orchestrator
- ► **SCORCHUSRERS**: The security group for Orchestrator users
- ► **SCOSQLSVC**: The service account for SQL

The prerequisite for System Center Orchestrator is .NET and you need 3.5 and 4.0. The IIS role is also needed, but the installation process of Orchestrator will solve this.

Add the SCORCHSVC account and the SCORCHUSERS user group to the local administrator group of the Orchestrator server.

How to do it...

The installation process for System Center Orchestrator 2012 R2 is divided into two steps:

- The installation of the backend SQL server
- The installation of System Center Orchestrator 2012 R2

Insert the SQL server media and run `setup.exe` as an administrator; the **SQL Server Installation Center** will start. Click on **Installation** followed by **New SQL Server stand-alone installation or add features to an existing installation**.

Setup Support Rules will run. Click on **OK** when it is finished.

Next is the **Product Key** step; enter your product key and click on **Next >** to continue.

In **License Terms**, select the checkbox next to **I accept the license terms** and click on **Next >** to continue.

The next step is **Product Updates**. Select the **Include SQL Server product updates** checkbox and click on **Next >** to continue.

In the **Install Setup Files** step, the SQL server installation will provide the installation bits for the installation process. Click on **Install** to continue.

The next step is **Setup Support Rules**, which will alert you if there are any prerequisites that are not fulfilled. Click on **Next >** to continue.

In the **Setup Role** step, choose **SQL Server Feature Installation** and click on **Next >** to continue.

In the **Feature Selection** step, choose the following features:

- **Database Engine Services**
- **Management Tools Basic and Complete**

Click on **Next >** to continue. The **Installation Rules** step will verify your selections and in the details view, you can verify any issues. Click on **Next >** to continue.

Next is the **Instance Configuration** step. Always use a named instance in SQL for its purpose. Choose the **Instance root directory** and click on **Next >** to continue.

Verify the **Disk Space Requirements** step and click on **Next >** to continue.

In the **Server Configuration** step, you start by adding the SQL service account credentials. Be sure to change **Startup Type** for **SQL Server Agent** to **Automatic**. Click on the **Collation** tab and verify that you have the SQL_Latin1_General_CP1_CI_AS collation. Click on **Next >** to continue.

Next is the **Database Engine Configuration** step; add your SA account for the SQL instance, or add the SCORCHUSRERS group. Click on **Next >** to continue.

Choose the **Install and configure** option in the **Reporting Services Configuration** step. Click on **Next >** to continue.

In the following two steps, click on **Next >** to continue and in the **Ready to Install** step, click on **Install** to start the installation.

You can follow the installation process in the **Installation Progress** step. When the installation of the SQL server instance is finished, you will see the **Complete** step, providing you with a summary of the installation.

Next, insert the System Center Orchestrator media and run setup.exe as an administrator. In the splash screen, choose **Install**.

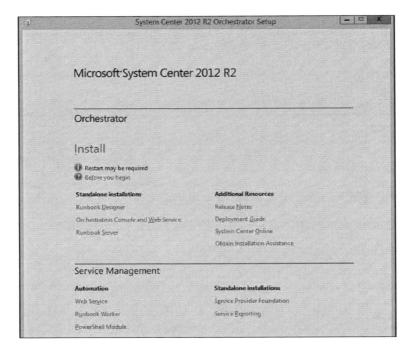

In the **Product registration** step, provide the information and click on **Next** to continue.

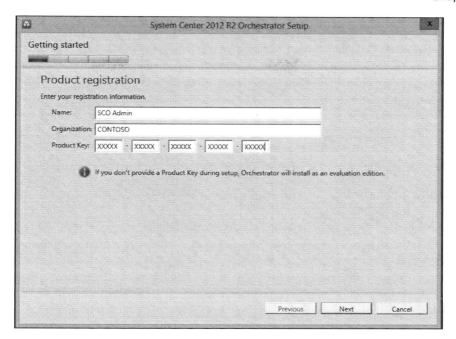

Accept the license term in the **Please read this License Term** step. Click on **Next** to continue.

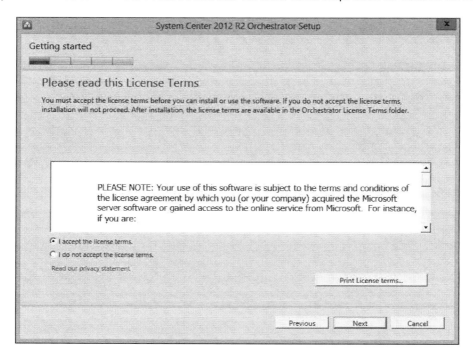

In the **Select features to install** step, choose to install all features and click on **Next** to continue.

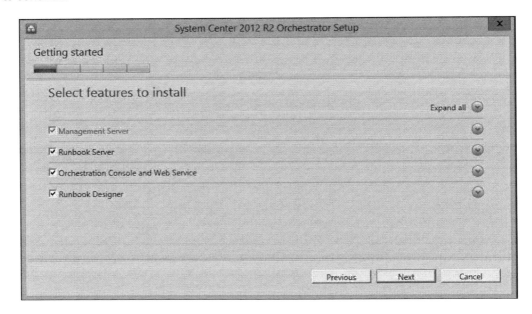

The installation will run a prerequisite check and prompt you with any missing roles that you may need. This information is presented in the **Setup will install these missing software prerequisites** step; click on **Next** to continue.

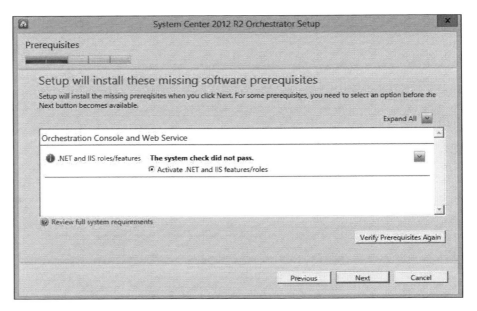

The installation will install the missing prerequisites and when it is finished, it will prompt you with this information: **All prerequisites are installed**. Click on **Next** to continue. The next step is **Configure the service account**, where you provide the credentials for your System Center Orchestrator service account. Click on the **Test** button to verify the credentials. Click on **Next** to continue.

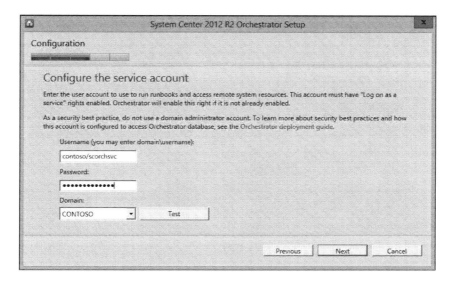

In the **Configure the database server** step, you type in the SQL server name and instance, followed by the **Port** number. Choose **Authentication Credentials** and click on the **Test Database Connection** button to verify the connection. Click on **Next** to continue.

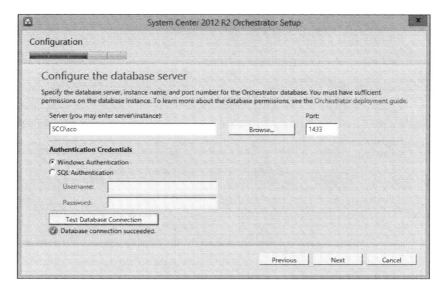

Next, select **Configure the database**, choose **New database**, and provide a name for it. Click on **Next** to continue.

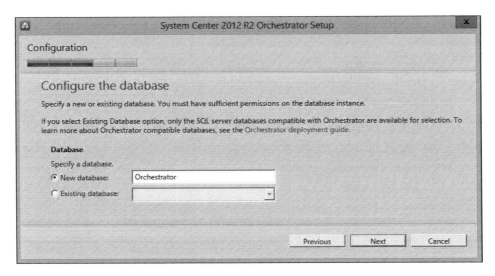

In the **Configure Orchestrator users group** step, enter the SCORCHUSERS user group and click on **Next**.

Provide the ports needed for the web services in the **Configure the ports for the web services** step. Click on **Next** to continue.

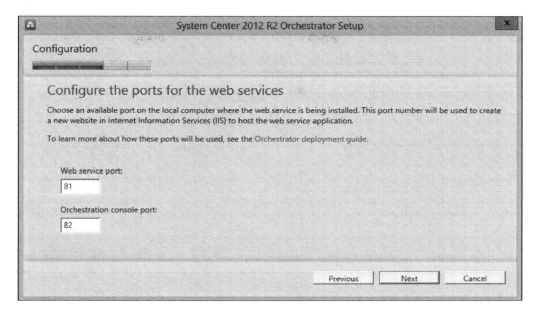

Next is the **Select the installation location** step. Choose the default location and click on **Next** to continue.

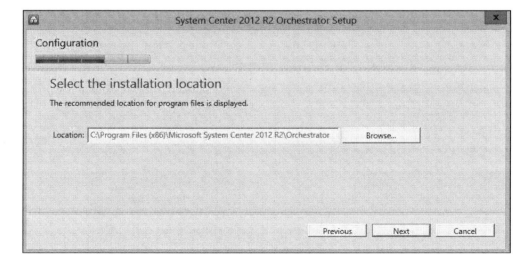

You can either update your System Center Orchestrator using **Microsoft Update**, or you can automatically apply the updates. This is not recommended. You must always be in control of when and what updates you apply. The default value in the **Microsoft Update** step is **On,** but it is recommended that you choose **Off**. Click on **Next** to continue.

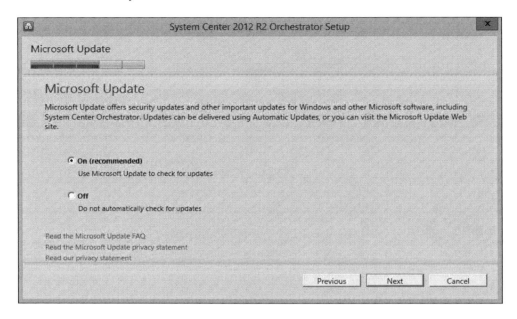

In the **Help improve Microsoft System Center Orchestrator** step, you can choose to either help out or not; either is fine. Select the option that you see fit and click on **Next** to continue.

Verify the configuration in the **Installation summary** step and click on **Install** to start the installation of System Center Orchestrator 2012 R2.

How it works...

System Center Orchestrator will connect to different solutions by using its integrations packs that are filled with all sorts of activities that you can use to automate your workflows.

There's more...

For more tips regarding cloud and automation, follow this blog: http://robertandthecloud.blogspot.com.

Installing the DPM Central Console

This recipe will cover how to install the DPM central console on your Operations Manager environment, so that you can manage and monitor multiple DPM servers via a single console.

Getting ready

The centralized console feature was something that the DPM team introduced in the release of the 2012 System Center stack. The purpose and intention of the centralized console is to be able to easily manage and monitor up to 100 DPM server or 50000 protected data sources per management group. This is done via the extension that the DPM team created in close interaction with the Operations Manager team in Redmond.

The prerequisite for the centralized console is .NET Framework 3.5 with Service Pack 1. The centralized console will need to use the TCP port 6075; this port is used for the scoped troubleshooting experience. For Operations Manager to be able to monitor and manage any DPM sever via the centralized console, you must first install an SCOM agent to the DPM servers.

How to do it...

To be able to get started with the centralized console feature for System Center Data Protection Manager 2012 R2, you must be sure to install both the console features on all management servers and console servers within your management group.

The installation process of the centralized console can be divided into three steps:

1. Install a SCOM agent to the DPM servers
2. Import the DPM management packs into Operations Manager
3. Install the server-side and client-side components on all management servers and servers hosting the console within the management group

The installation of an SCOM agent can be done either manually or via the SCOM console. For instructions on how to install an SCOM agent, read this guide: `http://technet.microsoft.com/en-us/library/hh230731.aspx`.

When the SCOM agent is installed and reports a healthy state, you can move on to the next step: the import of the DPM Management packs. The management packs are located in the DPM media. Be sure to have this inserted or mounted before you continue. In the SCOM console, go to **Administration** and on the left-hand side of the console, you will find **Management Packs**. Right-click on **Management Packs** and click on **Import Management Packs**.

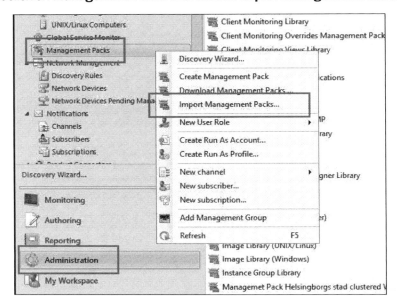

In the **Import Management Packs** window, click on **Add** and choose **Add from disk...** in the menu.

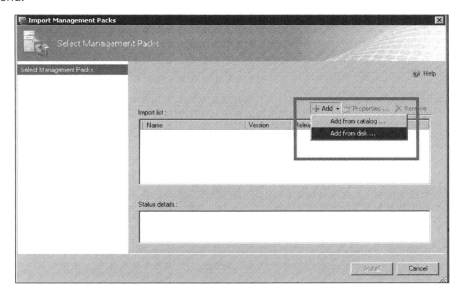

You will get a question asking whether you want to search the online catalogue for dependent management packs; click on **No** to continue.

 You must be very clear about what management packs you import to Operations Manager. Have a plan and a well-structured strategy that builds up your proactive monitoring and management approach.

Next, you must specify where you can find the management packs; open the DPM media, browse `CCX86\Management Packs\en-us`, and choose both management packs. Click on **Open** to continue.

Back in the **Import Management Packs** window, you now see the two selected management packs ready for import. Click on **Install** to continue.

You will get a question from Operations Manager, asking whether you want to install one of the management packs as the rules in it has write actions. This is okay and you should click on **Yes** to continue.

The management packs will now be imported into Operations Manager and you will start to discover the DPM servers that have an SCOM agent installed.

The next step is the installation of the central console; go to the management server that could also host the operations console. If your Operations Manager environment has a dedicated console server, just repeat this installation on these separate servers.

Start the DPM installation from the DPM media and on the splash screen, click on **DPM Central Console**. Accept all licensing terms by selecting the checkbox next to **I accept the license terms and conditions** and click on **OK** to continue.

Data Protection Manager Central Console Setup will start and present its first step, that is, the **Welcome** step. Click on **Next >** to continue.

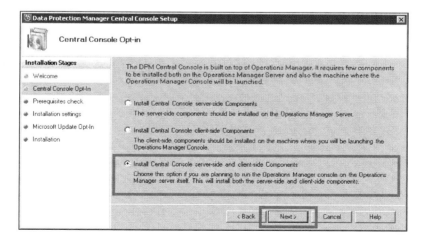

In **Central Console Opt-In**, choose the third option to install both server-side and client-side components. Click on **Next >** to continue.

Prerequisites check will verify the prerequisites and let you know whether there are any issues that you need to solve. If there are any, solve them and continue with the installation. Click on **Next >** to continue.

In the **Installation settings** step, verify the information and click on **Next >** to continue.

The next step is the **Microsoft Update Opt-In** step. Choose not to use Microsoft update and click on **Install** to start the installation.

The last step is the **Installation** step, where you can verify the installation when it has finished.

 The discovery of DPM data source will run between 06:00 a.m. and 06:00 p.m. every day. This value can be altered via an override.

How it works...

There are two components that build up the centralized console:

- ▶ Server-side components
- ▶ Client-side components

Server-side components are those components that will establish a connection to the DPM server from the management server and provide a centralized console experience.

If you want to be able to access multiple DPM servers from your client, you simply install the client-side components and you will be able to connect and have a DPM console on your client side, instead of working via RDP sessions.

 Currently, you are not able to install the client-side components if you have the DPM agent installed on the same client.

To get access to the centralized console, open the Operations Manager console and navigate to the management pack view of the DPM management packs, and via the server tasks provided in the management pack, you can access the centralized console.

There's more...

For more information regarding DPM, read this blog: `http://robertanddpm.blogspot.com`.

Understanding how to configure System Center Orchestrator for DPM automation

This section will cover how to connect your System Center Orchestrator server to DPM, so that you can start your automation journey.

System Center Orchestrator is a graphical automation tool that you can use to get started with your automation concepts. The automation concept for System Center Data Protection Manager is based on the fact that the integration pack for DPM uses Windows PowerShell remoting on the Runbook Designer and on the Runbook server to run commands on the DPM server.

The WinRM service is started automatically but has no listener configured; this is something that needs to be done before you automate DPM using Orchestrator.

Here are some steps to configure a successful connection between System Center Data Protection Manager 2012 R2 and System Center Orchestrator 2012 R2:

1. Add the SORCHSVC account to the local admin group of the targeted servers for automation
2. Enable Windows Remote Management trusted hosts
3. Change the execution policy
4. Enable remote connection settings
5. Configure the connection for DPM in Orchestrator

Add the SCORCHSVC account and the SCORCHUSERS user group to the local administrator group of the DPM servers that you want to automate.

To enable the Windows Management Framework, you must edit the Windows Remote Management trusted hosts policy on the System Center Orchestrator server. Open the Local Group Policy Editor by running `gpedit.msc` from Command Prompt or by hitting the Windows button. Expand **Computer Configuration**, **Administrative Templates**, **Windows Components**, **Windows Remote Management (WinRM)**, and **WinRM Client**, and then double-click on **Trusted Hosts**. You can either enter the IP addresses for the DPM servers that you want to automate, or you can provide an FQDN. Using the * wildcard, you can enter all servers that, for example, start with `DPM` in their FQDN, `DPM*`.

List all the DPM servers and click on **OK**.

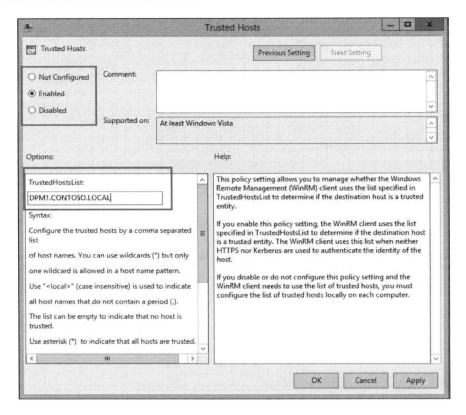

Next, you must change the execution policy; open a PowerShell (x86) console as an administrator on the Orchestrator server.

> It is important that you open a 32-bit version of the PowerShell console as currently, System Center Orchestrator is able to work only with the 32-bit version of the execution policy. If you change the execution policy in a 64-bit version of the PowerShell console, the changes will not apply.

Type the `set-executionpolicy remotesigned` command and answer `yes` when you are prompted.

Stay in the same console and configure the remote connection settings. Type the `ebable-psremoting` command and press *Enter*.

The last bit is to configure the connection in the System Center Orchestrator GUI. This recipe assumes that you have the integration pack imported and registered. For information on how to do this, read this guide: `http://technet.microsoft.com/en-us/library/hh420346.aspx`.

Go to the **Options** menu in the console, select **SC 2012 Data Protection Manager**, and click on the **Add...** button to add a configuration.

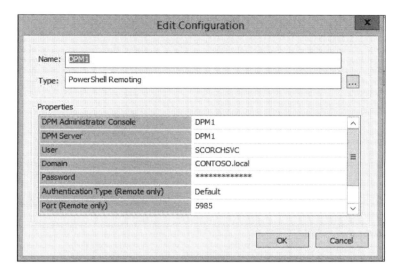

In the **Edit Configuration** window, you can configure the following parameters:

- ▸ **DPM Administrator Console**
- ▸ **DPM Server**
- ▸ **User**
- ▸ **Domain**
- ▸ **Password**
- ▸ **Authentication Type (Remote only)**
- ▸ **Port (Remote only)**
- ▸ **Use SSL (Remote only)**
- ▸ **Cache Session Timeout (min.)**

DPM Administrator Console should contain the name or IP address of the server that has both the DPM administrator console and the DPM Management Shell installed. **DPM Server** is the name of the DPM server that you would like to connect to.

User is the service account that you defined within Active Directory; it is important that this user is a member of the local admin group on the DPM server that you want to automate. **Domain** is the domain that the user account resides in. **Password** is the password for the specified service account listener in **User**.

Authentication Type is where you can list different authentication types for the DPM server and the Orchestrator runbook server. If you install the runbook server role on the DPM server, you need not authenticate, but this is not a recommended solution. The options that you can choose from are:

- **Default**
- **Basic**
- **Negotiate**
- **Negotiate With Implicit Credential**
- **Digest**
- **Kerberos**

Port is the TCP with which the clients connect to the WinRM service on the remote server.

Use SSL (Remote only) specifies whether you want to use SSL for the connection or not.

Cache Session Timeout (min.) is the number of minutes in which the session will time out.

When you have defined your connection, you are ready to get started with the automation journey. The best piece of advice is to start small and simple and then, from there, expand the automation concepts within your organization or company.

How it works...

System Center Orchestrator will use the runbooks you have built up and run its automation processes. As DPM can only be automated using remote management via PowerShell, it is very critical that the connection is verified and stable before entering a production state.

See also

- For more information regarding automation for clouds, follow this blog: http://robertandthecloud.blogspot.com.

Index

R

recovery goals
 Long-Term recovery goals 49
 Short-Term recovery goals 49
recovery points
 creating, manually 90-93
remote SQL server
 preparing, for DPMDB 22, 23
 used, for installing SCDPM 2012 R2 28-30
replica
 creating, manually 38-42
replication process
 from primary DPM server, to secondary DPM
  server 321, 322
replica volume 4
report management 54, 55
Restore as a Service (RaaS) 1, 155, 230
restore scenarios
 URL 271
runbook 346

S

Scale-Out File Servers (SOFS) 12, 35, 152
SCDPM 2012 R2
 about 1-3
 architecture 6, 7
 installing 24-27
 installing, with remote SQL server or
  cluster 28-30
 integrating, with SCVMM 156-158
 reference link 61, 230
 URL 4
 URL, for integration pack installation 377
SCVMM
 about 5, 156
 protecting 155
 SCDPM, integrating 156-158
secondary DPM server
 data, restoring 326-329
 DPM server, enabling 309-320
 primary DPM server, switching 322-326
Service Management Automation
  (SMA) 105, 226, 347
SharePoint
 about 166

individual objects, restoring 182-186
 maintenance tasks 187
 management tasks 188
 search, protecting 178
 VSS, configuring 167, 168
SharePoint farm
 configured with SQL aliases,
  protecting 178, 179
 protecting 168-178
 reference link 179
 restoring 180-182
short erase feature
 configuring 339
Short-Term recovery goals 49
single Exchange mailbox database
 protecting 198-208
SQL Server
 installing, on DPM server 18-21
 protection considerations 98, 99
 versions 98
SQL Server 2012
 configuring 99-103
 management tasks 104, 105
SQL Server 2012 AlwaysOn
 limitations 106
 protecting 105, 106
 used, for protecting Availability groups 107
 used, for protecting Availability Groups 107
SQL Server database
 protecting 108-116
 renaming 138, 139
 restoring 138, 139
 restoring, from Azure 145, 146
 restoring, from tape 146-148
 restoring, Latest feature used 148-150
 restoring, to alternative location 130-138
 restoring, to its original location 124-129
 restoring, to network location 140-144
stand-alone tape drives
 installing 333-335
Storage Area Network (SAN) 4
storage calculators
 URL, for downloading 14
supported Exchange server protection
 prerequisites 192, 193
supported file server protection
 prerequisites 64

Thank you for buying
Microsoft System Center Data Protection Manager 2012 R2 Cookbook

About Packt Publishing

Packt, pronounced 'packed', published its first book, *Mastering phpMyAdmin for Effective MySQL Management,* in April 2004, and subsequently continued to specialize in publishing highly focused books on specific technologies and solutions.

Our books and publications share the experiences of your fellow IT professionals in adapting and customizing today's systems, applications, and frameworks. Our solution-based books give you the knowledge and power to customize the software and technologies you're using to get the job done. Packt books are more specific and less general than the IT books you have seen in the past. Our unique business model allows us to bring you more focused information, giving you more of what you need to know, and less of what you don't.

Packt is a modern yet unique publishing company that focuses on producing quality, cutting-edge books for communities of developers, administrators, and newbies alike. For more information, please visit our website at www.PacktPub.com.

About Packt Enterprise

In 2010, Packt launched two new brands, Packt Enterprise and Packt Open Source, in order to continue its focus on specialization. This book is part of the Packt Enterprise brand, home to books published on enterprise software – software created by major vendors, including (but not limited to) IBM, Microsoft, and Oracle, often for use in other corporations. Its titles will offer information relevant to a range of users of this software, including administrators, developers, architects, and end users.

Writing for Packt

We welcome all inquiries from people who are interested in authoring. Book proposals should be sent to author@packtpub.com. If your book idea is still at an early stage and you would like to discuss it first before writing a formal book proposal, then please contact us; one of our commissioning editors will get in touch with you.

We're not just looking for published authors; if you have strong technical skills but no writing experience, our experienced editors can help you develop a writing career, or simply get some additional reward for your expertise.

Microsoft System Center Configuration Manager Advanced Deployment

Design, implement, and configure System Center Configuration Manager 2012 R2 with the help of real-world examples

Martyn Coupland

Microsoft System Center Configuration Manager Advanced Deployment

ISBN: 978-1-78217-208-6   Paperback: 290 pages

Design, implement, and configure System Center Configuration Manager 2012 R2 with the help of real-world examples

1. Learn how to design and operate Configuration Manager 2012 R2 sites.

2. Explore the power of Configuration Manager 2012 R2 for managing your client and server estate.

3. Discover up-to-date solutions to real-world problems in System Center Configuration Manager administration.

Microsoft System Center 2012 R2 Compliance Management Cookbook

Over 40 practical recipes that will help you plan, build, implement, and enhance IT compliance policies using Microsoft Security Compliance Manager and Microsoft System Center 2012 R2

Andreas Baumgarten   Ronnie Isherwood
Susan Roesner

Microsoft System Center 2012 R2 Compliance Management Cookbook

ISBN: 978-1-78217-170-6   Paperback: 284 pages

Over 40 practical recipes that will help you plan, build, implement, and enhance IT compliance policies using Microsoft Security Compliance Manager and Microsoft System Center 2012 R2

1. A step-by-step guide filled with practical recipes that will show you how to start your compliance project using Microsoft System Center and other supporting technologies.

2. Demystify the compliance deployment myth; bridge the gap between IT, audit, and compliance programs.

Please check **www.PacktPub.com** for information on our titles

System Center 2012 R2 Virtual Machine Manager Cookbook

Second Edition

Over 70 recipes to help you design, configure, and manage a reliable and efficient virtual infrastructure with VMM 2012 R2

Edvaldo Alessandro Cardoso [PACKT] enterprise

System Center 2012 R2 Virtual Machine Manager Cookbook

Second Edition

ISBN: 978-1-78217-684-8   Paperback: 428 pages

Over 70 recipes to help you design, configure, and manage a reliable and efficient virtual infrastructure with VMM 2012 R2

1. Create, deploy, and manage datacenters and private and hybrid clouds with hybrid hypervisors using VMM 2012 R2.

2. Integrate and manage fabric (compute, storages, gateways, and networking), services and resources, and deploy clusters from bare metal servers.

Microsoft System Center Configuration Manager

High availability and performance tuning

Deploy a scalable solution by ensuring high availability and disaster recovery using Configuration Manager

Marius Sandbu [PACKT] enterprise

Microsoft System Center Configuration Manager

ISBN: 978-1-78217-676-3   Paperback: 146 pages

Deploy a scalable solution by ensuring high availability and disaster recovery using Configuration Manager

1. Deploy highly available Configuration Manager sites and roles.

2. Backup, restore, and copy Configuration Manager to other sites.

3. Get to grips with performance tuning and best practices for Configuration Manager sites.

Please check **www.PacktPub.com** for information on our titles

Made in the USA
San Bernardino, CA
30 January 2016